PEOPLE
POWER

GEORGE WILLIAMS, one of Australia's leading constitutional lawyers and public commentators, is the Anthony Mason Professor and Foundation Director of the Gilbert + Tobin Centre of Public Law at the Faculty of Law, University of New South Wales. He is also an Australian Research Council Laureate Fellow and has held visiting positions at Osgoode Hall Law School in Toronto, Columbia University Law School in New York and University College London. He has written and edited many books, including *A Charter of Rights for Australia*, *Australian Constitutional Law and Theory* and *The Oxford Companion to the High Court of Australia*. He has also been appointed to major public inquiries into industrial relations, federalism and human rights, and practises as a barrister in the High Court of Australia and the Supreme Court of Fiji. George is a well-known media commentator on legal issues and writes a fortnightly column for the *Sydney Morning Herald*.

DAVID HUME is a Solicitor at Freehills and a Visiting Fellow at the University of New South Wales. He has worked as the Associate to Chief Justice Gleeson of the High Court of Australia and at the University of Melbourne. He graduated in 2009 with a Masters of Law from Harvard Law School, which he attended as a General Sir John Monash Scholar and Frank Knox Memorial Fellow. He has university medals in Law and Philosophy from the University of New South Wales.

PEOPLE POWER

THE HISTORY AND FUTURE OF THE REFERENDUM IN AUSTRALIA

GEORGE WILLIAMS
and DAVID HUME

A UNSW Press book

Published by
University of New South Wales Press Ltd
University of New South Wales
Sydney NSW 2052
AUSTRALIA
www.unswpress.com.au

National Library of Australia
Cataloguing-in-Publication entry
Author: Williams, George, 1969–
Title: People power: the history and future of the referendum in Australia/by
    George Williams and David Hume.
ISBN: 978 174223 215 7 (pbk.)
Subjects: Referendum – Australia – History.
        Constitutional history – Australia.
        Australia – Politics and government – History.
Other Authors/Contributors: Hume, David.
Dewey Number: 328.230994

Design Avril Makula
Cover Design by Committee
Back cover photograph Political banner outside a polling booth for the Republic
Referendum, Canberra, 1999, by Loui Seselja, National Library of Australia

CONTENTS

PREFACE

A book on referendums in Australia has been a long time coming. Despite the importance of these popular votes to Australia's national political life, they have not been the subject of a sustained historical, legal and political analysis. Our aim is to fill that gap. In this book, we explore Australia's referendum record, why success at the ballot box has been so rare and how referendums might be won in the future.

We approach this topic with a degree of understandable frustration. Australia's Constitution gives the people the power to change their system of government. This power was granted in 1901 with the clear expectation that it would be used to keep the Constitution up to date with contemporary best practice as well as popular values and aspirations. Decades-old problems in areas like federalism show how this goal has not been met. Successive governments have failed to navigate Australia's referendum machinery and to win the support of the people for important and urgent changes to the Constitution. As a consequence of not passing a referendum since 1977 and only a total of eight over more than a century, the community must pay the high price of having a second-best system of government. The costs of this can be seen in many areas, including in the billions of taxpayers' dollars lost each year due to a dysfunctional federal system and a lower standard of government services in areas like health and education.

We come from the perspective that Australia's long constitutional drought must be broken. We also believe that referendum success is achievable. The passage of many referendums held at the state level demonstrates that having the Australian people say Yes is not impossible. The key to getting to Yes is not just a matter of having good ideas, but of getting the process right. Australians want more than a chance to veto proposals at the ballot box; they want to be genuinely involved in a reform process that has broad political support.

The book has been written to be accessible to a general audience. It is also intended to be a comprehensive first point of reference for anyone interested in the law, history and politics of referendums in Australia. The focus of the book is upon national referendums to change the Australian Constitution. It covers: the philosophical, legal and political issues that result from placing constitutional change in the hands of the people (chapter 1); the path that the Australian Constitution sets out for holding a referendum to make constitutional amendments (chapter 2); how referendum campaigns are run (chapter 3); the referendum record (chapter 4); a detailed look at eight specific referendum campaigns from the first in 1906 to the most recent in 1999 (chapter 5); the factors that explain Australia's record in voting in referendums (chapter 6); and a path forward to referendum success (chapter 7).

In writing this book, we owe a great debt to our research assistants Keiran Hardy and Sophie Marjanac. They have tracked down obscure resources and compelling images and have helped us to produce a polished final work. We thank also the others who have read through early drafts of the chapters, particularly Gillian White and Kate Mason, and the people who agreed to share their experiences and observations through being interviewed for this book.

I

THE PEOPLE'S VOICE

Introduction

The Australian Constitution has been central to the daily debates of Australian politics for more than a century. It continues to have a profound impact in all areas of policy, including economic management, environmental protection and the delivery of services such as health and education. In these and other fields, the Constitution can promote good governance, as well as impose important limits and major obstacles. It can also be invoked as a powerful symbol in long-standing national debates, such as those on Indigenous reconciliation and whether Australia should become a republic.

At issue is not only what the Constitution now says, but what it should say in the future. Should it state that the Commonwealth runs the nation's hospitals and bears full responsibility for the nation's rivers and the Murray–Darling basin? Should the Constitution outlaw racial discrimination? Should there be fixed four year terms for the federal Parliament? In Australia, these questions cannot be finally resolved by the government of the day, nor by any Parliament. They can only be answered by a direct vote of the Australian people cast at a referendum to change the Constitution.

The Australian nation itself was brought about in a special way. When the Constitution came into force on 1 January 1901, it had a unique claim to popular authority. In what for the time was a radical experiment in direct democracy, the Constitution was approved by the people of the colonies in a series of referendums. Australians voted to constitute the new nation and to empower its system of government. In doing so, they also brought about a fundamental change in how successive generations would view their Constitution. The people of the colonies not only ratified the new law, they also entrenched the idea that alterations to it must be approved by a popular vote. Today, the idea that the Constitution can only be changed by the people voting at a referendum is a bedrock principle of Australian democracy.

The struggle to unite the Australian colonies under a new constitution spanned most of the 1890s. After appointees and then popular representatives painstakingly debated and drafted the terms of the Constitution at conventions held in 1891 and over 1897–98, debate shifted to the public at large. Newspapers canvassed the arguments of supporters and opponents at length, and public figures travelled the coasts and the countryside to debate the issues. The people of the six colonies – soon to become the six states – then considered and voted on whether to approve the Constitution and, in doing so, to become one nation.

The draft Constitution was supported by a majority of voters in each colony at referendums held over 1899 and 1900, before finally being enacted for the new nation by the United Kingdom Parliament. Australia's political leaders felt it necessary to have the new Constitution passed by the United Kingdom Parliament because, although they supported the idea of a popular vote, they were not seeking full independence from their colonial parent. The local referendums were an assertion of local sovereignty, but only within a framework that recognised Australia's continuing status as a subordinate part of the British Empire.

In line with the beliefs and values of the time, most women and Indigenous people were ineligible to vote in the referendums. Nevertheless, compared to anything that had come before, in Australia and worldwide, the Australian Constitution was brought about in a remarkably democratic way. The framers of the Constitution had put a vision of the future of the continent to a popular vote and the people had said Yes. As the United Kingdom legislation that formally adopted the Constitution triumphantly declared: 'the people … have agreed to unite in one indissoluble federal Commonwealth'.[1]

If the way in which the Constitution came about was radical, the way in which it was to be altered was equally so. Only if Parliament, the Crown and, most importantly, the people of the new nation agreed would the Constitution be amended. What the people had made, only they could unmake. Just as 'the people' had agreed to unite in a Commonwealth, so the Constitution said that any changes to that Commonwealth would need to be 'submitted' to them for approval. As was said at the 1897–98 convention by Isaac Isaacs, who later became Chief Justice of the High Court and the nation's first Australian-born Governor-General, 'the Constitution is being made for the people, not the people for the Constitution'.[2] This democratic principle was embodied in section 128 of the Constitution, the full text of which is set out in appendix 1. It states that Australia must hold a referendum to change its Constitution: change cannot be brought about by a government or Parliament acting alone.

When section 128 was being drafted, the framers initially only gave Australians the power to 'amend' the Constitution. But, as the drafting process continued, they changed this word to 'alter'. The purpose of this slight change was to make clear that the people's control over the Constitution did not extend only to minor amendments and petty tinkering. Instead, the power was to *alter* the Constitution – and that meant being able to do everything, including the most fundamental of rewrites. It is in this way that successive generations have been trusted with everything from the overarching principles to the narrow technical details of the Constitution. This point was summed up in 1901 by Andrew Inglis Clark, a former Tasmanian Attorney-General and a convention member who assisted in drafting the basic framework for the Constitution. He said that the Constitution

> must be read and construed, not as containing a declaration of the will and intentions of men long since dead, and who cannot have anticipated the problems that would arise for solution by future generations, but as declaring the will and intentions of the present inheritors and possessors of sovereign power, who maintain the Constitution and have the power to alter it, and who are in the immediate presence of the problems to be solved. It is they who enforce the provisions of the Constitution and make a living force of that which would otherwise be a silent and lifeless document.[3]

More than a century later, referendums are the only means of changing the words of the original constitutional compact. But, as for most aspects of government, the text of the Constitution tells only part of the story. In these first three chapters, we outline the broad concepts and fine details of referendums in Australia. The story brings together many of the key themes of Australian democracy and government since 1901.

What are referendums?

A REFERENCE TO THE PEOPLE

A referendum is held when the people cast a vote to accept or reject a question of law or policy, such as whether to amend a constitution or a piece of legislation. This might produce a binding legal outcome or just an advisory opinion. An example of the latter was the referendum held in New Zealand in 2009 on whether to ban the smacking of children by their parents.

Switzerland was the first country to make wide use of referendums. From the 1830s at the cantonal (or state) level in Switzerland, a referendum could be held to change a constitution or to repeal a law. At the federal level, a referendum for the revision of the Constitution was introduced in 1848. By 1874, any ordinary law could be repealed by referendum; and, in 1891, the Swiss Constitution allowed citizens to initiate a referendum to make a new law.

Referendums are also common in other countries, including for altering a constitution, changing an ordinary law and to determine whether a region should be granted independence. For example, in 1980 and 1995, people in the Canadian province of Quebec voted in a referendum on whether to secede from Canada. On both occasions, the vote was No, though in 1995 it was a close-run thing, with 50.6 per cent for No and 49.4 per cent for Yes. Recently, referendums have been held in many countries in Europe on whether to approve a new constitution for the European Union.

The idea of having a popular vote to change a constitution was adopted in Australia in the 1890s as momentum built towards Federation. Even though the term 'referendum' is not used anywhere in the Constitution, it has nonetheless come to describe the popular vote required to change that document or, on occasion, a state constitution. Such referendums are a way of having people directly involved in the making of laws, in this case a constitution, outside of the regular political path which involves a Bill being drafted and voted on just by elected representatives in Parliament. Referendums bring all voters directly into the process.

PLEBISCITES

In Australia, referendums to change a constitution are often distinguished from 'plebiscites'. The latter term can be used to describe non-binding votes of the people, or what are in effect giant opinion polls to test the public mood on an issue. An example is the Australian Republican Movement's proposal for a process to introduce a republic. It suggests holding a non-binding plebiscite on whether Australia should become a republic with an Australian head of state, followed by a second non-binding plebiscite on which model of a republic should be put to a referendum. These plebiscites could not change the law or require the government to act, but they could assist in building support for a republic and in determining what type of republic Australians would like to finally vote on when it comes to a referendum.

National plebiscites have been very rare in Australia, with only three held since 1901. Two were about whether to introduce conscription during wartime, and one was to choose a national anthem. The results are shown in table 1.1.

Even though voting was not compulsory in these plebiscites, the turnout was high. In fact, before voting in referendums became compulsory in 1924, the highest turnout in any Australian referendum or plebiscite was for the conscription plebiscite of 1916. The campaigns in the 1916 and 1917 plebiscites were fierce. In 1916, Prime Minister Billy Hughes issued a manifesto to all Australian soldiers in which he urged: 'Now is the hour when *our* race must prove itself worthy of *its* traditions and *its* heritage'. Hughes denigrated those advocating a No vote: 'they cover Australia with the mantle of eternal shame; the glorious name of Anzac becomes a tarnished and dishonoured thing'.[4]

TABLE 1.1 PLEBISCITES IN AUSTRALIA			
Question	Year	Vote	Result
Conscription	1916	Yes	48.39%
		No	51.61%
Conscription	1917	Yes	46.22%
		No	53.78%
National Song	1977	God Save the Queen	18.78%
		Advance Australia Fair	43.29%
		Song of Australia	9.65%
		Waltzing Matilda	28.28%

Sources: Australian Electoral Commission, *Australian Referendums 1906–1999* CD-ROM (2000) and *Parliamentary Handbook of the Commonwealth of Australia.*

THE STATES AND TERRITORIES

Referendums are not only a national event in Australia. They have also been held many times at the state and territory level. At this level, the distinction between the terms 'referendum' and 'plebiscite' is less clearly maintained, with many non-binding state and territory votes referred to as 'referendums'. The first example of putting a law to the people on the Australian continent was the South Australian plebiscite of 1896, which secured free, compulsory and secular education in public schools. This was also the first time that women were able to vote in Australia.

Unlike the Australian Constitution, the constitutions of the states can generally be changed through an ordinary Act of Parliament, without the need for a referendum. There are, however, exceptions, with some states requiring a referendum to change certain important parts of their constitution. For example, the New South Wales Constitution provides that the Upper House of its Parliament, the Legislative Council, can only be abolished by way of a referendum.

Most state votes have been advisory ballots on non-constitutional issues. For example, four of the 16 referendums or plebiscites in New South Wales have been on opening and closing hours for licensed premises. Many such votes have dealt with matters of great state and national importance. In 1933, Western Australians overwhelmingly voted Yes to secede (or withdraw) from the Commonwealth. The state then sent a petition to the British Parliament requesting independence. It got nowhere after the petition was ruled out of order because convention dictated that it be made by the Commonwealth and not an individual state. The Commonwealth opposed secession, and the issue quickly fell away. The most recent state ballot (in what nationally would be called a 'plebiscite') occurred in June 2009 when Western Australians voted against introducing daylight saving time.

The practice of state referendums and plebiscites varies widely. Some states only ask Yes or No questions; others have sometimes given voters an array of options, with the most popular option being the winner. For example, when New South Wales voted on closing hours for hotels in 1916, voters could select 6, 7, 8, 9, 10 or 11 o'clock (6 o'clock won, with more than 62 per cent of the vote).

Territory and local governments can also hold referendums and plebiscites. For example, a majority of Northern Territory voters narrowly rejected statehood in 1998, while the people of the Australian Capital Territory chose to adopt a system of proportional voting for their local Legislative Assembly in a 1992 referendum. In New South Wales, local councils are required to hold a referendum to change the way the Mayor is appointed, to change the number of councillors or their method of appointment and to divide the council into wards or abolish existing wards.[5]

CITIZEN-INITIATED REFERENDUMS

In Switzerland, New Zealand and many parts of the United States, referendums can be initiated by the people. These citizen-initiated referendums (CIRs) can be advisory (as in New Zealand or the European Union) or binding on government (as in California).

Australia does not have CIRs at the national, state or territory level. Nationally, the people get to vote in a referendum to change the Constitution, but the decision of whether to hold that referendum in the first place lies solely with the federal Parliament and the government of the day. Australia has debated whether to introduce CIRs. In the early 1980s, the Australian Democrats introduced Bills into the Senate to allow for them, and the Constitutional Commission discussed, but rejected, the idea in the late 1980s. In 2003, a Constitutional Convention in South Australia endorsed CIRs, but was split between supporters of a binding or merely advisory vote.

Supporters of CIRs argue that it is not enough to give the people a vote at a referendum when the people have no say on when referendums are held and what subject matters they deal with. They argue for a form of direct democracy in which the people are able both to initiate change to laws and constitutions and then to vote to reject or approve these changes.

Opponents argue that CIRs can lead to amendments that hamstring good government. In California, CIRs have locked the government into popular expenditure on items like education (indeed, up to a third of all expenditure by the Californian budget has been outside government control) while prohibiting it from making cuts or raising taxes to fund that expenditure.[6] CIRs can also be used against a minority group. Referendums, by definition, create a risk that the majority will support a law tailored to outlaw unpopular minority practices. In late 2009, for example, a CIR in Switzerland passed by 57 per cent of voters changed Swiss law to ban the building of minarets on Islamic mosques.

On other occasions, CIRs may be inappropriate because an informed vote is impossible unless the government releases confidential information. Opponents ask: could people really vote on something like national security policy when the government cannot fully disclose the information on which the policy is based?

Some of these risks can be mitigated by establishing good CIR processes. The threshold of public support for initiation could be set high and the referendum could be advisory only. Certain subject matters, such as foreign policy, could also be excluded from the CIR process. Nevertheless, even with such practices, real risks remain, such as the possibility that the opportunity to hold a CIR will be manipulated by the rich and powerful, including major corporate interests. In California, for example, signature-gathering firms can be engaged to collect the necessary signatures to initiate a referendum, whereas community groups without access to large sums of money can find it logistically impossible to get a CIR off the ground.

Referendums and the Constitution

A SPECIAL WAY TO CHANGE THE CONSTITUTION

In Australia, normal laws can be made or amended by a vote of both Houses of the federal Parliament and the assent of the Queen's representative, the Governor-General. The Constitution is not, however, a normal law. It sets the rules by which Australia is governed, and provides many of the most important checks and balances upon the exercise of public power by politicians, judges and other public office holders. To change the Constitution is to change the foundation stone of Australian government. It is not surprising, then, that a special, more difficult procedure must be followed if it is to be altered.

Section 128 of the Constitution states that, in addition to agreement by the two Houses of Parliament and the Royal Assent, an amendment must be approved within a short time frame by a double majority of: the people voting in a majority of the states; and a majority of people voting nationwide. In rare cases, majority popular support is also required in a particular state affected by the change. These processes and voting requirements are explored further below.

The framers of the Australian Constitution gave the people a say on any future amendment to the document. However, the people are not the only ones who can determine the outcome. Elected representatives in the Houses of Parliament can also say No, as can the Governor-General acting on the advice of the government of the day. Equally, if every one of these groups says Yes, the result is a law with unprecedented authority. It would have the support of every single political grouping in Australia: Parliament, the Executive (that is, the government and its departments) and the people both nationally and as residents of the states.

Donald S Lutz, an American professor of political science, has categorised the world's constitutions according to how difficult they are to amend. Lutz gives 'points' to constitutions based on how proposals are initiated, whether they require special legislative and executive approval and whether they require approval by referendum. These points are then added up to give an overall 'index of difficulty'. According to Lutz, Australia's Constitution is the fifth most difficult to amend in the world.[7] It seems, however, that Lutz did not take into account the full process that amendments to Australia's Constitution must go through. If these are included, Australia's Constitution jumps to the top of the list as the most difficult in the world to change![8] The difficulty of amending Australia's Constitution is reflected in the rate of amendment since 1901, with only eight of 44 changes put to the people in a referendum having been passed. Lutz's study shows that, among constitutions that had been in existence for more than 30 years, Australia's has the third lowest rate of amendment, beaten only by Denmark and Japan.

In this sense, Australia's amendment process has worked in a very conservative way. In 1967, Geoffrey Sawer, a leading Australian constitutional commentator, was referring to Australia's inability to rewrite its Constitution when he said that, '[c]onstitutionally speaking, Australia is the frozen Continent'.[9]

This assessment is a fair one if it is limited to changes to the text of the Australian Constitution. However, this can be too narrow a focus. Constitutional reform can occur not only through shifts in the words of the document, but also through changes in how institutions and people understand, interpret and apply that text. As we explore below, while the text of the Constitution has changed little since 1901, there have nonetheless been profound shifts in the way it operates in practice in areas like Australia's federal system of government.

In any event, the words of the Constitution actually say very little about how the Australian system of government operates. The Constitution does not, for example, mention the office of Prime Minister or the Cabinet. This means that much of Australia's system of government is defined outside the formal text of the Constitution, and so can be changed without the need for a referendum. For example, statutes that determine the operation of Parliament and its privileges, such as the Commonwealth *Parliamentary Privileges Act 1987*, are key elements of the constitutional structure. The constitutional significance of such statutes is as apparent in Australia as it is in nations like the United Kingdom that lack a written constitution, but they are not formally part of Australia's Constitution.

Australia's constitutional system is also defined by assumptions and practices from the Westminster system of government, which is derived from Britain. These assumptions and practices include a range of unwritten conventions, including that the Governor-General must act on the advice of the Prime Minister and that a Prime Minister must resign where he or she has lost the confidence of the House of Representatives. The fact that Australia's constitutional system includes elements such as unwritten conventions means that it is possible to engage in significant constitutional reform without ever holding a referendum. Referendums must be held to change the text of the Constitution, but are not required for any other form of change to Australia's system of government.

ARE THERE PARTS OF THE CONSTITUTION THAT CANNOT BE CHANGED BY A REFERENDUM?

The framers intended that the power to alter the Constitution by way of a referendum be a wide one. Through section 128, Australians can add to or subtract from any part of the Constitution. They can: delete anachronistic provisions; add new powers or subtract from existing ones; install something new, such as a constitutional Bill of Rights; remove, alter or codify constitutional conventions; and even change section 128 itself – for example, by doing away with the requirement that proposed amendments be put to referendum.

It is clear that the power is broad, but it arguably only extends to alterations to the text of the Constitution itself, and not to alterations of any other document. Hence, there is a view that section 128 does not extend to changing what are called the 'covering clauses' to the Constitution. The Act of the United Kingdom Parliament that set out the Australian Constitution (the *Commonwealth of Australia Constitution Act 1900*) first included a number of preliminary clauses. Indeed, what is now called the 'Constitution of Australia' does not appear in the United Kingdom statute until clause 9. The preceding 'covering clauses' state, among other things, that the Australian nation shall be an 'indissoluble federal Commonwealth'.

It may be that the referendum process in section 128 only applies to the Constitution set out in clause 9 of the United Kingdom statute and not to the preceding covering clauses. The argument runs along the following lines (emphasis added below):

- Section 128 of the Constitution sets out an amendment process that begins with the words: '*This Constitution* shall not be altered except in the following manner'.
- Clause 9 of the United Kingdom statute says: '*The Constitution* of the Commonwealth shall be as follows'.
- Therefore, it is argued, the referendum mechanism in section 128 only refers to the Constitution set out in clause 9 of the

United Kingdom statute, and cannot be used to amend any of the preceding 'covering clauses' of that statute.

No attempt has ever been made to amend the covering clauses by way of a referendum. As a result, this question remains unresolved and has not been the subject of a decision by the High Court. While there remains a difference of opinion, the stronger view is that the referendum mechanism could be used to change the covering clauses. This could be because the High Court would not impose limits on the popular sovereignty of the Australian people, as expressed in a referendum, to change any part of Australian law. Alternatively, it may be that the problem can be disposed of through clever drafting. A referendum might first be used to amend section 128 to provide that it not only extends to alterations to the Constitution, but also to the covering clauses to that document. This could well be a conclusive answer to the problem. Once section 128 has been amended in this way, the textual argument that it is limited only to alterations to the Constitution set out in clause 9 of the United Kingdom statute would likely fall away.

A further question is whether there are certain fundamental features of the Constitution that cannot be amended by the people because they go to the very root of the Constitution. It might be that there are some parts of the Constitution which are so fundamental that, if they were altered, it would no longer be a 'constitution' at all. Would, for example, an attempt to use a referendum to abolish the federal Parliament be a valid change under section 128? If the people are truly sovereign, then surely they can change any part of the Constitution that they like. However, if the effect of that change is to undermine their sovereignty, does this raise a paradoxical situation that calls into question the scope of the referendum power?

The Supreme Court of India has made a similar point in respect of the Indian Constitution, saying that there are certain 'basic features' of it that cannot be amended, because to do so would undermine the structure of the Constitution.[10] These may include the separation of powers, republican government, the separation of church and state, and other basic features. The Indian doctrine derives from the specific preamble and terms of the Indian Constitution, but it also makes sense in a nation that has a constitution which can be changed through a vote of two-thirds of the members of each of the Houses of the national Parliament, without the need for a popular vote. The rule operates to protect the interests of the people, and particularly minority groups, from being undermined by a vote of their elected representatives. On the other hand, it would seem very unlikely that similar structural limitations exist on what the Australian people can do through section 128; but this again has never been tested.

There is no accepted answer to these questions, but it seems clear that it would take a brave High Court to strike down any change to the Constitution passed by the people voting in a referendum. If the Court did so, it could well provoke a constitutional crisis. These are, in any event, hypothetical questions never likely to arise. The possibility that the Australian people would support a referendum proposal that destroyed their institutions of government and basic democratic principles is fanciful at best.

Constitutional change without a referendum

Since 1901, there have been major changes in the way Australia is governed. The Commonwealth operates in many more fields than it did in the past, while areas of state responsibility have declined. Today, the Commonwealth is primarily responsible for taxation, industrial relations, the regulation of companies and much more. The Commonwealth's role in health care, education, housing and even law enforcement − all traditional core areas of state responsibility

– is also growing and may soon surpass that of the states. All of this has come about without changing the text of the Constitution by referendum. This raises the issue of whether referendums are the only way in which Australians can change their Constitution.

There are two different ways of approaching this question. First, from a legal perspective, referendums may not be the only way of changing the actual words of the Constitution. Secondly, from a practical perspective, the effect of the Constitution can change even where its words stay the same: sometimes words can be given a new interpretation or applied differently over time. These possibilities are explored below.

A BACKDOOR WAY OF CHANGING THE CONSTITUTION?

There has long been debate about whether the Constitution can only be changed by referendum. The Constitution says in section 128 that '[t]his Constitution shall not be altered except in the following manner …'. And, if it is a fundamental legal document that is supreme over every other kind of law, that surely should settle the matter. There is, however, more to the debate. Two possibilities have been raised regarding how the Constitution might be amended in a way that bypasses the need for a referendum.

First, there is a legal argument that legislation enacted by the United Kingdom Parliament (and the Commonwealth and state Parliaments) since 1901 may permit the Australian Parliament to change the Constitution without submitting the matter to a referendum. In 1986, the *Australia Acts* were passed by all these Parliaments. Their aim was to provide the final legal recognition of Australia's independence from Britain and to increase the powers of self-government of the Australian states. One part of the Acts allows the Commonwealth Parliament to amend a United Kingdom law (called the *Statute of Westminster* of 1931) at the request or with the concurrence of the Parliaments of all the Australian states. The *Statute of Westminster* is significant because it states in section 8 that: 'Nothing in this Act shall be deemed to confer any power to repeal or alter the Constitution or the Constitution Act of the Commonwealth of Australia'. The argument thus runs that the *Australia Acts* provide a means by which the *Statute of Westminster* can be amended, and any such amendment could include revision of section 8 to provide a different means to amend the Australian Constitution. Hence, if all of Australia's Parliaments were able to agree to amend the *Statute of Westminster*, they might be able to amend or repeal the Constitution without a referendum.

Second, the United Kingdom Parliament itself might be able to change the Australian Constitution without a referendum. In 1900, it was widely thought that the people of Australia could not make a constitution by merely voting for it. After all, the six colonies, which became the six states, were the creations of the Parliament of the United Kingdom. How else could the colonies join together to become a nation other than through the body that had created them? At the time, Australians had a different conception of their place in the world. They saw themselves, and their new nation, as being much more reliant on, and subservient to, Britain. The result was that, after the Constitution was voted on by the Australian people, it travelled to England, where it was passed, after minor amendment, as an ordinary Act of the United Kingdom Parliament. Logically, because the Australian Constitution is part of an ordinary Act of the United Kingdom Parliament, the United Kingdom Parliament can amend or repeal the Constitution whenever it wants without holding a referendum in Australia. It would simply be a matter of that Parliament amending a law passed by it more than a century ago.

Both of these possibilities, while superficially plausible, run counter to the letter of section 128 (which insists that: 'This Constitution shall not be altered except in the following manner ...'), as well as the spirit of the document as expressed in the idea of 'popular sovereignty'. In any event, no Australian Parliament would now seek to bypass the people by way of the first option, while if the United Kingdom Parliament sought to amend or even repeal the Australian Constitution under the second, any such attempt would likely be ignored as an assertion of a now obsolete colonial power. Even in 1901, it was suggested by leading authorities on the new Constitution that an amendment of the document by the United Kingdom Parliament 'could only be justified by the gravest considerations of a most serious emergency'.[11] More than a century later, even if it theoretically had the power, it would be unthinkable for the United Kingdom Parliament to try to change Australia's Constitution. The result is that amendment of the Constitution now lies solely in the hands of the Australian people by way of a referendum under section 128.

The referendum requirement is a clear expression of the sovereignty of the Australian people. This concept of popular sovereignty has come to supersede the sovereignty of the United Kingdom Parliament in explaining why Australia's Constitution is authoritative. Not only is the Constitution accepted by the people and subject only to change by them, it also came to form the law of the land in the first place because it was developed by their representatives and supported by them at the ballot box. This view of Australian popular sovereignty came to be more widely accepted as Australia grew more confident and active on the international stage and as it has cut many of its legal and political ties with the United Kingdom.

Judges of the High Court of Australia, the final and authoritative interpreters of the Constitution, have supported this view. For example, former Chief Justice Sir Anthony Mason proclaimed in 1992 that the *Australia Acts* of 1986 'marked the end of the legal sovereignty of the Imperial Parliament and recognised that ultimate sovereignty resided in the Australian people'.[12] Two years later, Sir William Deane, a Justice of the High Court who later became Governor-General of Australia, stated that the present legitimacy of Australia's Constitution 'lies exclusively in the original adoption (by referenda) and subsequent maintenance (by acquiescence) of its provisions by the people'.[13]

CHANGE THROUGH INTERPRETATION AND PRACTICE

The Constitution is a written document. Its words have only ever been changed through a successful referendum. However, the *effect* of those words is marked by continuing change. Since 1901, the meaning attributed to the words of the Constitution has gone through enormous shifts without ever having been put to the people.

Such change is inevitable. Written words on a page must be interpreted; the Constitution is a long document, and the words it uses are sometimes vague or ambiguous. Notoriously, section 92 says that 'trade, commerce, and intercourse among the States ... shall be absolutely free'. This could mean a lot of things, but not likely what the words seem to suggest. If you were to take section 92 at face value, this might prevent legitimate quarantine restrictions or taxes on goods where they are sold interstate. Judges have grappled with the meaning of section 92 since 1901, and the accepted interpretation of it and other parts of the Constitution has changed many times. Language such as this has prompted agonising on the part of High Court judges, with Chief Justice Latham even going on to say in his retirement speech in 1952 that 'when I die, section 92 will be found written on my heart'.[14]

In other cases, a word may have had a clear meaning in 1901 when the Constitution came into force, but shifts in society and leaps in technology have meant that this can no longer be sustained. An example is the power of the Commonwealth in section 51(12) to pass laws with respect to 'currency, coinage, and legal tender'. The meaning of those words more than a century ago would not have contemplated the use of money in online transactions, but today would likely do so. Similarly, it is arguable that federal power over 'marriage' in section 51(21) might now extend to same-sex marriage, in addition to the 1901 conception of a marriage as being between a man and a woman.

The High Court usually has the final say on such questions. Since it first sat in 1903, the Court has changed the way it has interpreted many parts of the Constitution, and has implied some legal rules into it. These are not technically 'alterations' to the Constitution, but they do have the effect of reshaping how the Constitution is understood and applied. Critics of High Court decisions, or particular styles of judicial decision-making, often argue that this amounts to judges altering the Constitution in a way that usurps the power of the people. One example came in response to the High Court's broad reading in the 1980s of federal Parliament's 'external affairs' power so as to permit the making of laws for Australia implementing the nation's international treaty obligations. Academics Mark Cooray and Suri Ratnapala argued that there had been a 'transformation' of the Constitution, 'judicially executed … without the approval of the people' by 'an extraordinary legal subterfuge', which had brought about 'the translocation of substantial powers from the States to the central government'.[15]

As the High Court has handed down more and more decisions on the Constitution, its interpretations have built up to such an extent that many of the ways in which the Constitution now operates would be unrecognisable to Australians of 1901. This was anticipated by the framers of the Constitution. As Isaac Isaacs stated in 1898 during the debates on the draft Constitution:

> We are taking infinite trouble to express what we mean in this
> Constitution; but as in America so it will be here, that the
> makers of the Constitution were not merely the Conventions
> who sat, and the states who ratified their conclusions, but the
> Judges of the Supreme Court. Marshall, Jay, Storey, and all
> the rest of the renowned Judges who have pronounced on the

Constitution, have had just as much to do in shaping it as the men who sat in the original Conventions.[16]

In the area of federalism, for example, the Constitution was meant to secure the states' financial position and independence, and at Federation it was the states and not the Commonwealth that levied income tax. However, the demands of two world wars and the rise of a national economy, combined with some canny manoeuvring by the Commonwealth, left the states with no income tax revenue. The Commonwealth takeover of income tax was ratified by the High Court in the *Uniform Tax Cases* of 1942 and 1957. Other High Court decisions have stripped power away from the states to levy taxes on goods (such as taxes similar to the GST) and have recognised that the Commonwealth has a broad power to make grants to the states on strict conditions that enable it to micro-manage what had once been state functions. The impact of these changes in financial policy and practice and the series of High Court decisions has been profound. The relative positions of the Commonwealth and the states are almost the opposite of how they were conceived to be in 1901 by those who drafted the Constitution. This has been brought about despite there not having been any significant change in this area to the text of the Constitution.

It is sometimes said that High Court interpretation of the Constitution shows how Australia's system of government can adapt to new circumstances without the need for a referendum. The problem, though, is that it allows for what can amount to fundamental changes to Australia's constitutional structure without these having had the democratic stamp of approval by the people. While judges deserve credit for many changes that have updated and improved Australia's system of government, there are dangers in leaving constitutional reform solely to them. Court-initiated change is often a second-best solution. It can distance Australians from their governance and legal structures, and can contribute to the sense of alienation that weakens the democratic system and undermines the vision of the framers for popular involvement in constitutional change.

A further problem is that many reforms to the Constitution can only be brought about by changing the actual text of the Constitution at a referendum. There are important limits to what the judiciary can achieve: many of the most important reforms are beyond them and others can be seen as illegitimate. The High Court cannot, for example, interpret the Constitution to provide symbolic recognition of Indigenous people in a new preamble to the Constitution. Nor can it fix many of the most fundamental problems associated with Australia's federal system of government. In other areas, the court may simply have reached the workable limits of the text.

The High Court is also rarely capable of leading the debate to an effective conclusion. While it can bring about some changes in areas like federalism, there are also dangers it can lose touch with public opinion and political leadership. Ultimately, the Court also depends on other institutions to make its decisions work, and for the selection of its judges. While the High Court has a central role in Australia's democracy, section 128 of the Constitution reflects the fact that constitutional reform must be led by the community and its elected representatives. Such leadership is essential for successful reform, with many of the most important and necessary changes to the Constitution only capable of being brought about by means of a referendum.

Quite apart from judicial interpretation, change to Australia's system of government can be brought about without a referendum through changes in constitutional practice. The Constitution itself provides that states can refer extra power to the Commonwealth Parliament. This means that some or all of the states can agree to hand over control of an area to the Commonwealth Parliament. The referral mechanism that allows this lies in section 51(37) of the Constitution. It is now frequently used as a way of enabling national laws in areas that had previously fallen outside Commonwealth power. A prominent example was the 1996 referral by Victoria to the Commonwealth of wide-ranging power over industrial relations.[17] In 2009, all states except Western Australia followed this example and referred industrial relations powers to the Commonwealth in order to enable the federal Parliament to create a single, national system of industrial relations for the private sector.

The other major way in which the practice of the Constitution has changed is through cooperation between the Commonwealth and the states. By working together, the Commonwealth and states have been able to achieve uniform laws and policies across a number of policy areas. In recent times, much of this has been driven by the Council of Australian Governments (COAG), the peak intergovernmental forum comprising the Prime Minister, State Premiers, Territory Chief Ministers and the President of the Australian Local Government Association. As a result of intergovernmental agreements drawn up by this body and through a range of other less formal negotiations, Commonwealth and state government responsibilities in areas such as health, education and industry regulation have been greatly transformed since 1901.

2

THE PATH OF CONSTITUTIONAL CHANGE

Introduction

Section 128 of the Constitution, the full text of which is set out in appendix 1, sets out the steps that must be followed for the Constitution to be altered. A referendum of the Australian people on whether to approve the change is the most significant step, but it is only one of several. Each must be completed, in the order specified, if the text of the Constitution is to be amended. This ensures that any change to the Constitution has the broadest possible support. The people as a whole and as residents of their respective states must be in favour of the amendment, as must the federal Parliament and the Queen's representative, the Governor-General, as instructed by the government of the day.

This chapter sets out the stages of constitutional reform. It examines how ideas for change are generated, followed by their passage through Parliament, consideration by the Australian people and their assent by the Governor-General.

Generating ideas for constitutional change

Although passage through Parliament is the first step in the process of constitutional change specified by section 128, proposals tend to be debated, and sometimes even drafted, long before they reach that institution. Some ideas, like that of an Australian republic, may have been on the public agenda for years – and even decades – before reaching even the beginning of the process set down by section 128.

There are a host of ways by which ideas for constitutional change are generated and discussed. Many of them are informal, and involve debate along party lines: for example, Opposition Leader Tony Abbott announced in early 2010 that the Liberal–National Party Coalition favoured having the Commonwealth take over control of the Murray–Darling basin by way of a referendum in 2013. Other ideas are expressed regularly in newspapers and electronic media, while still more begin as the subject of discussion in the wider community. Proposals for constitutional change are never far from the surface of political debate in Australia, whether they be for fixing Australia's dysfunctional federal system, achieving an Australian republic or recognising Indigenous peoples or local government in the Constitution.

There are also a number of more formal means by which constitutional change can be considered. Such mechanisms have been used in the past as a way of generating considered debate, and ensuring that a broad range of people are involved in the discussion.

POPULAR CONVENTIONS

Popular conventions are an accepted way of debating changes to Australia's Constitution. They signal a serious intent to deal with major questions about Australian government, as well as respect for the democratic nature of the Constitution. By establishing an inclusive process that draws in people from across the nation, conventions can enable a broader range of voices to be heard than is normally the case when governments draft laws and develop new policies. Conventions can thereby bring popular legitimacy to the reform process, and in doing so focus national media and popular attention on a specific agenda.

Australia's Constitution was drafted at two conventions held in the 1890s, the second of which was comprised (except for the Western Australian delegation) of elected representatives. However, it took a century for Australia to return to the idea of a popular convention. The Liberal–National Party Coalition led by John Howard fought the 1996 federal election on the basis that it would, if elected, establish a convention to debate the republic issue. Upon the Coalition's victory, a convention comprised of 152 delegates was held over ten days in February 1998 in Old Parliament House in Canberra. Half of the delegates were elected by a voluntary postal ballot; the other half were parliamentary representatives and government appointees.

The Labor Party Opposition argued that the appointed delegates should be chosen by a parliamentary committee comprised of equal government and non-government members, who would make appointments by a two-thirds majority vote. The Howard government rejected this argument, and justified its power to appoint the delegates on the basis that it needed to ensure diverse representation from Indigenous groups, women and youth. The argument cut both ways. Nevertheless, Malcolm Turnbull, then leader of the Australian Republican Movement, recalls Opposition Leader Kim Beazley saying to him that 'the republic is in the hands of its enemies'.[1]

As a way of generating public interest, the convention on the republic was a success. Many Australians attended the convention in person, with some driving long distances; many others watched the proceedings live on ABC Television. The elections for half the delegates were prominent and, though voting was voluntary, turnout was more than 45 per cent. Although the convention failed to unite republicans around a single model, a majority of delegates did support a republican form of government in which an Australian president would be chosen by a two-thirds majority of the federal Parliament. This was the model that the Howard government then put to the Australian people at the failed referendum of 1999. Ironically, despite having been developed at the first popular convention in over a century, one of the most effective arguments against the move to a republic at that referendum was the idea that Australians should reject a 'politicians' republic'.

The key advantage of an elected convention is the democratic legitimacy it can bring to a proposal for constitutional reform. Elected conventions also extend and deepen the deliberative aspects of the referendum process: voters confront the issues when electing representatives to the convention, during the convention itself, and at the time of debating and voting on the final referendum proposal. The disadvantages of elected conventions include their cost, that representatives may not be especially knowledgeable about the issues and that representatives may not engage in genuine negotiations because they feel bound to their election platform.

INTERGOVERNMENTAL CONVENTIONS

Australia's longest ongoing review of the Constitution, the Australian Constitutional Convention, ran from 1973 to 1985. The Convention grew from a movement of the states. In 1970, the Victorian Parliament resolved to invite the other states to participate in discussions about the Constitution. These discussions were to focus on problems of federalism because the states were becoming increasingly resentful about growing Commonwealth power, and a number of High Court decisions were increasing this trend. The states met several times in 1972, but it became clear that Commonwealth participation was necessary if the discussions were to have any real effect. The Labor Commonwealth Government (under Prime Minister Gough Whitlam) joined in and, in 1973, the Australian Constitutional Convention was formed. It comprised representatives from Commonwealth and state Parliaments, local government and the territories.

The Convention began poorly. Whitlam announced on the first day that the Commonwealth intended to 'go it alone' regardless of any decisions of the Convention.[2] A view quickly crystallised that Whitlam had established the Convention to legitimise a preconceived, partisan agenda. Although the Convention came about in a spirit of consensus, it became increasingly divided as time passed, and proceedings degenerated into set-piece, party-line speeches.

Despite these setbacks, the Convention was still able to produce over 130 recommendations. Three of these – to give Territorians a right to vote in referendums, to set a compulsory retirement age for federal judges, and to hold simultaneous elections for the House and Senate – were put to referendum by the Fraser government in 1977. The first two of these were successful. One of the other 1977 proposals – to establish a set of rules for filling vacancies in the Senate – had originally been rejected by the Convention, but was eventually put to the people in satisfactory form. It also succeeded. Another recommendation of the Convention – on the interchange of powers between the Commonwealth and states – was put to the people by the Hawke government in 1984, but failed.

On other occasions, state governments have been involved in constitutional change without the need for a convention. For example, successful referendums were held in 1910 to give the Commonwealth power to take over state debts and in 1928 to allow the Commonwealth and the states to enter into financial agreements.

In both cases, the proposals were only put to the federal Parliament, and then the people, *after* the Commonwealth and states had reached agreement on the changes.

There have been moves to give the states a more formal role in initiating referendums. In 1975, the Australian Constitutional Convention debated, but rejected, a proposal to give states the power to initiate referendums. In 1988, the Constitutional Commission went one step further and recommended that half the states, representing a majority of Australia's population, should be able to initiate a referendum by petition. This recommendation has never been adopted by the Commonwealth, which continues to enjoy a monopoly on the power to initiate constitutional change.

COMMISSIONS

Australia has also turned to commissions of experts to generate reform proposals. In 1927, the government appointed a Royal Commission to review the Constitution chaired by Sir John Peden, a barrister and professor of law. The federal Labor Party refused to participate, but two state Labor representatives still took part. The Commission ran for three years and produced a comprehensive and considered final report. Many of the day's prominent lawyers gave evidence, including Sir Owen Dixon (a future Chief Justice of Australia) and Sir Robert Garran, a leading advocate of Federation who attended the 1897–98 Constitutional Convention as secretary to New South Wales Premier George Reid. Unfortunately, the Commission did not capture the public's attention, and failed to engender sustained political commitment. After the Scullin Labor government was elected in October 1929, the report was dropped from the national agenda. It remains a testament to the failed (but best) intentions of constitutional reform.

In 1985, Australia once more appointed a Commission to review the Constitution. The Constitutional Commission was established by Lionel Bowen (Attorney-General in the Hawke Labor government) and comprised of a range of political and legal luminaries, including former Prime Minister Gough Whitlam, former Governor-General Sir Zelman Cowen and future High Court Justice John Toohey. The Commission was chaired by Sir Maurice Byers QC, a former Commonwealth Solicitor-General. The Commission consulted widely and deeply, conducting public hearings in the capital cities and outside the major urban areas. It received close to 4000 written submissions. Its final report, delivered in June 1988, remains a comprehensive, landmark review of the Constitution. However, it has also largely been forgotten, partly because the Hawke government rushed some of its early proposals to the ballot box.

At the request of the government, the Commission delivered an interim report in April 1987, which made a number of preliminary recommendations. Bowen had requested the report early so that a referendum could be held in 1988, the bicentenary of the white settlement of Australia. Four proposals based on the interim report were put to the people on 3 September 1988. The first concerned four-year maximum terms for the federal Parliament; the second sought to guarantee both a right to vote and a 'one vote, one value' policy by requiring that the population of each electorate not deviate by more than 20 per cent from any other electorate; the third sought to recognise local government in the Constitution; the fourth sought to extend the operation of existing federal human rights guarantees in the Constitution to the states. Each of the four proposals was defeated nationally and in every state, with three of them being the most unsuccessful referendum proposals ever put to the Australian people.

The government's mismanagement of the Commission's Report was not the only problem. From the outset, the composition of the Commission attracted criticism: members were appointed, not elected, there were only two women, and many felt that the Commission had a Labor-bias. This led to staunch opposition from the non-Labor parties at Commonwealth and state levels, and indifference from state Labor leaders. The Labor government also never fully committed to the Commission or its recommendations. Prime Minister Bob Hawke took a back seat, perhaps concerned about expending his political capital on reforms that might not eventuate. So too did Treasurer Paul Keating, who instead focused on marshalling the major economic reforms of the 1980s. These problems were compounded by the government's management of the four 1988 referendums, which were rushed to the people before there had been any chance to properly consider and debate the final Report. After the unprecedented failure of the 1988 referendums, Bowen declared constitutional reform dead, saying: 'I think it's just impossible to bring about change until such time as some new civilisation develops'.[3] Labor Party Secretary Bob Hogg said that anyone in the Labor Party who proposed a referendum in 'the next 20 years ... would have a very short future'.[4] Leading political commentator Michelle Grattan also declared 'the cause of constitutional reform ... lost ... for a generation'.[5]

FIGURE 2.1 **Cartoon from the 1988 referendum**
Source: *The Australian*, 6 September 1988, p. 10. Reproduced courtesy of Graeme Dazeley.

The failure of the Constitutional Commission speaks more to inadequate political management than it does to problems with the commission model. A commission *could* be successful, but the lessons of 1988 show how important it is to select its members appropriately, find strong political backing and submit any proposals to full public debate before putting them to a referendum. Appointed commissions have the advantage of being relatively inexpensive and efficient because they can be small in size. Appointments can also be based on the skills that are needed and can represent a range of community interests. On the other hand, appointed commissions can appear elitist or, like the 1988 Constitutional Commission, partisan. That Commission sought to overcome its partisan image by undertaking community consultation, but this was only partially effective.

PARLIAMENTARY COMMITTEES

Parliamentary committees have played an important role in generating ideas for constitutional reform. From 1956 to 1959, the Joint Committee on Constitutional Review of the federal Parliament undertook a sustained and comprehensive review of the Constitution. The Committee was appointed by the Menzies government and involved politicians from all major parties. The Committee's proceedings were successful and, by and large, non-partisan. Its final report was also well received. However, the Committee never received support and commitment from the two people who had the capacity to make its findings meaningful: the Prime Minister, Sir Robert Menzies, and his Attorney-General, Sir Garfield Barwick. After its report, the government deferred action and national attention moved on. Ultimately, one of the Committee's proposals – to abolish the constitutional requirement for the size of the House to be twice that of the Senate – was unsuccessfully put to referendum in 1967.

Many of the Committee's recommendations for constitutional reform have inspired later referendums, including its recommendations for greater Commonwealth power over Indigenous affairs (1967), simultaneous elections for the House and Senate (1974, 1977 and 1984), making constitutional change easier to achieve (1974), codifying the convention regarding the filling of casual vacancies in the Senate (1977) and ensuring that members of the House of Representatives are chosen by a fair and democratic process (1974 and 1988).

Other reviews by parliamentary committees have been more specific. In 2008, the House of Representatives' Standing Committee on Legal and Constitutional Affairs coordinated a roundtable discussion on constitutional reform, inviting 14 experts to debate a range of issues. This led to a report discussing options for reform in a number of areas, including federalism, Indigenous recognition, citizenship and human rights.[6] Often, parliamentary committees have proposed a particular constitutional reform as part of a broader inquiry. On other occasions, they have looked specifically at one aspect of the Constitution. For example, the 1996 House of Representatives Standing Committee on Legal and Constitutional Affairs reported on the disqualifications for members of the federal Parliament set out in section 44 of the Constitution.

The advantage of ideas generated by parliamentary committees is that they may have a ready support base within Parliament, the only body that can initiate the referendum process. The disadvantages are that the ideas may be perceived to be partisan, responsive only to short-term political concerns, and in the interests of the Commonwealth rather than all Australians. Parliamentarians working in a committee may also be unwilling to compromise because they are bound to a pre-established party line.

Parliamentary committees can also review proposed laws to alter the Constitution before they are put to the people. In 1999, for example, Parliament established a Select Committee to review exposure drafts of the proposals to bring about an Australian republic and a new preamble to the Constitution. The Committee took public submissions and produced a report, which led to some minor changes.

GOVERNMENT

Governments, cabinets, party rooms, Prime Ministers and Attorneys-General have played important roles in generating (and occasionally in defeating) proposals for constitutional change. Each of these groups is guaranteed an important role in the constitutional reform process because the government of the day typically wields control over the House of Representatives. In practice, the House must approve reform proposals before they can be put to the people.

In 2003, for example, Prime Minister John Howard argued that the power of the Senate to defeat government legislation should be limited. He proposed that section 57 of the Constitution be amended to allow a government to call a joint sitting of both Houses of the federal Parliament to pass a law after the Senate had rejected a Bill twice, without the need for an intervening double dissolution election. The Prime Minister released a discussion paper and appointed a Consultative Group on Constitutional Change to talk with Australians about the reform. Although the Group reported that it was 'not convinced that the constitutional mechanism provided by section 57 is the best way of resolving legislative deadlocks', it also found that the Prime Minister's proposal 'received a rough passage in most of the Group's consultations', and that 'the option would have virtually no chance of community acceptance either now or in the foreseeable future'.[7] In view of these findings, the Prime Minister announced in 2004 that the proposal would not be put to a referendum.

NON-GOVERNMENT PARTIES

No proposal by a non-government party has been put to referendum, at least while the party has remained out of government. Nevertheless, the Opposition and minor parties have been fruitful sources of ideas for constitutional change. For example, in 1985 the Australian Democrats initiated a Bill to amend section 44 of the Constitution to change the circumstances in which people are disqualified from being a member of the federal Parliament. More recently, as Opposition Leader, Kevin Rudd proposed a referendum in 2007 to enable the Commonwealth to take over hospitals from the states (a position he maintained in government until the states agreed to his health reforms), while in early 2010 Opposition Leader Tony Abbott argued for a referendum to have the Commonwealth take control over the Murray–Darling basin.

INTEREST GROUPS

Many community and other interest groups have also promoted ideas for constitutional reform. Sometimes, lobbying by these groups has placed reform on the national agenda, and has played an important role in convincing the government to hold a referendum. An example of this was the 1967 referendum, which deleted racially discriminatory provisions from the Constitution and granted the Commonwealth power over Aboriginal peoples. It had been the subject of lobbying since at least the 1930s by groups including the Australian Aborigines' League and the Federal Council for the Advancement of Aborigines and Torres Strait Islanders.

More recently, the Australian Republican Movement played \a key role in securing the holding of the failed 1999 referendum on the republic, and continues to argue for another ballot. There has also been long-standing advocacy by local government to secure recognition of its existence in the Australian Constitution, which has led to unsuccessful referendums in 1974 and 1988. Undeterred, the Australian Local Government Association has sought a third referendum. Spurred on by a promise from the Rudd government to work towards constitutional recognition, it convened its own Constitutional Summit in December 2008, which was attended by approximately 600 delegates from local government bodies in every Australian state and the Northern Territory. The Summit generated strong support for constitutional recognition of local government, and proposed a number of ways in which this might be achieved.

Parliament

PARLIAMENT AS INITIATOR

In Australia's system of representative democracy, elected representatives in Parliament make and change the laws of the nation. It is not surprising, then, that alterations to the Constitution (which are still 'laws') involve a prominent role for the federal Parliament. Indeed, those who created the Australian Constitution gave Parliament sole control over the crucial first step in the formal process of constitutional reform. The federal Parliament has a monopoly on which ideas are put to a referendum.

Under section 128 of the Constitution, proposed laws to alter the Constitution must be passed by an *absolute majority* of each House of Parliament (subject only to the proposal being passed by one House twice in accordance with the deadlock provision examined below). It is not enough for a proposal to be passed only by a majority of people in each House who actually voted. Instead, a majority of the total number of representatives in the chamber must support the change, meaning that 76 votes out of 150 members in the House of Representatives and 39 votes from the 76 members of the Senate are required.

Once a proposed law to alter the Constitution has passed both Houses of Parliament, the Constitution states that the proposal 'shall be submitted' to the people voting at a referendum. Despite the apparently clear language, there is debate as to whether this need actually occur. The point has not been authoritatively settled, as it has never been challenged in court.

One view is that the Governor-General need not put the question to a referendum after it has been passed by Parliament if he or she is directed not to do so by the government. This occurred in 1915, 1965 and 1983.

In 1915, the Hughes government attempted to seek war powers by referendum, but these became unnecessary when the states agreed to refer the sought powers to the Commonwealth. In 1965, the government changed its mind about holding a referendum because incoming Prime Minister Harold Holt was less supportive of the proposals than outgoing Prime Minister Sir Robert Menzies. In 1983, the Hawke government decided to defer some of the proposals until 1984.

In 1965 and 1983, the Governor-General simply failed to issue a writ for the referendum. In 1915, the writ had already been issued, so, on the government's advice, the Governor-General revoked it by issuing a proclamation. To resolve legal doubts, Parliament then passed a law authorising the Governor-General's actions.

The framers of the Constitution had good reason to position the federal Parliament as the body that must initiate constitutional change. The framers were steeped in the British tradition of parliamentary sovereignty, and therefore expected the new Parliament to be strongly representative of the stakeholders in Federation. The people would be represented in the House of Representatives, which under section 24 of the Constitution was to be 'directly chosen by the people' on a population basis. The states, which were giving up a portion of their powers of self-government, would be represented equally in the Senate. It made sense that rejection by such a representative Parliament would be a good indicator of whether an idea should proceed to a referendum. Parliament would act as gatekeeper to save the people the cost and distraction of voting on proposals of dubious worth.

Parliament could also be expected to fully debate proposed constitutional amendments. One of the strengths of Parliament is that it reflects a range of views on an issue, and gives those views a full and public airing. By making Parliament the initiator of the referendum process, the founders were seeking to ensure that the people of Australia would be exposed to a broad discussion on the pros and cons of every amendment. Involving Parliament also meant that referendum proposals would benefit from its expertise. Parliament could be expected to be well versed in the process of drafting new laws and have a deep understanding of the operation of the Constitution.

Getting the federal Parliament on board was also important because the Commonwealth was likely to be affected by any constitutional amendment. The primary object of the Constitution is the creation of the Commonwealth itself. It was only sensible, therefore, to give the Houses of the federal Parliament a central role in proposals to change the Constitution. Of course, there are risks in giving a body the power to initiate changes to the rules that govern itself. It is no surprise that the Commonwealth Parliament has supported many changes that increase its own power, and has rejected proposals that reduce its power. Of the 44 referendum proposals put to the Australian people, 24 have sought to increase federal power, while only four would have reduced or checked that power.

Positioning Parliament as gatekeeper of constitutional reform means that many proposals have been 'Canberra-centric'. It also means that many proposals have been 'party-centric'. Often, what distinguishes a 'good idea' from an idea which becomes an actual referendum proposal is that the proposal suits the political strategy of one of the major political parties.

Sometimes, a referendum proposal may be motivated in part by a desire to cause dissent within another party or to force a political outcome. In 1951, for example, Prime Minister Robert Menzies knew that his referendum to ban the Communist Party would force the Labor Party to choose between its principles and appearing to support communism. Similarly, when Prime Minister Paul Keating proposed a vote on the republic in 1995, he knew that the Liberal Party would be divided between its more progressive and conservative elements. On other occasions, the Commonwealth Government has used a referendum proposal as a threat to force the states or the Senate to agree to change. In 1915, for example, the Hughes government threatened a referendum to centralise many powers, and used that threat to force the states to agree to refer those powers to the Commonwealth instead.

WHAT HAPPENS IF THE HOUSES OF THE FEDERAL PARLIAMENT DISAGREE?

The framers of the Constitution were pragmatists. By and large, they recognised that one of the first rules of politics is that it is very hard to get a group of politicians from across party lines to agree on anything. They also realised that the two Houses of Parliament would likely disagree on proposals for constitutional change, especially where the relative powers of the Houses were involved. For example, would the Senate ever agree to proposed amendments weakening its power in relation to the Lower House – even if it were in the national interest? Would the House of Representatives ever agree to a similar reduction in its power? In such cases, the framers asked whether a majority of representatives in just one House – perhaps motivated by self-interest – should be able to choke off important changes to the Constitution.

Prompted by these concerns, the framers introduced a deadlock provision into the referendum process. The idea for this came from the colonies (which became the states). After a Premiers' Conference in 1899, the Premiers requested the insertion of a provision intended to ensure that neither House of the federal Parliament acting alone (particularly the House of Representatives) could veto constitutional change. Under this part of section 128 of the Constitution, the agreement of just one House is sufficient to initiate a referendum. This is the case where an absolute majority of one House has passed a proposal to change the Constitution and the other House 'rejects or fails to pass it, or passes it with any amendment to which the first-mentioned House will not agree', and, after an interval of three months, this occurs a second time. The idea is that, if the Houses of Parliament disagree twice on the same proposal, the tiebreaker should be the people of Australia voting at a referendum.

In 1901, this deadlock provision might have been thought to be a powerful weapon in the hands of one of the Houses of Parliament. For example, the Senate could (as the states' House) pass a Bill over the objections of the Lower House to amend the Constitution so as to address state grievances. However, the deadlock provision has not been used in this way, even where the Senate has been under the control of the Opposition, minor parties and independents. Similarly, governments lacking control of the Senate have not generally sought to bring on a referendum by using their majority in the House of Representatives. In fact, only one set of referendums has gone ahead under the deadlock provision. These were the four unsuccessful referendum questions put forward by the Whitlam government in 1974. Of those four, the Senate had twice rejected two (a proposal to introduce 'one vote, one value' Australia-wide, and a proposal to allow the Commonwealth to borrow money on behalf of and lend money to local governments), once rejected and once failed to pass another (a proposal to introduce simultaneous elections for the House and Senate) and twice amended the fourth (a proposal to change the double majority requirement for referendums). No referendum has gone ahead with the support only of the Senate.

There are two reasons why the deadlock provision has played only a minor role. First, there is legal uncertainty about the scope of the provision. It only operates when one defiant House 'rejects or fails to pass' the proposed amendment, and there is dispute about what this means. If the Bill is listed for debate but, because of manipulation of procedural rules, never comes for debate or a vote, has it failed to pass the House? What if the House that does not want to pass the amendment Bill sends it to a committee for lengthy consideration as a delaying tactic? In practice, it may be possible for the objecting House to delay voting on the Bill until the existing parliamentary session expires and the deadlock provision is spent. The same questions arise in regard to double dissolution provisions in section 57 of the Constitution, and there also have never been satisfactorily resolved.

Secondly, the deadlock provision uses words that make it seem as though the Governor-General can decide whether or not to proceed with the referendum. The deadlock provision says that the Governor-General '*may*' submit the question to a referendum; whereas, when the law is passed by both Houses, the Constitution says that the question '*shall*' be submitted to the people. As set out above, there is a view that the Governor-General has a power not to submit a proposal even where it has been approved by both Houses. Because of the difference in language, this argument is even stronger in the case of the deadlock provision. If so, in line with the principle of responsible government, the Governor-General would not need to submit a proposal passed under the deadlock provision if so advised by the government of the day. The effect is devastating for the Senate because a government lacking a majority in the Senate can still use one of the levers of executive power to deny a referendum.

Both of these reasons help explain what happened in 1914. The Senate, which was controlled by the Labor opposition, twice passed a set of proposals to amend the Constitution. The proposals sought to give the Commonwealth power over trusts, industrial matters, railway disputes, monopolies, corporations and trade and commerce. (These same proposals had already been put to the people on 31 May 1913.) Although the proposals had the support of the Senate, the Governor-General, acting on the advice of the government, declined to put the question to a vote of the people. Others pointed out that there was also a doubt as to whether, for technical reasons, the House of Representatives had failed to pass the proposals for a second time. Either way, the deadlock provision will ordinarily be a dead letter in the hands of the Senate, and will rarely be used in the hands of the House of Representatives.

Another unresolved debate about the deadlock provision is about what, exactly, should be submitted to the people. The Constitution says that the Governor-General can submit the proposal agreed to by one House, *and* 'either with or without any amendments subsequently agreed to by both Houses'. In other words, the Constitution contemplates that, after passage twice through one House, the other House might decide that it wants to have some say by way of an amendment to that proposal before it is put to the people. The language used in this section of the Constitution is obscure and difficult to apply. It may mean that the Governor-General can submit the proposal, but only as amended by both Houses. This makes practical sense, because it means that the people are ultimately voting on something that has had the input of both Houses of Parliament, and therefore has greater legitimacy and parliamentary support. Or, it may be that the Governor-General can decide whether to submit the law with or without the amendments. This view fits better with the language used in the Constitution, but it also gives the Governor-General (or, in practice, the government) a power to go against the will of Parliament in deciding what to put to the people. This is inconsistent with the basic purpose of the provision that, when there is disagreement, neither Parliament nor the Governor-General should decide the outcome. Instead, it should be left to the people.

PARLIAMENT'S POWER TO FILL IN THE DETAILS

All referendums begin with a Bill passed by Parliament. The Bill provides the basis for the referendum, with the people voting on whether to accept the changes to the Constitution set out in it. Because Parliament determines the content of the Bill, it also decides on what the people will vote. Parliament could decide to include only one small change in a Bill, or a series of major changes across the whole Constitution. Either way, the people just get a Yes or No vote on the Bill as a whole. This was recognised by the High Court in the case of *Boland v Hughes*, when it was said that 'there is much force' in the view that 'it is for Parliament to decide … the content of the proposed law'.[8] The result is that Parliament can incorporate as many different ideas and proposals as it wants in the one Bill and, therefore, in the one referendum question.

Parliament has often sought to introduce many changes in the one question. An example of this was in 1944, when, in one referendum question, the Commonwealth sought more than ten new powers. On the other hand, a question might deal with only one subject matter, but involve a large number of textual changes to the Constitution. Hence, the 1999 question on the republic only dealt with the question of whether Australia should become a republic, but would have involved 69 separate changes to the Constitution. Many of these changes were semantic, involving the replacement of 'Governor-General' with 'President'.

Parliament also gets to decide the wording of the question asked on the ballot paper. It does so now in accordance with the *Referendum (Machinery Provisions) Act 1984* (Cth) (Referendum Act).

The form of the ballot paper has changed over the years. For most of the 20th century, voters were asked one lengthy, complicated question. For example, in the 1951 referendum, voters were asked:

> Do you approve of the proposed law for the alteration of the
> constitution entitled 'Constitution Alteration (Powers to deal
> with Communists and Communism) 1951'?

Since 1974, changes to the law have meant that a simpler (though still convoluted) format is used. It first sets out the short title of the Act, and then asks whether voters approve the law. For example, in 1974, the ballot read:

Proposed law entitled –

'An Act to alter the Constitution so as to ensure that Senate Elections are held at the same time as House of Representatives Elections'

Do you approve the proposed law?

The Referendum Act requires the question on the ballot to include the short title (for example, 'An Act to alter the Constitution so as to ensure …') of the proposed law passed by Parliament. That short title is determined by Parliament, which means that Parliament, and in effect usually the government, gets to decide the wording of the question put to the people.

Governments have sometimes been criticised for using misleading titles to describe the proposal. An example of this was in 1988 when the proposal was to entrench the principle of 'one vote, one value' (which was designed to ensure that electorate sizes would be of roughly comparable size) for Commonwealth and state elections. The question asked voters to approve a law '[t]o alter the Constitution to provide for fair and democratic parliamentary elections throughout Australia'. Critics said that the proposal would, at best, only provide for a small part of what goes to producing fair and democratic elections, and that the title was a tactic used to artificially inflate support at the referendum.

In 1999, the Republic referendum question was more evenly balanced. Polling showed that more voters supported a republic when primed to think about the monarch than when primed to think about the Governor-General. The short title and the question included references to *both* the Queen and the Governor-General. Voters were asked to mark their ballot papers Yes or No to:

A proposed law: To alter the Constitution to establish the Commonwealth of Australia as a republic with the Queen and

Governor-General being replaced by a President appointed by a two-thirds majority of the members of the Commonwealth Parliament.

The ballot paper does not set out the text of the proposed change to the Constitution. The Referendum Act presumes that, by the time voters enter the ballot box, they are already familiar with them. As we examine in the next chapter, the proposed changes are included in the official pamphlet sent by the Australian Electoral Commission to every voter.

Parliament also gets to decide how many questions are asked on each referendum day. Australians have gone to the polls for a referendum 19 times to answer 44 questions. On 14 of those occasions, Parliament asked the people more than one question. The most common number of questions has been two. On one occasion, in 1913, Parliament asked the people six questions on the same day. Where multiple questions are asked on the same day, they are all printed on one ballot paper unless the government makes a special request to the Electoral Commissioner.

CALLING THE REFERENDUM

After Parliament passes the Bill to amend the Constitution, the Governor-General issues a writ for the holding of a referendum. The writ sets out the day for the closing of the rolls of electors, the day for voting (which must be a Saturday), and the day for the returning of the writ with the results of the referendum.[9] The writ must also set out the text of the proposed law, the text of the provisions of the Constitution that are to be altered, and the text of the proposed alterations.[10] The day for voting must ordinarily be between 33 and 58 days from the time that the writ is issued[11] and the day for the returning of the writ must ordinarily be no more than 100 days after the writ is issued.[12] The Governor-General can extend these times by publishing a notice in the Government Gazette.[13]

When there is a vote at a referendum, it happens on the same day all around Australia. Referendums can be held on the same day as a Commonwealth election, but they cannot be held on the same day as a state election. Exactly half of the referendum questions put to the Australian people (22 out of 44) have been asked at the same time as a Commonwealth election.[14]

One advantage of holding a federal election and referendum concurrently is that it reduces cost, because there is no need to organise and pay for a separate ballot. However, when governments have decided to hold referendums and elections on the same day, they have been criticised for politicising the referendum, or distracting voters from properly considering the issues. An example of this was the 1946 referendum, which was held on the same day as the general election. The Liberal and Country Parties expressed concern that the referendum proposal to give the Commonwealth power over social services was politicised by the fact that a major plank of the Chifley government's election campaign was to roll out a national medical scheme, in part pursuant to the new power it was seeking.

The people

SUBMISSION TO THE PEOPLE

Once Parliament passes a proposal, it faces its most difficult and important step: submission to electors across Australia. The people play a special role in lawmaking when it comes to constitutional change. Ordinarily, after a law passes through the Houses of Parliament, it goes to the Governor-General for the Royal Assent. In the case of referendums, the Constitution places the people between the Houses of Parliament and the Governor-General. In this sense, they are a third 'House'.

The first draft of the Australian Constitution prepared in 1891 did not directly involve the people in the process of constitutional change. One delegate to the 1891 Convention, Charles Kingston, who was later to become Premier of South Australia, proposed the use of the popular referendum for both constitutional amendment and, in certain circumstances, for ordinary legislation. Another delegate, Richard Chaffey Baker of South Australia, also canvassed these ideas in a booklet that he provided to other delegates, but ultimately rejected the idea of popular referendum because he believed that it would undermine the representative principles of what was to become Australia's political system. At the 1891 Convention, popular referendum was excluded from the draft Constitution. Instead, the draft adopted the United States' model, in which proposals for constitutional change need approval from conventions of elected representatives (and not directly from the people).

As the framers consulted more widely over the 1891 draft, it became clear that representative democracy would not be sufficient when it came to adopting, and later changing, the Constitution. There was precedent for the alternative idea of putting such questions to the people, with the Swiss Constitution permitting constitutional amendments to be made by majority vote, and South Australia having successfully trialled a popular referendum in 1896. At first, there was strong opposition to such a radical idea. Sir Henry Parkes, the father of the Federation movement, was concerned that referendums placed the Constitution in the hands of a 'mob of people'.[15] Sir Samuel Griffith, the first Chief Justice of Australia, argued that a direct vote would be impractical: how, he asked, could a question possibly be put to 'millions of people'?[16] Despite such eminent opposition, the push for direct democracy by way of referendum ultimately proved stronger, resulting in the present section 128 of the Constitution.

The Constitution sets out who votes on a constitutional amendment only in broad terms. In 1901, the Constitution provided that the proposal had to be submitted to the people of every state qualified to vote in elections for the House of Representatives. In 1977, a referendum was passed that rewrote the words of section 128 to extend the vote to electors in each territory as well (however, these new voters are only to be counted for the purpose of the national tally, and not the separate vote of the people of each state). Territory voters first participated in a referendum in 1984.

The referendum proposal must be submitted 'in each State and Territory to the electors qualified to vote for the election of members of the House of Representatives'. Under section 24 of the Constitution, the House of Representatives must be 'chosen by the people of the Commonwealth'. Within that broad constraint, Parliament decides who can vote. Since 1901, the group of people eligible to vote for the House of Representatives, and so in referendums, has greatly expanded. At the time of Federation, most women and Indigenous Australians could not vote. Soon after, the *Commonwealth Franchise Act 1902* extended the franchise to women, but (in section 4) denied the voting rights of 'aboriginal native[s] of Australia'. It took until 1962 to amend the *Commonwealth Electoral Act 1918* to extend universal adult suffrage to Aboriginal people. Even then, full equality at federal elections for them did not occur until 1983, when the Act was amended to make enrolment for and voting in federal elections compulsory for Indigenous people as it is for other Australians. In 1973, the voting age was lowered from 21 to 18 years.

Today, a person of at least 18 years of age who is an Australian citizen (or a British subject enrolled to vote in Australia before 26 January 1984) can vote in a referendum. There are exceptions for: people who are of unsound mind and cannot understand the nature and significance of enrolment and voting; people who have been convicted of treason or treachery and have not been pardoned; and prisoners serving a sentence of three years or longer. Of course, people can only vote if they have taken the trouble to join the electoral roll. That roll closes three working days after the issue of the writ for the referendum.[17]

The Referendum Act has been drafted to ensure that everyone who is entitled to vote can in fact vote. If people are going to be out of the country, they can enter a postal vote. The law even sets out a way for Australians who are in Antarctica to vote.

Voting in referendums is compulsory. In fact, the law does not just say that it is compulsory; it states that it is a *duty*. In other words, it is part of what comes with being a citizen of Australia. If a person breaches this without a legitimate excuse, they can be fined $20, with the penalty rising to $50 if the person contests the fine. In practice, the duty to vote is really a duty to attend the polling booth: the ballot is secret, so voters cannot be penalised for not voting, or voting informally, so long as they attend.

Because constitutional changes can alter Australia's democratic structure, it can be argued that the duty to vote in referendums is greater than the duty to vote in ordinary elections. Reflecting this, in 1915, the Hughes government initiated compulsory voting on an experimental, temporary basis for referendums, but not for elections. The idea was to have compulsory voting at referendums to be held in 1915, but they were never held. In 1924, compulsory voting was made permanent for both referendums and elections.

Even before voting became compulsory, turnout at referendums was reasonably high. The lowest turnout was for Australia's first referendum in 1906, where just over 50 per cent of electors voted. But turnout was generally between 60 per cent and 70 per cent until 1924. Today, under the system of compulsory attendance, the turnout rate is extremely high. In the 1999 referendum, for example, turnout was 95.1 per cent, a slightly higher rate than the 2007 House of Representatives election, for which turnout was 94.8 per cent.

The law makes clear that voting at referendums is to be free of harassment, intimidation and undue influence. It is an offence to bribe a voter to vote in a particular way, to take advantage of people who are sick or old, or to interfere more generally with the liberty of someone to vote in a referendum.

DELIBERATION

When Australians vote in a referendum, they are being asked to make long-term decisions about how the nation is run and how power is to be exercised on their behalf. Constitutions are meant to endure, and voters in a referendum are asked not just to make a decision for their generation, but also for the generations that will follow. The framers recognised that such decisions should not be made lightly, and only after careful consideration and extensive debate. Their own experience reflected this, with the debate over Federation running for much of the second half of the 19th century, with a particular intensity during the 1890s.

Initially, the framers set down that referendums should be put to the Australian people between two and three months after the proposed change had been passed by Parliament. This was later changed to between two and six months. The historical record is not clear on why the period was extended. A leading constitutional scholar from the early 1900s, W Harrison Moore, said that these times were fixed 'to afford sufficient time for the electors to inform themselves of the issue and to prevent undue delay'.[18] The idea was that people should cast a vote on the basis of full information and free from the heat of the moment. Only then could Australians not just *vote* in referendums, but actually *deliberate*. The framers did not set out a detailed scheme in the Constitution for how this deliberation was to take place: they left that to Parliament. We set out in the next chapter the scheme enacted by Parliament for this purpose.

In the spirit of deliberation, the Referendum Act contemplates that Australians will come together in public meetings to discuss the referendum proposals, and tries to ensure that those meetings are effective and that everyone can participate. Under section 134 of the Act, it is an offence, punishable by a fine of $500, to try to disrupt a public meeting held in relation to a referendum. The Act even gives the chair of the meeting a power to ask a person who is disrupting a meeting to leave under police escort. Someone who disobeys such a direction can be fined $1000 or be jailed for six months.

The deadlock provision (which enables a constitutional change to be put to the people where it has been approved by only one House of Parliament) does not include a minimum and maximum period within which a referendum must be held. Section 128 says only that the Governor-General may submit the proposal to the electors. One view is that the same time limits as for other proposals are implicit. But it seems more likely that there is no limitation. It is difficult to work out why the framers incorporated different time periods according to whether an amendment has been approved by one House of Parliament or two. Maybe they thought that, if it has only been approved by one, but rejected by the other, there would have been more debate in Parliament – so there was no special need to create a separate period of debate for the people. Alternatively, the lack of a specified time period may simply be a drafting oversight. This may be exactly the type of omission that the framers thought would be corrected by a future referendum. If so, more than a century later, the problem persists.

THE 'DOUBLE MAJORITY'

Once it was decided that the people's approval would be the critical step in the process of constitutional change, the question became: what degree of support from the people should be sufficient? Too little and the change could not truly be said to have won endorsement from the people. Too much, such as a two-thirds majority, and the Constitution would become almost impossible to change.

The framers sought to balance out these concerns by requiring more than a simple majority of the people voting at the referendum. They imposed instead a double majority requirement. For a referendum to be approved, a proposed change to the Constitution must receive support from:

- a majority of voters Australia-wide (a *national majority*); and
- a majority of voters in a majority of the states (a *state majority*).

Only a resounding endorsement from the people of the nation and the people of the states is sufficient to amend the Constitution. The referendum process thereby reflects both the *national* and *federal* elements of Australian democracy.

Since 1977, as a result of a constitutional amendment, referendum questions have been submitted to voters in the territories as well as the states. However, there is no requirement that a referendum be approved in the territories as part of the state majority requirement, meaning that territory votes only count towards the national majority.

VOTING

Voting at a referendum occurs in the same way as for a general election: people mark their ballot paper in secret in a booth and place their completed vote in a ballot box. A vote is cast by writing 'Yes' or 'No' in the space provided on the ballot paper. This means the process is even simpler than that for ordinary elections, where voters write numbers next to what can be a long list of candidates' names. The words 'Yes' and 'No' have been the recognised ways of voting in referendums since 1967. Until the 1926 referendum, electors put a '✗' next to 'Yes' or 'No' to indicate their vote. In referendums from 1928 to 1951, electors put a '1' and '2' next to 'Yes' and 'No'.

Even though the Referendum Act requires voters to write 'Yes' and 'No' on their ballot paper, it also requires the electoral officials who count the votes to give effect to the intentions of the voter. This means that a vote can be counted as Yes or No even though the voter does not use those words.

The Australian Electoral Commission produces a guide before referendums about which ballot papers count as formal and which count as informal. For the 1999 referendum, a vote was counted as Yes if the voter wrote 'Yes', 'Y', 'OK', 'sure', 'definitely' or if the voter drew a '✓'. A person could vote No by writing 'No', 'N', 'never' or 'definitely not'. A '✗' did not count as either Yes or No and was considered informal. This was because a cross mark can be used both to indicate support *and* disapproval, and so does not provide a clear intention on the part of the voter. In 1988 in the lead-up to the referendum held that year, the Hawke government sought to have a Bill passed that would have counted all ticks and crosses as informal, but this did not occur after it was opposed by the Coalition and the Democrats. On the eve of the 1988 referendum, the Opposition sought to pass the same Bill, but this was opposed by the government on the grounds that some people had already voted. The result was that a '✓' was counted as Yes, but a '✗' did not count at all.

The practice of the Australian Electoral Commission (and its predecessor, the Commonwealth Electoral Office) since 1906 has been to not count informal votes towards determining whether a majority of voters approve or disapprove the change to the Constitution. The effect of this can be explained by an example. Suppose 49 per cent of electors voted Yes, 46 per cent voted No and 5 per cent voted informally. The practice is to consider that proposal as having been approved because a majority of votes formally cast were in favour of the proposal. This practice has never been tested in the courts. Section 128 states that a proposal is passed if 'in a majority of the States a majority of the electors voting approve the proposed law, and if a majority of all the electors voting also approve the proposed law'. It might be argued that an informal vote is still a 'vote' and so should be counted as being a No for the purposes of determining whether there is a majority for the Yes case. If this approach were taken, it would make success at a referendum much more difficult, and in our example above would mean that the referendum would fail 51 per cent to 49 per cent.

Referendum votes are counted by Commonwealth officials. The Governor of each state, the Chief Minister of the Australian Capital

Territory, and the Administrator of the Northern Territory may appoint a scrutineer to verify the results of voters within their jurisdiction[19] and may request a recount.[20] The power of the states to appoint scrutineers has been part of Australia's referendum process since the first referendum in 1906,[21] and reflects the state and territory interests at stake when Australians vote on the Constitution.

The states

When Australia became a nation in 1901, it also became a federation of states. As stated in the preamble to the United Kingdom statute that enacted Australia's Constitution, the people of the colonies agreed to 'unite in one indissoluble Federal Commonwealth'.

Getting agreement from the colonies (which became the six states) was a necessary step in the formation of Australia. The colonies were being asked to hand over much of their power to a new central government. For example, they would no longer have control of what and who came in and out of their state: customs and trade policy would be something for the Commonwealth to decide. The Commonwealth could tax their citizens, and it could spend the money in other states, or on the Commonwealth itself. Interpreting the Constitution, and determining what the Commonwealth and states could and could not do, would be the High Court of Australia – a Court full of judges appointed and paid by the Commonwealth.

The states were handing over a lot, and feared that they would be forced to hand over even more in the future. This was why it was seen as essential that the Constitution give the states, and particularly the small states, a special say in any attempt to amend the Constitution. This is reflected in section 128, which does not conceive of Australia as one, undifferentiated whole, but rather as a nation comprised of state units. Hence, the section operates on the basis that a proposal to change the Constitution is submitted not to the people voting as a whole, but shall be submitted to electors 'in each State and Territory'. The protections provided to the states by section 128 are set out below.

THE STATE MAJORITY REQUIREMENT

The first protection for the states is the double majority requirement. The six original states remain the only states of the Commonwealth; therefore, a majority of the people voting Yes in at least four of the six states is required for the referendum to succeed. The framers had expected the number of states to increase, perhaps as subdivisions of existing states, through the incorporation of territories, or even as a result of the expansion of Australia into the broader Pacific region. If any of these had occurred, it might have become slightly easier to satisfy the 50 per cent-plus-one in a majority of states requirement. For example, if just one more state is added (such as if the Northern Territory achieves statehood), approval in four states would still be sufficient for a referendum to succeed, but this could be achieved by a Yes vote in 'four out of seven' states, as opposed to the current 'four out of six'.

The effect of the state majority requirement is that any three states currently have a veto over constitutional change. If a majority of voters in favour of change fails to materialise in three states, this determines the outcome even if there is a clear national majority. This happened in the 1977 referendum to introduce simultaneous elections for the Senate and House of Representatives. A substantial majority of the nation approved the change (62.2 per cent), but it failed when there was not a majority in support of change in Tasmania, Queensland and Western Australia.

SPECIAL PROTECTIONS FOR THE STATES

The framers decided that the state majority requirement was not enough to secure state interests, particularly those of the small states. In particular, there was concern that four or more states might band together to pass a referendum that badly affected the interests of the people of another state. Without special rules, the other states could, for example, change the Constitution to abolish the state of Tasmania or Western Australia, and divide up its people, land and resources among the rest of the states. The framers sought to meet this concern by incorporating special requirements for the approval of particular types of amendments that affect a state.

The special requirements are triggered for the following types of amendments:

1   Changes 'diminishing the proportionate representation of any State in either House of the Parliament, or the minimum number of representatives [currently set at five] of a State in the House of Representatives';
2   Changes that 'increase, diminish, or otherwise alter the limits of the State';
3   Changes 'in any manner affecting the provisions of the Constitution in relation thereto' (that is, in relation to the state).

In any of these circumstances, the amendment to the Constitution only succeeds if in addition to the double majority requirement it receives majority approval in the affected state.

None of these special protections have ever been invoked. The closest Australia came was in the 1977 referendum to give Territorians the right to vote in referendums. There was a view that this proposal, by changing the calculation for determining what amounts to the success at a referendum, could have engaged the last of the special protections in respect of every one of the six states. If this had been the case, a No vote of any one state could have killed the proposal. Ultimately, all six states voted Yes, and the scope of these protections was not tested. Nevertheless, they remain important to constitutional reform, and can exert a powerful influence over the kinds of proposals that the Commonwealth believes have a realistic chance of success in a referendum.

The reason for the first protection is clear. It deals with the risk that states might try to increase their power at the Commonwealth level by reducing the representation of other states in the federal Parliament. The protections would, for example, apply to a proposal to replace the equal representation of each state in the Senate with a system based on each state's relative share of the Australian population. In such a case, the first protection would require approval of the change by a majority of voters in every state whose proportionate representation in the Senate would be reduced (that is, likely every state except New South Wales and Victoria).

This first protection has never been in issue because Australians have not been asked to vote on a measure that would change state representation in the Houses of Parliament. This is despite the fact that there have been complaints that the Senate is unrepresentative because it gives Tasmania (with a population of 503 000) the same number of Senators as New South Wales (with its population of 7 100 000). (Former Prime Minister Paul Keating, for example, famously described the Senate as 'unrepresentative swill'.[22]) The fact that no such proposal has ever been put to a referendum reflects the unlikelihood that it would be passed by the people of the affected state, and thus that the special protection for states placed in section 128 is achieving its desired effect.

The second protection applies to amendments changing a state's territorial boundaries. Again, no referendum has ever been put that would have engaged this protection.

The last protection has been the subject of much debate, in part because it uses technical, outdated, legal language. However, even in the language of lawyers, it is not clear what this last protection means. One option is that this third protection should be read as part of the second, so that the words 'in relation thereto' mean only 'in relation to the limits of the State'.

It can also be argued that this protection applies to proposals that would amend:

- any provision of the Commonwealth Constitution, no matter which section, where that amendment would affect, in some way, the subject matter of the special protections set out in section 128;
- any of the special protections themselves (but not other provisions of the Constitution); or
- the Commonwealth Constitution in a way that would affect state constitutions.

There are good reasons for adopting any one of these views. The text of the Constitution certainly fails to supply a clear answer. Each interpretation would give substantial protection to states against attempts to change the Constitution in a way that affected their fundamental interests. The fact that the scope of this protection remains unclear is problematic. Governments may be deterred from putting referendum proposals to the people where any one of these interpretations may be invoked.

The Executive

After a proposal to change the Constitution has been passed by Parliament and supported by the necessary popular majorities at a referendum, it has only one more stage to pass. It must also be presented to the Governor-General for Royal Assent. This is largely a formality. The principle of responsible government means that the Governor-General must, with only rare exceptions, act on the advice of the government of the day. In practice, the government will ask the Governor-General to assent to an amendment that has been approved by the people.

This last formal step is symbolically significant. When the Governor-General, as the head of the Executive, and representing the Crown in Australia, gives his or her approval to a referendum, it means that the measure has been approved by two of the three branches of Australia's government and by the people. Only the courts have not had to approve the change – a fact that reflects their independence from political matters.

There are two unlikely scenarios under which the Royal Assent might be more than just a formality. First, a referendum might be passed at the same time that an election is held, and that election produces a change of government from one that supports the proposal to one that opposes it. Second, the proposal might have been put to the people at a referendum without the support of the government after being twice passed by the Senate. In either case, the government could, at least in theory, require the Governor-General to refuse assent to the change. However, it is very unlikely that a government would instruct the Governor-General to withhold assent to a proposal that has gained the support of the nation and of the people of enough states.

The judiciary's special role

Of the three branches of government – Parliament, the Executive and the judiciary – only the judiciary has no formal role in approving constitutional change. There is a good reason for this: the judiciary has a special role in policing the process of constitutional change and interpreting amendments once they have been made.

The High Court has interpreted constitutional amendments in the same way as other parts of the Constitution. It first looks at the text itself. What words are used? Do they have a clear and ordinary meaning? Does the context in which the words are used help explain their meaning? Particular attention is also given to the parliamentary debates surrounding the Constitution Alteration Bill, the official referendum publications and the meaning of the words at the time of the referendum.

What happens when referendums fail? If a referendum proposal is rejected, should the High Court be reluctant to interpret the Constitution to achieve the goals of the failed referendum? The High Court squarely confronted this issue in the *WorkChoices Case* of 2006.[23] The issue was whether Parliament could rely on its power over corporations to make laws about industrial relations. The people had, on several occasions, voted No to referendums that sought to give the Commonwealth a power of that kind. It was argued that the High Court should now interpret the Constitution in a way that mirrored the views of the people. The High Court rejected this argument. In its view, failed referendums are of no use. They can fail for many reasons, and it cannot be unequivocally said that a referendum proposal was rejected because Australians believed that the change should not be made. For example, a failed referendum to give the Commonwealth a new power might simply suggest that Australians believed that the Commonwealth already had that power. Further, there is a problem of equivalence. The question to which Australians voted No is almost always different, even if only in subtle ways, from the question confronted by the Court. In any event, the High Court found that the view of the Australian people of what the Constitution does or ought to say is irrelevant. Under the Constitution, the judges of the High Court, and not the people, have ultimate responsibility for interpreting the Constitution.

Updating the Constitution

After a proposed law to alter the Constitution receives the Royal Assent, it is no longer a *proposed* law: it is a law holding special status as part of the Constitution. Having been created through the referendum process, it can then only be changed through that same process. It is difficult to change the Constitution; it is just as hard to change it back.

Once the amendment becomes law, it is traditional in Australia to present the Constitution as one consolidated document, with the amendment appearing intermixed with the original text of the Constitution. The Constitution is thus presented as one consistent, coherent legal instrument.

This is a stylistic choice. The country on which Australia based much of its Constitution – the United States – does things differently. The United States Constitution is displayed by first setting out the text of the original 1789 Constitution followed by the amendments to it in the order of their making (hence, the amendments are referred to at the end of the document as the First Amendment, Second Amendment and so on). Because the amendments to the United States Constitution are shown in chronological order, and have often been made in response to events of high national importance, the United States Constitution shows the arc of American history.

When the Australian Constitution is read from beginning to end, the broader context of its amendments is only implicit. But this broader context should not be forgotten. Australians have found it necessary to amend the Constitution on eight occasions in more than a century. Some of these have reflected the need to make minor corrections to deal with small issues, such as the retirement age of High Court judges. Others have reflected the need to respond to the High Court interpreting the Constitution in unexpected or inconvenient ways. One referendum in particular – the referendum in 1967 on Aboriginal peoples – reflected a fundamental change in national attitudes. What is common to each, however, is that they all resulted from a remarkable concurrence on the merits of the reform proposal between key institutions of government and the people voting at a referendum, both as Australians and as residents of the several states.

3

REFERENDUM CAMPAIGNS

Introduction

For a referendum to succeed, Australians must resoundingly vote Yes. The task of persuading Australians to do this has typically fallen to a Yes campaign composed of politicians, interest groups and others who support the change. Ranged against the Yes campaign, a No campaign has typically argued for the status quo. Both can be well-oiled political machines, with the cash and expertise to target swinging voters with an effective message. This chapter is about the Yes and No campaigns that have been a feature of Australian referendums since the early 20th century, the kinds of arguments they have made, and the ways they have gone about persuading Australians to support their point of view.

Yes campaigns have generally been spearheaded by the government of the day. Typically, the government has initiated the idea, provided it with parliamentary support and penned the official Yes case. The No campaign has often lacked an identifiable figurehead. Sometimes the Opposition has managed the No campaign, as was the case in 1988 when Peter Reith, the Shadow Attorney-General, marshalled disparate groups into a united and highly effective front against the four referendum questions put that year. On one occasion, in 1951, a particular member of the Opposition (HV Evatt) was the figurehead of the No campaign. On other occasions, the No campaign has been managed by a loose coalition of opponents. This was the case for the No campaign to the Simultaneous Elections proposal in the 1977 referendum, which was managed by Senators across major and minor parties. In addition to these groups, Australian referendums have attracted support and opposition from a broad range of interest groups.

Parliament gave official recognition to the Yes and No campaigns for the first time in the 1999 republic referendum, when it enacted temporary legislation to establish and fund official Yes and No committees. Appointed from participants at the 1998 Constitutional Convention, the committees were charged with overseeing the Yes and No campaigns. Each received $7.5 million in public funding, and was prohibited from accepting donations or raising other funds. All advertising materials produced by them were subject to oversight by the Ministerial Council on Government Communications.

In 1999, the government also established a 'Neutral' campaign committee with $4.5 million in public funding. This campaign was charged with preparing a 'Neutral' pamphlet to be distributed to voters. This pamphlet – entitled 'Know Your Facts' – was prepared by a panel of five eminent Australians and contained information on Australia's system of government, referendum processes and background information on the referendum questions. The panel was chaired by Sir Ninian Stephen, a former Governor-General and High Court Justice.

Advertising

Parliament has been reluctant to restrict public debate about referendums. In part, this reflects Parliament's long respect for free speech. The High Court has also said that there are constitutional limitations on the extent to which Parliament can restrict speech during the time of a referendum. In 1997 in *Lange v Australian Broadcasting Corporation*,[1] a unanimous Court said that:

> [s]ection 128, by directly involving electors in the States and in certain Territories in the process for amendment of the Constitution, necessarily implies a limitation on legislative and executive power to deny the electors access to information that might be relevant to the vote they cast in a referendum to amend the Constitution.

Referendums, the High Court said, require the 'informed decision' of the people, and the government and Parliament should generally only intervene in the process to help achieve that aim.[2]

Consistent with this aim, the *Referendum (Machinery Provisions) Act 1984* (Cth) (Referendum Act) makes it an offence to print, publish or distribute any information likely to mislead or deceive electors in relation to their vote at the referendum. However, the authorities have found it difficult to enforce this rule. The boundary separating misleading from non-misleading information, especially when it comes to matters of opinion, is unclear. Because courts are reluctant to restrict speech, they err on the side of allowing the publication of information in such cases. In fact, the courts have never applied the prohibition on misleading information during a referendum campaign; but, they have considered the prohibition in the context of an *election* campaign. There, courts have said that the prohibition is very limited in applying only to statements that affect the physical casting of a person's vote.[3] The result is that the prohibition does not apply to statements intended to influence who or what people vote for.

COMMONWEALTH GOVERNMENT ADVERTISING

The Commonwealth Government is limited in how much money it can spend on referendums. Under section 11(4) of the Referendum Act, it is limited to funding:

- the preparation, printing, posting and translation of the official pamphlets containing the Yes and No cases; and
- the Australian Electoral Commission (AEC) to provide information relating to the proposal or its effect.

Beyond this, the Commonwealth cannot spend money on arguments for or against a referendum proposal. This means that, unless special amendments are made to the Referendum Act (as occurred for the 1999 referendum so as to permit funding of the Yes and No campaign committees), the government cannot fund advertisements on television, radio and the Internet giving arguments for and against the proposal, or even just information to explain the changes (other than through the AEC). These restrictions only apply to the Commonwealth Government: state and local governments, political parties and major interest groups have no restriction on what they can spend.

The High Court gave a strict interpretation to these limits on the Commonwealth in its 1988 decision in *Reith v Morling*.[4] Peter Reith, the plaintiff, was the Shadow Attorney-General and the spearhead of the No campaign. He challenged two government-funded advertisements about the 1988 referendums that the government argued were 'neutral'. One advertisement said that the proposed amendments had been developed after wide consultation with the public, after many public meetings and on the basis of many public submissions. The second advertisement informed voters that, in the referendum, 'you have the opportunity ... to review our Constitution'. The Court held that both advertisements encouraged

IF THERE CAN be said to be a father of our Constitution, it would be Sir Henry Parkes.

But in fact, the draft Constitution was the work of many men.

And as many points of view.

People from each of the Australian colonies took part, each putting forward the view of the people they represented.

However, before the Constitution was adopted, it was approved by the people.

By referendum.

The same requirement applies today.

Before any amendments can be made to the Constitution, they too must gain the approval of the people.

That is why on September 3, you will be asked to say yes or no to the four proposed amendments.

1

A Proposed Law: To alter the Constitution to provide for four-year maximum terms for members of both Houses of the Commonwealth Parliament.

2

A Proposed Law: To alter the Constitution to provide for fair and democratic parliamentary elections throughout Australia.

3

A Proposed Law: To alter the Constitution to recognise local government.

4

A Proposed Law: To alter the Constitution to extend the right to trial by jury, to extend freedom of religion, and to ensure fair terms for persons whose property is acquired by any Government.

FIGURE 3.1 Government advertising from the 1988 referendum

Source: *The Advertiser*, 27 August 1988, p. 24. Reproduced courtesy of Commonwealth of Australia.

people to vote for the proposal and that the government could not fund them. During that same referendum, it was even suggested that government printing and distribution of copies of the Constitutional Commission report from which the reform proposals came would have been against the law.

The Referendum Act allows the AEC to provide information on the effect of the proposal, but this is generally understood in a narrow way. In 1984, when introducing the Bill for the current Referendum Act, Senator Gareth Evans said that the information was to be impartial, meaning 'an explanation of what a particular proposal does. It does not mean arguments for or against a proposal'.[5]

Under the Referendum Act, the government is required to print copies of the proposed alterations and make them available at AEC offices around Australia. The government must also take out advertisements in newspapers around Australia explaining that these copies are available, and where they can be viewed.

In addition to these responsibilities, in 1999, the AEC conducted a broad public education campaign. The campaign was divided into three phases: encouraging enrolment, explaining voting services and explaining how to vote formally. To this end, the Commission spent approximately $7.5 million and produced six television commercials, eight radio commercials and seven print press commercials. The commercials were translated into 17 different languages in the ethnic press; 25 languages for ethnic radio; 11 languages for ethnic television; and 20 Indigenous languages. Key information about the referendum was available in Braille and large print. The AEC also maintained a telephone inquiry service to answer questions about the referendum.

OTHER ADVERTISING

Groups outside the Commonwealth Government have often played a major role in the referendum debates. These groups are not covered by the funding restrictions that apply to the Commonwealth.

State governments in particular have played a prominent role, both for and against referendums. In 1928, state governments issued official statements urging voters to support the proposal to allow the Commonwealth and states to enter into agreements about borrowing money. More often, states have opposed referendums. For example, state government opposition was important in securing the defeat of the 1944 referendum to secure a range of temporary powers for the Commonwealth to assist with postwar reconstruction.

The media has also played a prominent role in referendum campaigns. Newspapers around Australia editorialised in favour of voting Yes at the 1999 referendum on a republic. The *Daily Telegraph*, the main Sydney tabloid newspaper, went so far as to distribute 'Vote Yes' stickers with copies of the paper.

There are few legal limits on non-Commonwealth Government advertising. When such advertising appears in traditional media, such as newspapers, the Referendum Act requires that it include the name and address of the person authorising it. This prevents anonymity becoming a shield for misleading or defamatory statements. Beyond that, there are no special restrictions, with political and other interests of all kinds entitled to spend as much money as they wish advocating a Yes or No vote.

When the advertising is contained in non-traditional media, there are even fewer restrictions. In the case of the Internet, there is no need to authorise material appearing as part of general commentary on a website. There is also no need to authorise material on t-shirts, badges, pens, balloons and a host of other advertising paraphernalia.

The official pamphlet

Since 1912, the Referendum Act has allowed the government to distribute an 'official pamphlet' containing Yes and No cases to all

FIGURE 3.2 **Liberal Party advertisement in the 1951 referendum on communism**
Source: *Sydney Morning Herald*, 16 September 1951, p. 8. Reproduced courtesy
of the Liberal Party of Australia.

electors. The pamphlet was introduced by the Fisher Labor government, which had been stung by the heavy defeat of its 1911 referendum proposals (neither of which achieved more than 40 per cent of the national vote). The government believed it had lost the referendums because of an exaggerated and uncontrolled No campaign. The purpose of the pamphlet was to inject a rational element into the debate, thereby increasing the chances of referendum success. Attorney-General William Hughes envisaged the case for either side being put in an 'impersonal, reasonable and judicial way', and appealing to 'reason rather than to the emotions and party sentiments',[6] while Prime Minister Andrew Fisher was optimistic about the Yes/No pamphlet, remarking: 'I have no doubt at all that the case will be put from both sides impersonally and free from any suggestion of bias or misleading on the one side or the other'.[7]

FIGURE 3.3 Image from the cover page of the 1999 official Yes/No pamphlet
Source: 1999 Yes/No pamphlet. Reproduced courtesy of Commonwealth of Australia.

The law provides for the Yes and No cases to be authorised by the members of Parliament who voted for and against the proposal. A majority of the parliamentarians who approved the Bill may authorise the Yes case and a majority of those who opposed the Bill may authorise the No case. Unanimous consent is not needed, leaving some parliamentarians with no input into the official pamphlet. This happened in 1946 when the Labor government did not consult with the members of the Liberal and Country parties who supported the three referendum Bills. In 1999, the Labor Party voted against the Preamble Bill in Parliament, but chose to withdraw its opposition before the drafting of the No case. This left Independent MP Peter Andren as the only parliamentarian who had voted against the Bill remaining in active opposition. The law refers to authorisation of the Yes and No case by those who voted for or against the Bill *and* who 'desire' to forward an argument to the AEC. Andren relied on the position that, although the Labor Party had voted against the Bill, it no longer sought to put an argument against it, and so he was entitled to take sole responsibility for drafting the official No case.

The parliamentarians who authorise the case need not actually draft the arguments themselves. For the 1999 republic referendum, the Yes and No cases, although ultimately authorised by parliamentarians, were drafted by the respective Yes and No committees.

The law does not require an official pamphlet for each referendum. The requirement only applies if the members of Parliament *want* the pamphlet to be produced. In 1919, 1926 and 1928, no official pamphlet was produced. In 1919, the government said that there was insufficient time to prepare the pamphlet. In 1926, supporters were so divided in their reasons for support that it was impossible to produce one coherent argument. In 1928, support was so widespread that the government believed a pamphlet was unnecessary. On two occasions – the 1967 referendum on Aboriginal people and the 1977 referendum on a retirement age for federal judges – there was a Yes case but not a No case.

The word limit for each of the Yes and No cases is 2000 words (with no provision for images, diagrams and the like). The cases are allocated the same amount of words regardless of how much parliamentary support there was for the proposal. This means that, even if only one parliamentarian votes against the proposal, the No case still has the right to the same amount of space as the Yes case.

If there are multiple referendums on the one day, then all the arguments for and against are printed in the one pamphlet. The word limit for each proposal can be added together to form one overall word limit, and there are no word limits for the individual proposals. This means that, if five proposals are put on the same day, the total word limit will be 10 000 words for each side; and, if desired, 5000 of those words could, for example, be used for the first proposal with fewer words allocated to the others.

The Yes and No cases need not use up all of their allotted space. In 1999, for example, the Yes case used far fewer than its allotted words. Because the Yes and No cases were printed on opposing pages, the second half of the pamphlet had a series of blank left-hand pages where the Yes case could have been.

Once they are ready, the arguments are forwarded to the Australian Electoral Commissioner. The Commissioner must print them to create an official pamphlet and post the pamphlet to all the electors at least 14 days before the voting day. The official pamphlet must also show the proposed textual alterations and additions to the Constitution. In 1999, because of the number of proposed changes to the Constitution, the official pamphlet set out the Constitution in full with the proposed changes marked up in the text. The law is explicit that the official pamphlet must be printed and posted to each elector. The Referendum Act has never been updated to provide for other means of distribution, such as by email. In 2009, a parliamentary committee recognised the 'vast array of media forms and communication that did not exist 10 years ago, much less in

Tell Canberra NO.

There is a common theme to this referendum — more power to the central government in Canberra.

The Government is trying to undermine the independence of the Senate, one of the pillars of our democracy, and which has proved its worth in protecting Australia from the excesses of Government, such as the ID card. The Government is also trying to gain the power to order the States how to conduct their own elections. And the Government is tampering with rights – such as freedom of religion – which have been entrenched in the Australian Constitution for 87 years.

There is much more to this referendum than meets the eye.

The case for and against each question is set out clearly on the following pages. They show why you should vote NO to all 4 questions.

AUSTRALIA HAS A STRONG CONSTITUTION.

WHY WEAKEN IT?

FIGURE 3.4 Summary page for the No case in the 1988 official Yes/No pamphlet
Source: 1988 Yes/No pamphlet. Reproduced courtesy of Commonwealth of Australia.

1912', and recommended a more flexible approach to the distribution of such information.[8]

In 1988, the Australian Electoral Commissioner permitted drafters of the official Yes and No cases to send 'camera-ready' copy of their cases to the Commissioner, prepared for printing in their own choice of format. However, this method of preparing the cases caused concern that this could advantage one case over the other, so this was abandoned for 1999. In that referendum, the Commissioner published *Guidelines for Members of Parliament preparing the arguments to be sent to Electors*. Those Guidelines set out detailed requirements specifying required font, size and layout. The Commissioner permitted the pamphlets to be colour-coded such so that the Yes case was in green and the No case in red.

According to a survey by Eureka Strategic Research on the 1999 referendum, more than 80 per cent of people reported having received the official pamphlet by referendum day, but only 51 per cent said they had read some or all of it.[9]

Persuading the people

THE OFFICIAL PAMPHLET

The first official pamphlet[10] was produced for the 1913 referendums, by which the Fisher Labor government sought a range of new powers for the Commonwealth Parliament, including powers over trade and commerce, corporations, industrial matters, railways and monopolies. The pamphlet sincerely set out to achieve the aim of bringing an air of rationality to the debate. The Yes case began and concluded with:

> In order that the people may understand the reason for our attitude we here set forth the position as it appears to us.
>
> …
>
> Here, then we leave the question. We have done our part; it is for the electors to do theirs. The responsibility is theirs, and in their hands alone is the remedy.[11]

The Yes case, in language that could easily be used by proponents of constitutional reform today, urged that the Constitution was meant to change. It stated that

ours [is] a living Constitution, capable of being adapted to suit
the changing requirements of the people ... New conditions
have arisen, and no means exist to deal with them. The Federal
Parliament cannot deal with the most important problems that
confront modern society ... The States are quite unable to deal
with these [problems]; the national Parliament is powerless.
But the people must be protected and in order to protect them
the Constitution must be amended.[12]

The No case, however, hinted that the future of the official pamphlet
would involve charged language, exaggeration and mischaracterisation. It began:

This is an appeal of citizens to fellow citizens, in their common
interest and for the sake of Australia against the rash, reckless
and unreasonable wrecking of the Federal Constitution which
must result, unless the people's answer is a resounding No.[13]

The No case attacked each of the proposed powers in unrestrained,
highly emotive language. It argued that the proposed power over
trade and commerce would result in the 'nationalisation ... of all
the means of production, distribution and exchange',[14] that the
proposed corporations power was 'ruthless and reckless'[15] and that
the proposed industrial matters power would 'effectually dispose of
[the] Federation'.[16] The proposed railways power also threatened
'not only the satisfactory working and future of the Railways, but
the financial stability of the States'.[17] The proposed power over
monopolies was perhaps the most dangerous: 'if adopted, [it would]
pave the way for the introduction and adoption of ... Socialism'.[18]
The No case concluded:

[If the referendums were successful], [a] Socialistic
Government ... would pose and preside as our Dictator, while
living upon the captured earnings and savings of the whole
people, until finally the bubble project bursting plunges all

concerned into inevitable disaster …

Put into plain words, these amendments mean that the Federal Government, if Labor gets its way in the Referendum, will be enabled to become master of all the businesses in Australia and employ every person connected with them on terms fixed by its Parliament. The result would be that everybody would ultimately be a public servant dependent upon the Government which would be at the head of a universal Public Service … The electors are counseled to [vote] … with a clear, conscientious, deliberate, and final No.[19]

Despite the stridency of the No case, the introduction of the official pamphlet seemed to help the government in 1913. All six referendum questions failed, but each received more than 49 per cent of the vote and succeeded in three states (Queensland, Western Australia and South Australia). Two of the same questions had been asked two years previously, in 1911, and had received less than 40 per cent of the national vote and a majority only in Western Australia. For many observers, the official pamphlet could have been considered a success.

Almost a century on, opinions about the official pamphlet are lukewarm at best. The referendum record may also suggest that the Yes and No cases have done more to hinder than assist constitutional reform. As figure 3.5 shows, approximately one in seven referendums (including those which were so popular that a No case was not produced) have been successful where there has been an official Yes/No pamphlet. On the other hand, more than two in seven referendums without a pamphlet have been passed.

YES AND NO CASES

Since the first official pamphlet in 1913, there have been 34 Yes cases produced and 32 No cases. The subject matter of the referendums has differed, but the themes have been strikingly similar to that of the first pamphlet.

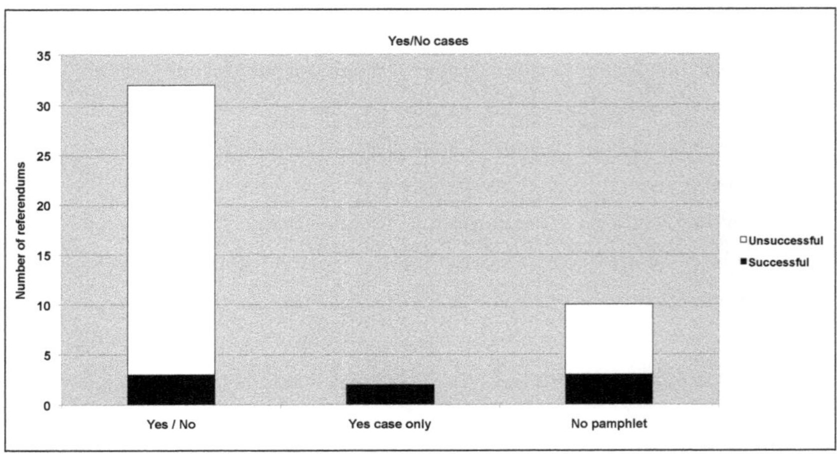

FIGURE 3.5 Success rate of referendums with and without official pamphlets

FIGURE 3.6 Most used words in official Yes/No pamphlets (larger words are used more often)

Two themes have recurred in the Yes case. First, that circumstances have changed so as to render constitutional amendment necessary. An example of this was the 1937 Yes case for the referendum seeking Commonwealth power over aviation. That case was based on the revolution in air transport which had taken place in the 36 years since the Constitution had been adopted. The Yes case stated:

> In 1900, when the Constitution was established, nobody except a few singularly prophetic authors had thought of that conquest of the air with which we are now so familiar … [A]s the least 'airminded' pedestrian knows, aeroplanes have to-day achieved the most phenomenal speed and may, in another few years, have made the existing records almost snail-like in comparison … Opposition [to the amendment] can come only from those who have failed to realize that we live in a world of vast growth and rapidly increasing complexity, and that in such a world it is an act of great folly to regard any Constitution as immutable or, for that matter, any system of government as eternal.[20]

Second, where possible, the Yes case has been at pains to emphasise that the question is not partisan, or has been produced by a process of consultation. For example, the Yes case to the 1967 proposal to break the link between the sizes of the House and Senate concluded with a statement that

> [t]his case … was prepared by the Prime Minister, the Rt Hon. Harold Holt, Leader of the Federal Parliamentary Liberal Party; by the Deputy Prime Minister, the Rt Hon. John McEwen, Leader of the Australian Country Party; and by the Leader of the Opposition, Mr Gough Whitlam, Leader of the Australian Labor Party.[21]

Three themes have recurred in the No case. First, No cases have repeatedly characterised the proposals as threatening Australian traditions and have urged voters to stick with the less risky course, the status quo. In 1951, the No case to the Communist Party referendum argued that:

OUR ADVICE — TAKE NO RISK …
Play safe and preserve the Constitution as it now stands …
PLAY SAFE BY VOTING … NO …
WARNINGS!! When in doubt say NO.[22]

This language is strikingly similar to that used in the No case for the 1999 Republic referendum:

Don't Know? Vote No
Those who don't know – should vote No – because that is the
only safe way to go …
Keep the status quo! – Vote No
Those who value the certainty and stability of our current
Constitution – should vote No[23]

Second, No cases have claimed (often with good reason) that the proposals are about centralising power in Canberra, or increasing the power of politicians. An example of the former is the 1946 No case. In that referendum, the Chifley Labor government sought powers over social services, the marketing of primary products and industrial employment. The No case claimed that the referendums would result in a nationwide army of public servants answering every question with 'I must refer it to Canberra'.[24] Reams of red tape would result, with

> huge Departments at Canberra, largely manned by people with
> no practical experience of industry or production [who] control
> our industrial [and] productive activities … To put such matters
> entirely into the hands of Canberra would be disastrous.
> Local … industries can only be handicapped … by the creation
> of a new mass of Canberra rules and regulations and boards.[25]

Similarly, in a series of capitalised exhortations, the 1988 No case urged:

Tell Canberra NO …
NO MORE POWER TO CANBERRA. VOTE No …
REJECT ANOTHER CANBERRA POWER GRAB …
DON'T LET CANBERRA RUN YOUR STATE …
STOP CANBERRA'S POWER GRAB[26]

The 1999 Republic referendum No case led with the argument that the referendum was a power grab, not by Canberra per se, but by politicians. 'The politicians will appoint the President, not the people',[27] the No case said, urging: 'Vote No to the politicians' republic'.[28]

Third, the No case has increasingly focused on an assertion that the Yes case and the proponents of reform are trying to *deceive* Australians into supporting a change that is really just about political self-interest. (Of course, many commentators have pointed out the irony of a No case authorised by politicians arguing that politicians simply cannot be trusted.) This argument is designed to tap into public distrust of politicians.

In 1977, the Simultaneous Elections referendum No case was headed: 'An Exercise in Deception'.[29] It intimated that the government was 'deliberately attempting to deceive the people of Australia' and that 'the Bill was a fraud'.[30] It concluded:

DON'T BE DECEIVED
VOTE NO[31]

In 1988 and 1999, the theme of deception was elevated to a mantra. In 1988, for example, sections of the No case were headed:

WHAT IT REALLY MEANS …
WHAT LABOR REALLY WANTS[32]

Repeatedly, the 1988 No case in the official pamphlet asked whether the government's intentions were 'sincere' or 'fair dinkum'.[33] Opponents tied the idea that the Hawke government was being deceptive to the claim that the referendum was just about giving more power to politicians:

> There is more to this proposal than meets the eye. It has hidden and dangerous consequences which would forever remove the essential checks and balances in our democratic system of government. It means more power for the Prime Minister and the Government, and less power for the States …
> *DON'T BE DECEIVED BY CANBERRA … VOTE No.*[34]

UNSCRUPULOUS CAMPAIGNING

Paul Kelly, editor-at-large of *The Australian*, has said that the 'technique of scaremongering reaches its highest political art form in the field of constitutional alteration'.[35] The official pamphlet has been one forum for this. In 1937, the No case to the proposal to give the Commonwealth power over aviation said that a Yes vote would 'wreck the State's railway systems', 'bankrupt country towns' and 'mean dearer freights and dearer food'.[36] In that same pamphlet, the No case to a referendum on giving the Commonwealth power to market goods argued, absurdly, that it was an attack on democracy. Under the heading 'Whittling away democracy', it urged:

> Once again democracy is attacked … [L]title by little control over the things that matter is stolen from the people … Here, under the cloak of technical and ambiguous language, upon the pretext of an emergency is another attempt to whittle away our self-government …

> Protect the freedom which the Constitution guarantees: Defend the 'Seamless Garment' of Australian unity: Resist every attack upon Democracy.[37]

The official No case has often been criticised for scaremongering and exaggeration. So too has the Yes case, though less often. In 1944, the Yes case argued that serious consequences would follow unless the Commonwealth were granted temporary postwar reconstruction powers. It argued that 'temporary powers must be granted now, or chaos will result'.[38] It promised a Yes would end society's ills:

> *ABOLISH POVERTY AND UNEMPLOYMENT*
> The Commonwealth Parliament, armed with these powers …
> can prevent unemployment; maintain stable prices and markets;
> and increase the comfort, security and happiness of every
> Australian family …
> *NO MORE DEPRESSIONS*
> When the Commonwealth gets these … powers, it will guard
> against another depression …
> A No vote is a vote for unemployment and depression.
> A Yes vote is a vote for full employment and prosperity.[39]

Sometimes, the official cases have been accused not only of exaggeration, but also of blatant deception. In 1946, the No case to the Social Services proposal quoted selectively from a High Court judgment to argue, contrary to expert opinion, that the Commonwealth already had the power it was seeking. This prompted a retort from the Minister for Health, Senator Nicholas McKenna, that opponents were 'guilty of the worst type of suppression'.[40]

Outside the official pamphlet, exaggeration and mischaracterisation have been even more blatant. In 1948, the Country Party leadership argued that giving the Commonwealth power over prices would establish a socialist state in Australia.[41] In 1988, the National Party claimed that extending the prohibition on establishing a religion to the states might prevent the ABC from broadcasting religious services and prevent religious people from ministering to the sick in government-run hospitals. The Reverend Fred Nile, New South

Wales state parliamentarian and then leader of the Call to Australia Party, went even further. He released a statement suggesting that religious rights could lead to legal protection for the self-immolation of widows, stoning of adulterers, amputation of thieves' limbs and female circumcision. Nile suggested there would be 'Hindu idols in Martin Place' and that the 'Imam of Lakemba' would be required to 'bless the colours of an Australian battalion'.[42] During the 1999 Republic referendum, in response to a suggestion that British citizens should not be entitled to vote in the referendum, then leading monarchist Tony Abbott suggested that it would constitute 'ethnic cleansing' of the right to vote.[43] Meanwhile, the Director of the

FIGURE 3.7 **Example of advertising by opponents of the 1999 Republic referendum**
Source: *Courier Mail*, 3 November 1999, p. 9. Reproduced courtesy of the
Australian National Flag Association – Qld.

No campaign, David Elliott, suggested that an Australian republic would be akin to a 'Hitler-style dictatorship'.[44]

Proponents of constitutional reform are now well aware that any referendum will likely attract scaremongering by those in opposition. In response, the proponents have increasingly used the official Yes case to set out pre-emptive rebuttal. In 1988, half of each of the four Yes cases comprised sections variously entitled:

WHAT A YES VOTE DOES NOT MEAN

…

WHAT THE CHANGES WILL NOT DO[45]

In 1999, the Yes case to the Republic proposal also felt compelled to set out a list of things the referendum would not do:

It would not change the flag or the national anthem.
It would not change the number of public holidays.
It would not mark a break with our tradition of stable, parliamentary democracy.
It would not alter the day-to-day operation of the Commonwealth Parliament.
It would not give the President more or different powers to those of the Queen's representative in Australia, the Governor-General.
It would not create an office of President that is more grand or expensive than that of the current Governor-General.[46]

The cost of referendums

Referendums can be expensive for the public purse. Pamphlets must be printed and posted to every elector in Australia. The government also advertises widely to ensure that as many Australians as possible turn up and vote. In 1999, the government had the further cost of funding the Yes and No campaigns. Events such as conventions, held to debate and draft referendum proposals, can also come with a significant cost. With only a couple of exceptions, each referendum Australia has held since 1901 has been more expensive in nominal terms than the last. Table 3.1 sets out a sample of the costs borne by the AEC in running referendums.[47]

In 1999, the total cost to government was even higher once the costs of the Constitutional Convention ($28 million), the official Yes and No campaigns ($15 million) and the 'Neutral' campaign ($4.5 million) are included. This gave a total public cost of approximately $114 million.

Why has the cost of referendums increased? Part of the increase is explained by inflation. For example, at 1999 rates, the 1967 referendum cost $7.9 million. Part of the increase is also explained by an increase in the number of enrolled electors. In 1967, there were just over 6 million electors; in 1999, there were nearly 12 and a half million. However, even taking account of both inflation and an increase in the number of electors, the 1999 referendum ($5.34 per elector) was still more than four times more expensive than the 1967 referendum ($1.28 per elector). The 1999 referendum was also more than two and a half times more expensive than the 1974 referendum ($2.01 per elector). The 1984 referendum was particularly expensive, working out at $7.25 per elector at 1999 rates. The rising cost of referendums reflects a range of factors, including rising real

TABLE 3.1 AEC COSTS IN RUNNING REFERENDUMS

Referendum	Cost
1906	£48 177
1951	£222 704
1967	$1 041 000
1974	$3 166 000
1984	$38 430 000
1999	$66 233 682

Source: Commonwealth of Australia, *Australian Referendums 1906–1999* CD-ROM (2000).

wages, greater use of expensive public communications such as television on the part of the government and the AEC, and a commitment to ensuring that Australians can vote regardless of whether they are in remote areas or overseas.

In 1999, the AEC's main cost was actually running the ballot on referendum day – at approximately $33 million, it accounted for almost half of its expenditure. Other significant costs were the production of the official pamphlet (approximately $17 million or $1.30 per enrolled elector) and advertising (approximately $7 million). In 1999, the AEC printed and posted 12.9 million pamphlets, making it the largest mailout in Australian history. The AEC has estimated that, if a referendum on one question had been held in 2009, the mailout would have cost approximately $25 million, or $1.80 per enrolled elector.[48] That same year, a parliamentary committee recommended amending the Referendum Act so that the official pamphlet need only be sent to each household, rather than to each elector.[49]

_4_

THE RECORD

Australia's referendum record

The Australian people have been asked to vote on 44 referendum questions to change the Australian Constitution since 1901. Just eight of these have been passed after gaining a Yes vote from a majority of people voting in a majority of the states and a majority of people voting nationwide. Whichever way it is analysed, Australia's referendum record shows a very low rate of success, with less than one in five referendums having been successful. For the proponents of constitutional change, the record is dismal, with very few proposals having been passed, and none since 1977.

The headline figures are underpinned by some broad trends. Some states like to vote Yes, others No. Some subjects have proven popular, others not. These trends have changed over the course of the 20th century. The figures also obscure some important information, such as the many proposals to alter the Constitution that have never been put to a referendum.

In this chapter, we analyse the referendum record in detail, drawing out some important themes and conclusions. We examine everything from the rate at which referendums have been held, to which referendum proposals have been the most successful, to the record of individual states, including which are most likely to support and to oppose constitutional reform.

Australia's first referendum was held in 1906, and the most recent in 1999. Table 4.1 sets out each referendum to change the Australian Constitution, with successful referendums shaded.

Proposals to change Australia's Constitution are often made, but very few are ever put to the people at a referendum. One bottleneck has been the difficulty of first securing the support of the federal Parliament. Of the 137 Bills to amend the Constitution introduced into Parliament, 58 have been passed by both Houses or twice by the House of Representatives (with 44 being put to a referendum, and 14 not progressing to that stage[1]). With only eight proposals having succeeded at a referendum, only one in 17 of the Bills introduced in Parliament have ended up changing the Constitution.

Of course, an even larger number of proposals for constitutional reform never make it to the floor of Parliament. Many worthy proposals, such as those having the support of the states, or commissions or committees appointed to review the Constitution, are never introduced into that body.

How often are referendums held?

On average, the Australian people have been asked to vote on a change to the Constitution every 2.4 years since Federation. However, because multiple questions can be asked on the one day, Australians have only been to the polls for a referendum 19 times. This amounts to a referendum day every 5.7 years since Federation. As of 2010, it has been more than 11 years since the most recent referendum. This is the longest period between referendums since

TABLE 4.1 REFERENDUMS TO CHANGE THE AUSTRALIAN CONSTITUTION				
Year	Proposal	Government submitting	States approving	National Yes vote (%)
1906	Senate Elections	Protectionist	6	82.65
1910	Finance	Fusion	3 (Qld, WA, Tas)	49.04
	State Debts	Fusion	5 (all except NSW)	54.95
1911	Legislative Powers	ALP	1 (WA)	39.42
	Monopolies	ALP	1 (WA)	39.89
1913	Trade and Commerce	ALP	3 (Qld, WA, SA)	49.38
	Corporations	ALP	3 (Qld, WA, SA)	49.33
	Industrial Matters	ALP	3 (Qld, WA, SA)	49.33
	Railway Disputes	ALP	3 (Qld, WA, SA)	49.13
	Trusts	ALP	3 (Qld, WA, SA)	49.78
	Nationalisation of Monopolies	ALP	3 (Qld, WA, SA)	49.33
1919	Legislative Powers	Nationalist	3 (Vic, Qld, WA)	49.65
	Nationalisation of Monopolies	Nationalist	3 (Vic, Qld, WA)	48.64
1926	Industry and Commerce	Nat–CP	2 (NSW, Qld)	43.50
	Essential Services	Nat–CP	2 (NSW, Qld)	42.80
1928	State Debts	Nat–CP	6	74.30
1937	Aviation	UAP	2 (Vic, Qld)	53.56
	Marketing	UAP	0	36.26
1944	Post-war Reconstruction and Democratic Rights	ALP	2 (WA, SA)	45.99
1946	Social Services	ALP	6	54.39
	Organised Marketing	ALP	3 (NSW, Vic, WA)	50.57
	Industrial Employment	ALP	3 (NSW, Vic, WA)	50.30
1948	Rents and Prices	ALP	0	40.66
1951	Communism	Lib–CP	3 (Qld, WA, Tas)	49.44
1967	Parliament	Lib–CP	1 (NSW)	40.25
	Aboriginals	Lib–CP	6	90.77
1973	Prices	ALP	0	43.81
	Incomes	ALP	0	34.42

1974	Simultaneous Elections	ALP	1 (NSW)	48.30
	Mode of Altering the Constitution	ALP	1 (NSW)	47.99
	Democratic Elections	ALP	1 (NSW)	47.20
	Local Government Bodies	ALP	1 (NSW)	46.85
1977	Simultaneous Elections	Lib–NP	3 (NSW, Vic, SA)	62.22
	Senate Casual Vacancies	Lib–NP	6	73.32
	Referendums	Lib–NP	6	77.72
	Retirement of Judges	Lib–NP	6	80.10
1984	Terms of Senators	ALP	2 (NSW, Vic)	50.64
	Interchange of Powers	ALP	0	47.06
1988	Parliamentary Terms	ALP	0	32.92
	Fair Elections	ALP	0	37.60
	Local Government	ALP	0	33.62
	Rights and Freedoms	ALP	0	30.79
1999	Establishment of Republic	Lib–NP	0	45.13
	Preamble to Constitution	Lib–NP	0	39.34

Source: Commonwealth of Australia, *Australian Referendums 1906–1999* CD-ROM (2000).
Note: Shading indicates a successful referendum.

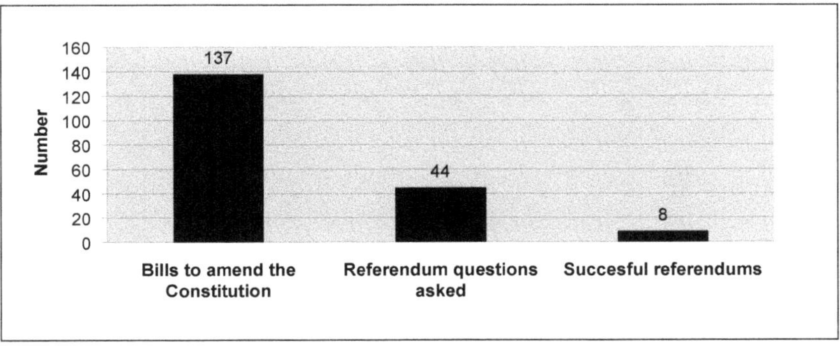

FIGURE 4.1   The gauntlet of constitutional reform

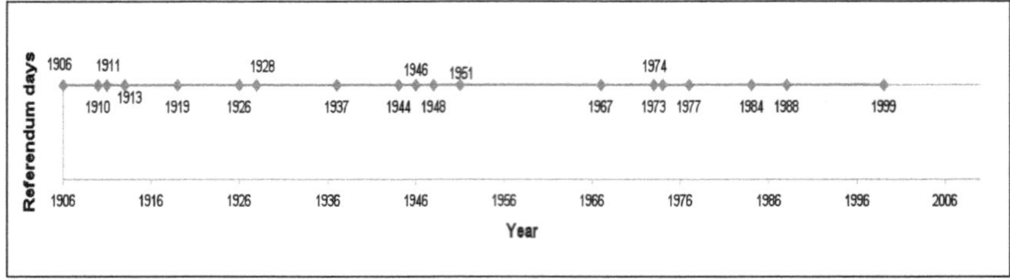

FIGURE 4.2   Referendum days, 1901–2010

the 16-year gap between the 1951 and 1967 referendums. Figure 4.2 sets out the years in which referendums have been held.

The periods of greatest activity were the first 20 years after Federation and the 1970s. There was only one referendum question asked during the life of the Menzies government from 1949 to 1966, the unsuccessful 1951 referendum on the banning of communism. Figure 4.3 sets out the number of referendum questions asked per decade.

The Commonwealth has shown no preference for asking referendum questions mid-term (22 questions) or on election day (22 questions). Referendum days have, however, more often been held mid-term (11 times) than on election day (eight times). There has been a strong movement away from holding a referendum in

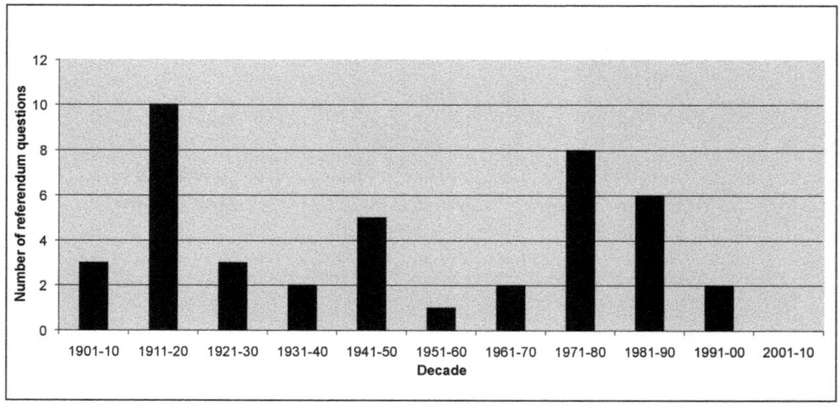

FIGURE 4.3   Number of referendum questions asked per decade.

conjunction with an election over recent decades. Since the Second World War, seven of ten referendum days (1948, 1951, 1967, 1973, 1977, 1988 and 1999) have been mid-term.

The success rate

Eight of 44 referendum proposals have been successful, the last being in 1977. As at 2010, 33 years have passed since Australia changed its Constitution. This is approximately one-third of the life of the Australian nation and is by far the longest period that Australia has gone without amending its Constitution. The next longest period was the 21 years between the 1946 and 1967 referendums.

By 2014, when it is estimated that half of Australia's population will be 37 or younger, a majority of Australians will not have been alive at the time that Australia's Constitution was last amended. This will be the first time this has happened in Australian history.

Since 1901, almost 226 million formal votes have been cast in referendums, with 110 857 642 Yes votes and 114 898 246 No votes. This amounts to 4 040 604 more No than Yes votes, or an overall No vote of 50.9 per cent. The trend has been very different since

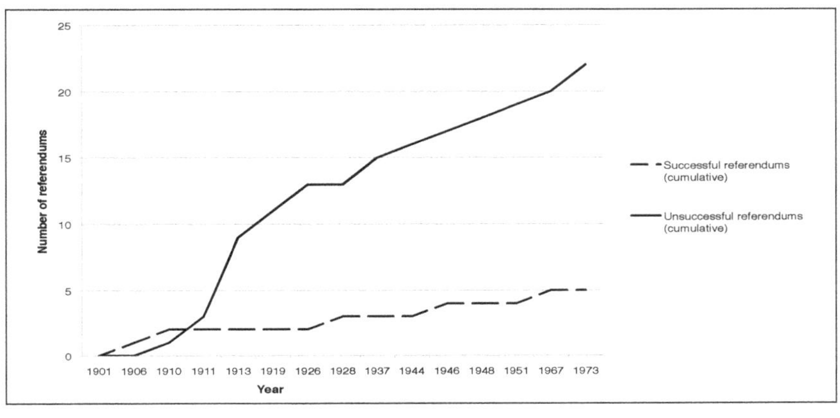

FIGURE 4.4 Success rate of referendums

TABLE 4.2 REFERENDUMS BY SUCCESS

Year	Proposal	National Yes vote (%)
1967	Aboriginals	90.77
1906	Senate Elections	82.65
1977	Retirement of Judges	80.10
1977	Referendums	77.72
1928	State Debts	74.30
1977	Senate Casual Vacancies	73.32
1977	Simultaneous Elections	62.22
1910	State Debts	54.95
1946	Social Services	54.39
1937	Aviation	53.56
1946	Organised Marketing	50.57
1984	Terms of Senators	50.64
1946	Industrial Employment	50.30
1913	Trusts	49.78
1919	Legislative Powers	49.65
1913	Trade and Commerce	49.38
1951	Communism	49.44
1913	Corporations	49.33
1913	Industrial Matters	49.33
1913	Nationalisation of Monopolies	49.33
1913	Railway Disputes	49.13
1910	Finance	49.04
1919	Nationalisation of Monopolies	48.64
1974	Simultaneous Elections	48.30
1974	Mode of Altering the Constitution	47.99
1974	Democratic Elections	47.20
1984	Interchange of Powers	47.06
1974	Local Government Bodies	46.85
1944	Post-war Reconstruction and Democratic Rights	45.99
1999	Establishment of Republic	45.13
1973	Prices	43.81
1926	Industry and Commerce	43.50
1926	Essential Services	42.80
1948	Rents and Prices	40.66
1967	Parliament	40.25

1911	Monopolies	39.89
1911	Legislative Powers	39.42
1999	Preamble to Constitution	39.34
1988	Fair Elections	37.60
1937	Marketing	36.26
1973	Incomes	34.42
1988	Local Government	33.62
1988	Parliamentary Terms	32.92
1988	Rights and Freedoms	30.79

Source: Commonwealth of Australia, *Australian Referendums 1906–1999* CD-ROM (2000).
Note: Shading indicates a successful referendum.

1980. Before 1980, there were 79 734 530 Yes votes to 67 493 883 No votes, equating to a 54.2 per cent Yes vote. After 1980, there were 31 123 112 Yes votes cast to 47 404 363 No votes; that is, a Yes vote of just 39.6 per cent. Since Australia last said Yes in 1977, Australians have proved much more likely to vote No.

The most successful referendum was the 1967 proposal to grant the federal Parliament power to make laws with respect to Aboriginal peoples and to delete discriminatory references to Aboriginal peoples from the Constitution. It secured a 90.8 per cent Yes vote. The least successful was the 1988 proposal to extend certain guarantees of rights and freedoms to state law. Most questions have clustered around or just below a 50 per cent national Yes vote. Table 4.2 sets out Australia's referendum questions, from most successful to least successful. Questions passed at a referendum are shaded.

Timing

When a referendum is held on election day, it is often thought that this necessarily politicises the question and that hopes for bipartisan and cross-community support may be defeated. Indeed, No campaigns have often relied on the coincidence of referendum

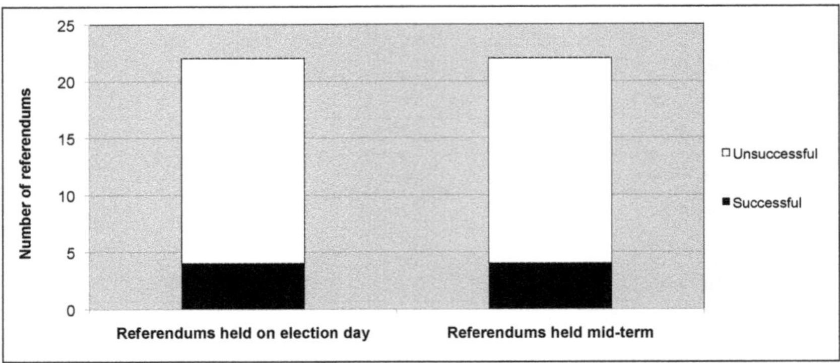

FIGURE 4.5 Success of referendum questions by day of referendum

and election days to argue that the choice of day demonstrates the government's intent to hustle through constitutional change under the cover of a general election.

The record does not, however, bear out the proposition that referendums are less likely to be successful when held on election day. Since 1901, the success rate of the two has been identical, with half of Australia's eight successful referendums occurring mid-term, and the other half on election day.

There has, however, been a gap of more than 60 years since the last successful election day referendum, the 1946 (Social Services) referendum.

The states and territories

The most common referendum result (occurring 13 times) has been a deadlock, with the people of three states voting in favour of the change and people of the other three states voting against. A 3:3 result guarantees the defeat of the referendum because section 128 of the Constitution requires that a majority of the states support the change. Figure 4.6 sets out the number of referendum questions that have had zero, one, two, three, four, five and six states in favour.

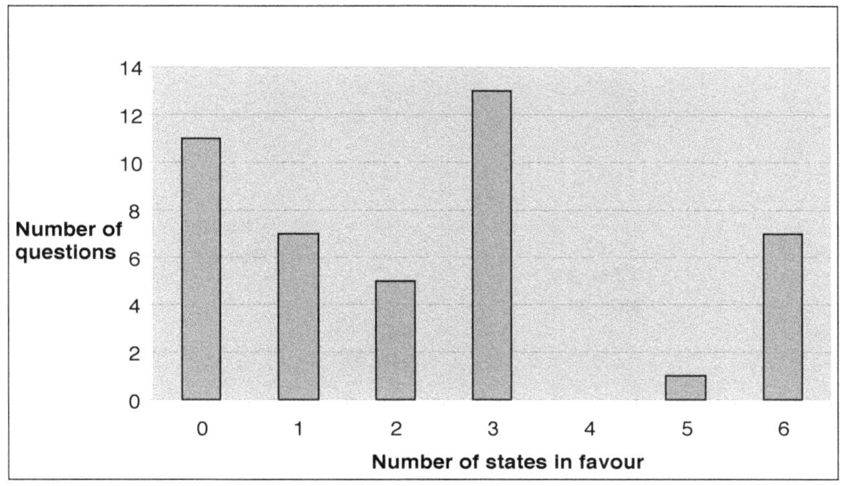

FIGURE 4.6   Number of states in favour of referendum questions

Eleven referendum questions have been supported in no states; seven have been successful in all six. The referendum that secured support in five states was the 1910 (State Debts) referendum, which lost in New South Wales but succeeded overall when it won a majority in both a majority of the states and the nationwide vote. This means that, since 1901, there has only been one occasion on which a successful referendum has been rejected in any state. Typically, successful referendums have attracted broad support across the whole of Australia.

Every state, with the exception of Western Australia, has voted No in more than half of all referendums. Figure 4.7 shows the number of times each state has voted Yes and No since 1901.

Since 1901, Western Australia has been the state most likely to support constitutional change, voting Yes to 23 referendums. Queensland has been the second most likely, voting Yes 21 times. This reflects strong Western Australian and Queensland support for Labor proposals to centralise power in the early years of Federation. Tasmania has been the most reluctant to embrace change, voting Yes just ten times. This may reflect an inherent constitutional

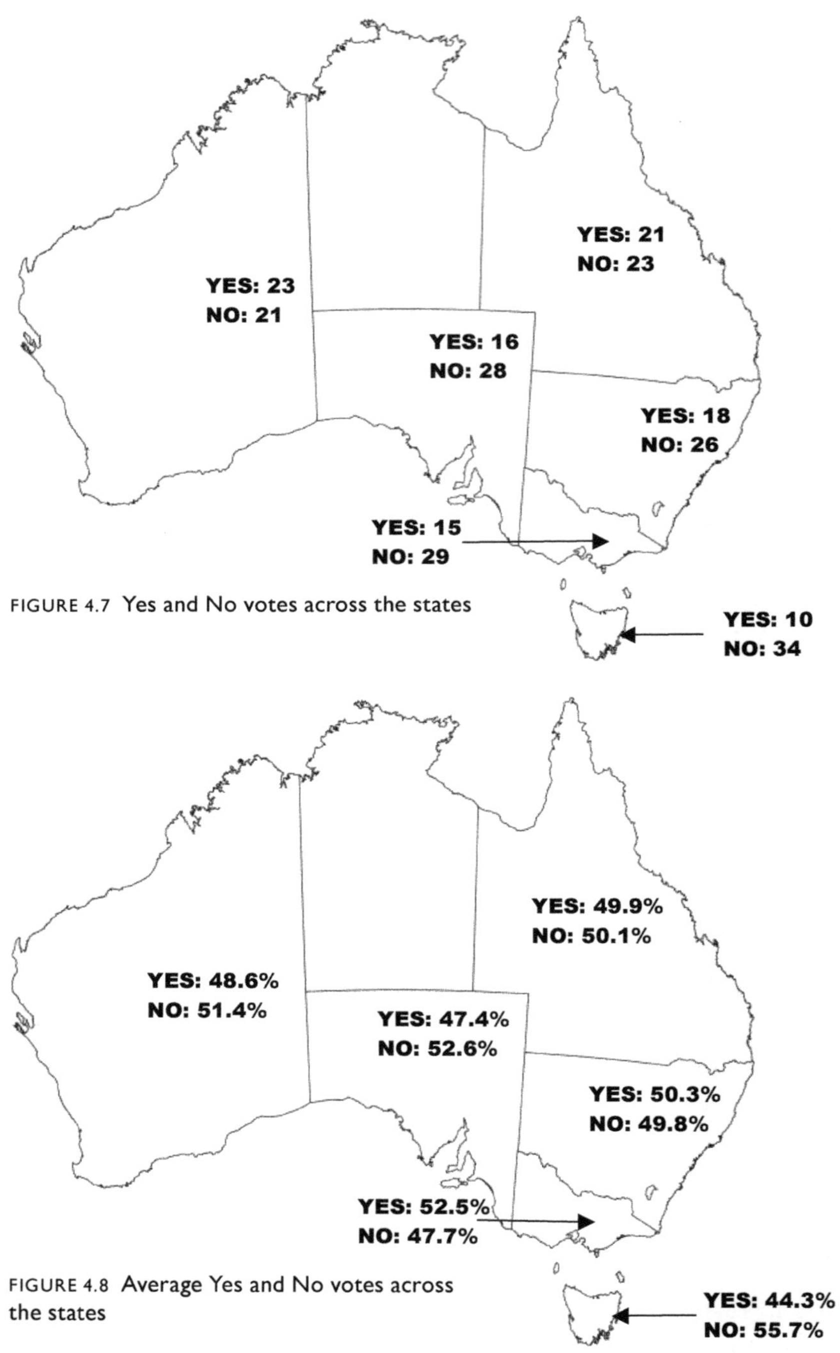

FIGURE 4.7 Yes and No votes across the states

FIGURE 4.8 Average Yes and No votes across the states

conservatism or a view that proposals emanating from 'Canberra' must necessarily be contrary to the interests of Australia's smallest state. This result also means that Tasmania has been the state that has most often voted in a way which reflects the ultimate outcome of the referendum. Only in the 1910 (Finance) and 1951 (Communism) referendums (in both of which a majority of Tasmanians voted Yes) did that state's vote not match the outcome of the referendum.

No federal electoral district has voted Yes or No to every single referendum. (The Australian Electoral Commission collects data on voting in referendums by reference to the districts used to elect members of the House of Representatives.) In the 1906 (Senate Elections) and 1967 (Aboriginals) referendums, every single district in Australia voted Yes. There has been no referendum in which every district voted No. Only one district (Melbourne) voted Yes to the 1988 (Rights and Freedoms) proposal.

Although there are substantial differences in the number of times states have voted Yes and No to referendums, there is less difference between the average Yes and No votes of the states.

Tasmanians are the most reluctant to amend the Constitution, with 55.7 per cent saying No on average. Victorians have been the most supportive of change, with 52.5 per cent, saying Yes on average. Across the 44 referendums, New South Wales (50.3 per cent) and Queensland (49.9 per cent) have been very finely balanced. This reflects the fact that many votes have been a close-run thing: though a state may vote Yes or No, it is rare for it to vote overwhelmingly one way or the other.

The end of the Second World War marked a turning point in the approach of many states to voting in referendums. Between 1901 and 1945, Australians were asked 19 referendum questions. Western Australia voted Yes to all of the first 13 referendums, while Queensland voted Yes to 15 of the first 17. By contrast, neither Western Australia nor Queensland (nor South Australia and Tasmania) have supported a referendum since 1977.

Before 1945, three of the six states (Queensland, Western Australia and Victoria) had average Yes votes of more than 50 per cent. Queensland had an astonishing average Yes vote of 55.4 per cent. South Australia and New South Wales were the most reluctant to support change, with 46.3 per cent and 46.8 per cent average Yes votes respectively.

In referendums since 1945, New South Wales (52.9 per cent) has become easily the most supportive of constitutional change. Victoria (51.8 per cent) also remains supportive. The biggest changes have been in Queensland (55.4 per cent pre-1945 to 45.8 per cent post-1945) and Western Australia (52.0 per cent pre-1945 to 46.0 per cent post-1945). Tasmania has become even less supportive, dropping from an average Yes vote of 47.7 per cent before 1945 to one of just 41.7 per cent since 1945. Figure 4.9 shows the number of Yes votes for each state before and after the end of the Second World War.

The clear theme is that, in recent times, the big states (New South Wales and, to a lesser extent, Victoria) have supported constitutional change, while the smaller states have opposed it. This reflects the fact that the bigger states, by virtue of their population, control the lion's share of the seats in the House of Representatives and,

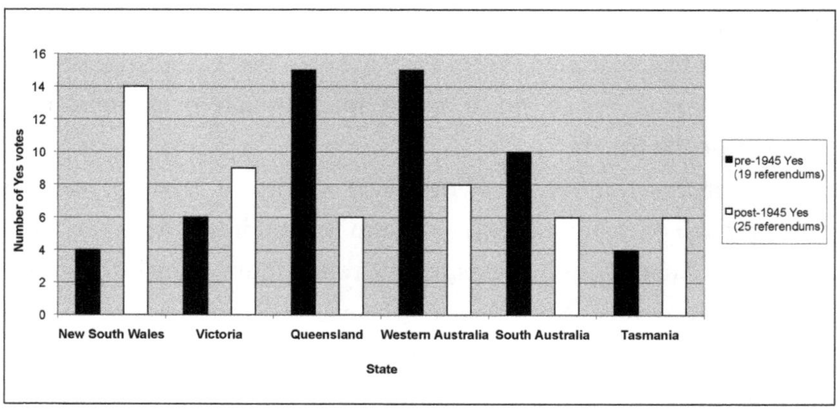

FIGURE 4.9 Number of Yes votes pre-1945 and post-1945 by state

consequently, have the greatest say in which proposals to change the Constitution are put to the people.

Since 1977, the territories have been able to vote in referendums. The first referendum at which Territorians cast a vote was in 1984. In general the Australian Capital Territory (ACT) has been far more supportive of constitutional change than other jurisdictions. The ACT has voted Yes in four of its eight referendums. During those eight referendums, only New South Wales, Victoria and the Northern Territory (all once) have voted Yes. In the period since 1980, when Australians have tended to overwhelmingly vote No to referendums, the ACT has recorded an average Yes vote of 49.7 per cent and the Northern Territory 43.1 per cent.

What have Australians voted on?

Most of the proposals put to the Australian people to change the Constitution have sought to grant the Commonwealth additional powers. This reflects the fact that the Commonwealth controls which proposals are put to the people. Indeed, Australians have never been asked to vote on granting the states a new power. However, the Commonwealth has not sought a new power by referendum since 1973. This reflects the low success rate of such proposals and the fact that the Commonwealth already has extensive powers due to broad readings of its existing constitutional powers by the High Court.

Australians have generally been unwilling to approve changes that give extra power to the Commonwealth. Just three of 24 such proposals have been successful. Australians have been relatively willing to vote Yes to changes to the federal system (three from eight) and also to the structure of Parliament (two from seven). As we set out in chapter 6, successful changes to the federal system and the

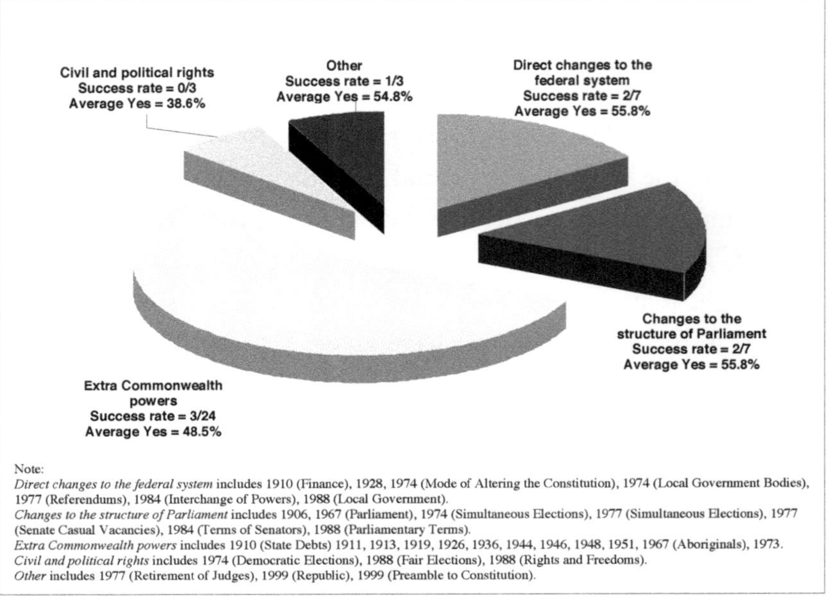

Note:
Direct changes to the federal system includes 1910 (Finance), 1928, 1974 (Mode of Altering the Constitution), 1974 (Local Government Bodies), 1977 (Referendums), 1984 (Interchange of Powers), 1988 (Local Government).
Changes to the structure of Parliament includes 1906, 1967 (Parliament), 1974 (Simultaneous Elections), 1977 (Simultaneous Elections), 1977 (Senate Casual Vacancies), 1984 (Terms of Senators), 1988 (Parliamentary Terms).
Extra Commonwealth powers includes 1910 (State Debts) 1911, 1913, 1919, 1926, 1936, 1944, 1946, 1948, 1951, 1967 (Aboriginals), 1973.
Civil and political rights includes 1974 (Democratic Elections), 1988 (Fair Elections), 1988 (Rights and Freedoms).
Other includes 1977 (Retirement of Judges), 1999 (Republic), 1999 (Preamble to Constitution).

FIGURE 4.10 **Success rate of referendums by subject matter**

structure of Parliament have tended to either be incremental or have been built upon a foundation of Commonwealth–state consensus.

The Commonwealth has sometimes put the same proposal (sometimes with slightly different wording) more than once. Subsequent referendums on the same proposal have never been successful. Governments have asked multiple times for extra power over monopolies (three times), marketing (twice) and industrial relations (twice).[2] Governments have also sought three times (albeit with slightly different proposals) to introduce simultaneous elections for the House of Representatives and Senate.

It has sometimes been thought that proposals have a lower chance of success the second time around. Voters may have reform fatigue or perceive that the government is trying to win by persistence, not merit. No campaigns have often tried to turn the fact that the proposal is a repeat proposal against the government by arguing that it is not listening to the people.

The results do not, however, bear out the claim that repeat referendums fare worse (though of course the record also does not show that such proposals succeed on a subsequent occasion). For example, in 1974, 1977 and 1984, the government put versions of the Simultaneous Elections proposal. It achieved respectively 48.3 per cent, 62.2 per cent and 50.6 per cent of the vote. In 1977, had just 9211 votes gone the other way in Western Australia, the proposal would have succeeded. There were similar improvements (or insignificant deteriorations) in support for proposals on Monopolies/Nationalisation of Monopolies (39.9 per cent in 1911; 49.3 per cent in 1913; 48.6 per cent in 1919), Marketing/Organised Marketing (36.3 per cent in 1937; 50.6 per cent in 1946) and Industrial Relations/Industrial Employment (49.3 per cent in 1913; 50.3 per cent in 1946). The fact that a proposal is a repeat proposal may be relevant to some people's vote; but the results suggest that it does not guarantee a proposal's defeat. If anything, the results suggest that *more* people vote Yes the second time around, perhaps reflecting a better understanding of the proposal or a feeling that they have had time to get used to the idea.

Political parties

The Labor Party has been, by far, the political party most likely to champion constitutional reform. Twenty-five of 44 proposals (about 57 per cent) for constitutional change have been put by Labor governments, despite Labor having been in office for less than a third of Australia's federal political history. This translates to more than seven proposals for every ten years the Labor Party has been in power, and about two and a half proposals for every ten years non-Labor parties have been in government.

Labor's unease with the Constitution, at least in the early years of the new Federation, may have sprung from the fact that the labour movement played only a marginal role in its development. Only one delegate – William Trenwith, a member of the Victorian Parliament and former bootmaker and trade union organiser – participated in the 1897–98 Constitutional Convention, and by then he had already distanced himself from the Labor Party. The Labor Party also ran strong campaigns against the Constitution in each state. Labor was not opposed to the idea of Federation, but rejected the terms on which it was proposed. The Labor Party's concerns centred on the powers given to the Commonwealth and to be wielded by the Senate, the role of the Governor-General and the difficulty of amending the Constitution.

It is not, however, the case that all attempts to centralise power in Canberra have come from the Labor side of politics. Between 1910 and 1937, non-Labor governments sponsored a series of referendums seeking new Commonwealth powers. These were the 1910 (Fusion government), 1919 (Nationalist government), 1926 (Nationalist–Country Party government) and 1937 (United Australia Party government) referendums. In 1951 and 1967, the Menzies and Holt Liberal governments also sought new powers for the federal Parliament. Of 24 questions seeking new powers, nine have been asked by non-Labor parties.

Proposals sponsored by Labor governments have almost always been unsuccessful. Just one of 25 Labor proposals – the 1946 (Social Services) referendum put by the Chifley government – has succeeded, a failure rate of 96 per cent. By contrast, seven of 19 non-Labor proposals (36.8 per cent) have been passed. This may reflect the fact that many non-Labor proposals have been perceived to be incremental or minor changes to the Constitution (for example, all three of the successful 1977 proposals). By contrast, non-Labor has often criticised Labor proposals as being radical and risky (for example, Labor's four 1988 reforms).

The overall record

The results reveal a complex picture, but with a clear recent trend. Few proposals for constitutional reform have actually passed the gauntlet of section 128. Success has also become far less likely over time. Indeed, it is not just a matter of referendums being less likely to succeed as time has gone on, but that over recent history referendums have been unlikely to be put to the people at all.

While Australians have voted in referendums regularly since Federation, the decade just past is the first since 1901 without any such poll. The period since 1980 has also seen Australians vote No in record proportions, with fewer than four in ten votes being cast for constitutional change. This has occurred despite the grant of the referendum vote to Territorians in 1977, which has seen the ACT become, by far, the jurisdiction most supportive of constitutional change.

Recent trends also show that the big states (New South Wales and Victoria) – the regions which together dominate membership in the Lower House of the federal Parliament – tend to support reform. By contrast, the other states have tended to overwhelmingly say No.

Since 1901, Australians have most often voted on whether to give the Commonwealth new powers. Such questions have generally been rejected. When it comes to political parties, Labor has been, with only a single exception, unable to sponsor constitutional reform. A proposal put to the people by a non-Labor government has been more than nine times more likely to succeed than one put by a Labor government.

These raw results hide the many subtleties that have coloured each and every one of the 44 referendum questions that have been put since 1901. It is to these subtleties, the overarching political and strategic context and the details of the debate to and fro, which we turn to in the next chapter.

5

EIGHT
REFERENDUMS

Introduction

Having examined the overall referendum record in chapter 4, we now look in more detail at eight of the most important referendums held in Australia since Federation. Our aim is to tell their story, including how the proposals were generated, how the referendum was conducted and the response of the people at the ballot box.

1906 – Australia's first referendum

It took just under six years for Australians to change their 1901 Constitution. The change, however, was not momentous. At a referendum held on 12 December 1906, the people voted to amend section 13 of the Constitution to make Senators' terms begin on 1 July instead of 1 January. The hope of the Deakin Protectionist government was that this would lead to the holding of elections in March, and not the end of the year (as had happened in 1903 and 1906). Elections in the last quarter of the year brought two problems: they clashed with the harvest, making it difficult for farmers to vote; and, because of a convention that a new Parliament did not commence sitting until the next June, it left a period of six to nine months of parliamentary inactivity. The government also hoped that changing the beginning date of Senators' terms would facilitate the holding of simultaneous elections for the Senate and the House of Representatives.

The referendum process of 1906 was unrecognisable from that of today. Enrolment and voting were voluntary, with voters needing to be over 21 years of age, resident in Australia continuously for six months and a subject of the King of England. Unless falling within special exceptions, Indigenous Australians and natives of Asia, Africa or the Pacific Islands (except New Zealand) were denied the vote. Debate on the referendum proposal was virtually non-existent, and there was no Yes or No case distributed (this was not introduced until six years later). Australians were also not asked to vote by writing Yes or No. Instead, they were required to place a '✗' in either box.

By placing a '✗' on their ballot paper, Australians wielded their power to alter the Constitution for the first time. For many, the response was one of indifference. Just over 2.1 million people were enrolled to vote, which was just over half of Australia's total population of 4.1 million. Barely half of those enrolled actually voted. Even then, the turnout of 50.2 per cent was no doubt inflated by the fact that the referendum took place on the same day as the 1906 general election.

The result of the referendum was never in doubt. It was carried overwhelmingly, with a national Yes vote of 82.7 per cent. Queensland (76.8 per cent) had the lowest approval, while South Australia (87.0 per cent) had the highest.[1] The result may have left

COMMONWEALTH OF AUSTRALIA

REFERENDUM

Submission of a **PROPOSED LAW** for the Alteration of the Constitution, entitled the

CONSTITUTION ALTERATION
(SENATE ELECTIONS) 1906.

HOW TO VOTE

If you **APPROVE** of the proposed **LAW** make a **CROSS** in the **SQUARE** opposite the word "**YES**," thus:—

| ☒ | **YES.** |
| ☐ | **NO.** |

If you **DO NOT APPROVE** of the proposed **LAW** make a **CROSS** in the **SQUARE** opposite the word "**NO**," thus:—

| ☐ | **YES.** |
| ☒ | **NO.** |

Chief Electoral Office for the Commonwealth,
Melbourne, 15th October, 1906.

BY AUTHORITY: J. KEMP, ACTING GOVERNMENT PRINTER, MELBOURNE.

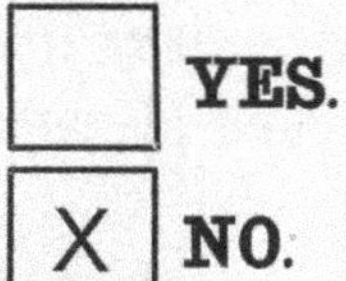

FIGURE 5.1 **How-to-vote card from the 1906 referendum**
Source: National Archives of Australia: A406, E1906/7720 Part 2.

some with the idea that constitutional amendment in Australia was easy to accomplish.

Sir Robert Menzies, Australia's longest serving Prime Minister, was later to put the success of the 1906 referendum down to the fact that 'the average voter … does not care how frequently a Senator rotates'.[2] The *Sydney Morning Herald* even considered the referendum proposal a waste of valuable parliamentary time, and speculated that it was part of a government tactic to distract Parliament from considering more important issues. Its report on the parliamentary debate preceding the referendum was scathing:

> Last night's protracted sitting thoroughly demoralised the House of Representatives. A handful of Opposition members, a little knot of Labour members, and one or two ministerialists, maintained the semblance of a deliberative assembly, whilst the other members whose physical presence was necessary for the maintenance of a quorum, bandaged their eyes as protection against the electric light, and slept away the time on the benches.[3]

Neither during this parliamentary debate, nor in the weeks before the referendum itself, does the media record show any significant debate on the proposed change to the Constitution. The referendum was no doubt overshadowed by the general election on the same day and other pressing issues.

The 1906 referendum set an important precedent. It established that referendums were not to be reserved for fundamental changes to the Constitution. When debating the proposal, some Senators vigorously argued that it was insufficiently important to justify a referendum. Senator James Drake, a member of the Protectionist Party, a leading Federation activist and Australia's first Postmaster-General, labelled the proposal as mere 'tinkering'.[4] According to Drake, constitutional amendment required 'an overwhelming case' for change.[5] In his view:

> This … Bill … ought to be approached with great
> deliberation and caution. We ought to be extremely chary
> of making alterations in the Constitution … [Our] powers
> of amendment … should be used whenever a case of
> overwhelming necessity arises, and the wellbeing of the whole
> people is concerned. But, if we err at all, we should err in the
> direction of overcautiousness.[6]

These voices, eminent though they were, did not carry the day. Some of the leading Senators stood up for the right of Australians to change their Constitution for whatever reason they thought fit. In the words of Tasmanian Labor Senator David O'Keefe:

> [T]he Constitution itself prevents us from making alterations
> in an ill-considered manner. Every proposed amendment
> has not only to be fully considered by both Houses of the
> Parliament, but has also to be accepted by the people when
> submitted to them. If it can be shown that it will in any way
> improve our legislation and our manner of performing our
> duties to make the alteration proposed, that is, I think, a
> sufficient justification for the Bill.[7]

The argument was this: it was not for Parliament to decide what amendments were unnecessary; that was a job given by the Constitution to the people.

The 1906 referendum also showed several risks that would attend other efforts at reform. First, some Senators raised the charge of political self-interest against the proposal, a call that would haunt many later referendums. Senator Drake put the argument simply: 'It is unfortunate that the first amendment proposed in the Constitution … [is] one involving an extension of the term of honorable Senators.'[8] Even Senator O'Keefe, a supporter of the proposal, recognised the risk: 'I do not say that we are here to suit the convenience of Members of Parliament. We have to consider the convenience of the people.'[9]

Second, the 1906 referendum underscored the need to get the proposal right. A principal aim of the amendment was to facilitate the holding of simultaneous elections of the House and Senate. In introducing the Bill to the Senate, Senator John Keating (a Protectionist, who was elected at 28 as the youngest member of the first Parliament) argued that the Bill would help ensure, as far as possible, that House and Senate elections would occur on the same day, thereby saving tens of thousands of pounds. Immediately, Senator Edward Millen, a Free Trader, pointed out that the proposal would only ensure simultaneous elections if the House always ran to its full term. If the House were dissolved earlier, one of two things would happen from then on. Either the Senate would be elected well before the new Senators took their seats (the only condition being that the election could not happen more than a year in advance) or the elections of the House and Senate would not be held at the same time. In the words of Senator Millen:

> We are now asked to take the serious step of altering
> the Constitution to secure an advantage which might be
> limited absolutely to one election … We are being asked
> to amend the Constitution … for an entirely imaginary
> advantage, it being assumed that a dual election which has
> taken place once only in our Federal history will continue
> indefinitely.[10]

Millen lost the argument, but was proven right, and later governments would try repeatedly, but unsuccessfully, to amend the Constitution to guarantee simultaneous elections.

Third, Senators recognised the inherent difficulties in educating voters about constitutional change. In part, this difficulty was born from the challenge of explaining to the people the meaning and effect of what was a highly technical amendment. According to Senator Drake:

By adopting the form of proposing the striking out of certain
words and the insertion of other words [in the Constitution],
no human being, unless he has the Constitution before him …
will know what is meant.[11]

Senator Millen was even less hopeful:

I am certain that no honorable senator will contend that any
considerable number of the electors will have the slightest
chance of giving an intelligent vote on the proposition to be
submitted to them … They will have to state their view of
what is intended by the document placed before them from the
varying interpretations placed upon it by the different candidates
who address them. In expressing an opinion upon a proposed
amendment of the Constitution, it is not desirable that the
electors should have to rely for advice in casting their votes on the
varying interpretations of different individuals … [I]n preparing
a proposed amendment of the Constitution it should be framed
in such a way as to be clear, not only to the mind of a lawyer and
draftsman, but to every man and woman in the country.[12]

In part, the difficulty was one of party politicking, fear and scaremongering. Drake lamented that '[w]hen we are dealing with such
a thing as an amendment of the Constitution, we should rise above
party', but in practice:

Who will explain this measure to the people? Some who are
opposed to the proposed amendment … might tell the electors
that what is meant is that those going up for election will get
six months added to their term of service. Others may tell them
that what it means is that the Senate elections will take place in
November instead of December.[13]

Australia's first referendum was, from the perspective of the Yes
vote, an overwhelming success. But storm clouds were brewing.

1928 – Paying state debts

On 17 November 1928, Stanley Melbourne Bruce's Nationalist–Country Party government, with the support of the Labor Opposition and the governments of all the states, asked the Australian people to support a proposal to fix a fundamental problem with Australia's federal system. The problem was complex, and so was the proposed remedy. This posed a challenge: Australians had said Yes to two referendums, one in 1906 and one in 1910. But, on both of those occasions, enrolment and voting were not compulsory. By 1928, things were different. Australians had only voted at one referendum with compulsory enrolment and voting. That was in 1926, when Australians had decisively said No to two straightforward referendum questions on granting the Commonwealth power over industry and commerce, and over essential services, both of which had won bipartisan support. In 1928, the issues were far more complicated: how the Commonwealth and states should cooperate when it came to getting the best deal on the domestic and international debt markets.

The proposal was to insert a new section 105A into the Constitution to give the Commonwealth power to enter into agreements with the states about state debts and state borrowing. The section would also validate any agreement entered into by the Commonwealth and states prior to the referendum. The proposal was motivated by common sense, and its purpose was simple: by coordinating borrowing and allowing the Commonwealth and states to act as one unit in the debt markets, Australian governments could borrow at cheaper rates and, if necessary, spread the risk of default.

The proposal was a response to the Commonwealth and the states vigorously competing for capital, and thereby pushing up interest rates, when the Commonwealth was trying to pay off its war debt and the states were escalating spending on infrastructure. At the 1923 Premiers' Conference, the Commonwealth and state governments had agreed to form a voluntary Loan Council to coordinate the timing and price for the issue of debt and other securities. In 1927, this arrangement was formalised, with the Commonwealth and states agreeing to establish a new body, the Australian Loan Council, to coordinate borrowing. Doubts emerged about whether the Commonwealth actually had the power to do this. Nothing in the Constitution said that it could enter into agreements with the states about debts and give effect to those agreements by creating a Commonwealth bureaucracy. The result of these doubts was a push, led by the Commonwealth Attorney-General (and later Chief Justice of the High Court) John Latham, for a referendum to, in effect, retrospectively ratify the agreement that had already been reached and implemented.

The proposal to add section 105A to the Constitution sailed through Parliament, with 43 in favour and only three against in the House of Representatives. James Scullin, then leader of the Labor Opposition, criticised the government for pushing the referendum Bill through Parliament before the Royal Commission into the Constitution (which sat from 1927 to 1929) had reported. Scullin also sniped at the Bruce government's general policy on Commonwealth–state financial relations but, ultimately, Scullin and the majority of the parliamentary Labor Party supported the proposal. The *Sydney Morning Herald* described Scullin's speech criticising the government's general policy, but still supporting the referendum, as 'about as effective as blowing soap bubbles at an aged rhinoceros'.[14]

Political support for the referendum was widespread. The Labor Premier of Victoria, Edward Hogan, issued a strong statement urging voters to vote Yes. So too did Philip Colier, the Labor Premier of Western Australia. No official Yes/No pamphlet was produced, reflecting the strong support for the change at the national parliamentary level. The media also aligned behind the referendum, with *The Age* pointing out that the referendum was 'advocated by all political parties [and] in fact, the issue is entirely non-party'.[15] Only two prominent figures opposed the referendum: Jack Lang, leader of the Labor Opposition in New South Wales, and Sir William Mitchell, leader of the Nationalist Opposition in Western Australia.

Widespread support at the Commonwealth and state levels was reflected in the outcome.[16] All six states voted Yes, with a national Yes vote of 74.3 per cent. Queensland led the way, recording its highest Yes vote since 1901 of 88.6 per cent. Only four electoral districts – all Labor strongholds in New South Wales – voted No.

Why did Australians vote Yes in such large numbers? Two factors were at play. The first was the consensus achieved between three important stakeholders in the referendum process: the Commonwealth Government, the Commonwealth Parliament and the states. This consensus flowed over to the fourth key stakeholder – the people – resulting in Australia's fifth most successful referendum. The Commonwealth and the states had identified a defect of the federal system: there was a need for coordinated borrowing, but the Constitution apparently gave the Commonwealth insufficient power to achieve this end. The agreed solution was also in everyone's interest: it increased the power of the Federation as a whole, without taking anything away from any one part.

The second reason for success was that the referendum posed no threat to the status quo. Its immediate effect was to ratify an existing agreement. Any new agreements entered into under the new power required the agreement of the Commonwealth and the states involved. By applying to an existing agreement, and requiring consent to any further agreements, the proposal did not pose a threat to 'states' rights'. The incremental nature of the proposal did not mean it was without practical effect. In 1936, the Commonwealth and the states extended the agreement to debt issued by a broader range of government bodies, while the Australian Loan Council went on to play a major role in Australian history (including in the 1950s as one of the major mechanisms for the delivery of the Commonwealth's macroeconomic policy by reducing government borrowing levels so as to reduce inflation).

Given the conjunction of these factors, commentators asked: how could more than 25 per cent of voters, or 773 852 Australians, have voted No? *The Age* speculated:

> Perhaps the majority of 'No' votes were cast by the same people who have always tried to defeat referendums because they did not understand what was proposed, and thought it surer to leave things as they were. Then again, many may have voted 'No' on account of that strange streak of perversity in human nature which tempts people to vote 'No' simply because they are told to vote 'Yes'.[17]

Whatever reasons people had for voting No, it is clear that the 1928 referendum was an overwhelming success. It showed that the Federation can be reformed. It also showed that the Commonwealth and states can, through negotiation and agreement, followed by concerted effort, bring about constitutional change that will be supported by the people of Australia.

1946 – Labor's referendum

On 28 September 1946, Australians went to the polls. It was a special day: Australians had not voted in peacetime for nine years. The day saw both a general election, at which the Chifley Labor government was re-elected, and a referendum in which Australians handed the Labor Party its first referendum victory in ten attempts. More than six decades later, it remains Labor's sole referendum victory, despite Labor now having made 25 attempts at constitutional change.

In late 1946, Australia was wedged between the end of hostilities in the Second World War and a Cold War in its early stages. Wartime rationing lingered; and the modern welfare state was in its infancy. During the Second World War, under its defence power, the Commonwealth had taken on vast responsibilities (such as the collection of income taxation) that had, until then, been in the hands of the states. Once the war was over, the Commonwealth showed little intention of giving these powers back.

In 1944, through the unsuccessful Post-war Reconstruction and Democratic Rights referendum, the Curtin Labor government had sought to continue Commonwealth power in the areas it had taken over from the states during the Second World War. So long as the War continued, the Commonwealth had the power to do those things pursuant to its power to look after the nation's 'defence'. Once the war ended, that 'defence' power would wane, leaving the Commonwealth without the powers it wanted.

The 1944 referendum was unsuccessful; but Australians were nonetheless increasingly turning to the Commonwealth as a primary source of assistance for the problems of daily life: food, jobs, family, health care and disability. Between 1940 and 1946, the Curtin and Chifley governments had introduced benefits for the unemployed, the sick, widows and dependants of the disabled. The governments had also presided over unprecedented increases in pensions for the disabled and the elderly, and in child endowment benefits. Similar efforts were occurring internationally. By 1946, President Roosevelt's New Deal – with its emphasis on national spending – was entrenched in the United States, while New Zealand had nationalised its medical services and the United Kingdom was debating whether to do so.

This momentum in Australia struck a snag. In 1945, the High Court declared invalid a Commonwealth law that sought to bring about a national pharmaceutical benefits scheme.[18] It was believed that the result called into question more generally the validity of the social services schemes built up by Labor governments since 1940; and the government had been advised by various King's Counsel that welfare for parents, children, the unemployed, the sick, the disabled and the old were all at risk. It was in this context that Prime Minister Ben Chifley put three proposals to the people. First, the Social Services proposal sought to insert a new section 51(23A) into the Constitution to permit the Commonwealth to make laws for:

> The provision of maternity allowances, widows' pensions, child endowment, unemployment, pharmaceutical, sickness and hospital benefits, medical and dental services (but not so as to authorize any form of civil conscription), benefits to students and family allowances.[19]

Secondly, the Organised Marketing proposal sought to allow the Commonwealth extra power to legislate for the organised marketing of primary products. Thirdly, the Industrial Employment proposal sought to allow the Commonwealth to legislate for industrial conditions, but not so as to authorise industrial conscription.

The three proposals were adopted by the Labor caucus on 12 March 1946. On Cabinet's recommendation, it was decided to hold the referendums on the same day as the election due to be called later that year. The three Bills to implement the proposals were introduced into Parliament and, in debate on 4 April, the Country Party's Earle Page foreshadowed amendments to the Social Services proposal to prevent conscription of the medical and dental profession. On 10 April, Robert Menzies, leader of the Liberal Opposition, pressed a version of Page's amendment. Evatt accepted this and the qualification 'but not so as to authorise civil conscription' was added to the change. As so amended, the proposal passed the House with 54 votes for and just one vote against. The No campaign to the Social Services proposal was ultimately led by three South Australians: Keith Cameron, a Liberal and Country League member of the House, and Liberal Senators James McLachlan and Edward Mattner. These three took responsibility for drafting the official No case.

The non-Labor parties had greater concerns with the Organised Marketing and Industrial Employment proposals. The Marketing

Bill received significant Opposition support, passing 48 votes to eight. Opposition to the Industrial Employment Bill was stronger. It passed with 41 votes for and 15 against, but gained more detractors over time. On 8 May, the Federal Council of the Liberal Party authorised members to vote according to their conscience. By 20 June, when the Bills were voted on by the Senate, opposition had solidified. The Social Services Bill retained support, with only two Opposition Senators voting against. But Opposition support for the other two Bills had fallen away. Government Senators were joined by just one member of the Opposition on the Organised Marketing Bill, with the Opposition voting as a block against the Industrial Conditions Bill. Despite this opposition, the Bills passed Parliament and the date for the referendum and the general election was set for 26 September.

The Yes and No campaigns quickly stepped into gear. For the Yes campaign, the referendums were about bread-and-butter domestic issues: social services, full employment and stable markets. The question was simple: should the Commonwealth have the power to legislate to those ends? Or should the Constitution continue to inhibit the Commonwealth from bringing about social progress?

The No campaign coalesced around broad themes that suggested that the Australian way of life was under attack. It was argued that the proposals gave rise to three threats: totalitarianism, communism and unification. People were asked, who do you want to control your job, basic necessities and health care? Do you want it to be the *Government* (totalitarianism)? Do you want it to be *Labor* (communism)? Do you want it to be *Canberra* (unification)? For opponents of the referendums, the proposals, in one swipe, risked all three. The official No case pamphlet to the Industrial Conditions proposal directly tied the proposals to the rising communist threat, saying in capitals:

*THE COMMUNISTS ARE OUT TO SMASH OUR
ARBITRATION SYSTEM. THEY HAVE MADE NO
SECRET OF THEIR OPPOSITION TO IT.*[20]

The No case to the Organised Marketing proposal emphasised the problems of unification:

> The word 'uniformity' may turn out to be our greatest curse,
> rivalling even the rabbits. Why should every citizen in
> Australia be subject to the same dull and uniform collection of
> rules?[21]

Meanwhile, a newspaper advertisement funded by a group calling itself the Vote No Campaign said:

> DON'T BE FOOLED. If the Federal Parliament wins even
> one of the three points, it will have forged a strong link in its
> desired chain of national dictatorship.[22]

Outside these broad themes, the campaign went back and forth. Opponents argued that the proposals were unnecessary because the High Court decision was confined to its facts and did not call other benefits into question. Repeatedly, opponents reminded Australians that, despite the decision, benefits continued to flow. Proponents parried that this was a misrepresentation of the High Court's decision, and they tendered lawyers' opinions in support of their view. For opponents, the extra powers (other than the social services power) were also already exercisable through cooperation with the states. Proponents replied that cooperation was difficult, time-consuming and could not guarantee success.

Proponents argued that the questions were not a party issue. They relied on three claims. First, that the Liberal and Country parties had, by and large, supported Labor's legislative efforts to expand the welfare state during the 1940s.[23] Second, that both of these parties had supported the proposals in the House of

FIGURE 5.2 **Advertisement for the No campaign in the 1946 referendum**
Source: *Sydney Morning Herald*, 27 September 1946, p. 4.

Representatives; and, thirdly, that the powers were for the federal Parliament and not for the Labor Party. Once the Constitution had been amended, the powers could be used, for better or for worse, by any Parliament. Opponents replied that, despite the government's claims, the proposals had been inevitably politicised by the fact that the referendum was being held in conjunction with a general election. Further, they said that the referendums were about topics that, from Labor's point of view, had always been political, such as the Commonwealth's power over industrial relations. The *Courier-Mail* deplored Labor's 'deliberate confusing of a referendum with a general election' and, in reply to Labor's assertion that it was non-party, said: 'Unfortunately, the Referendum has a great deal to do with party politics. It is an attempt to obtain for the Federal Parliament new powers wanted by the Federal Labour [*sic*] Party'.[24]

Opponents relied on two other arguments. First, Labor was proceeding too hastily. For the Country Party in particular, the referendum was flawed because it had not proceeded from a non-partisan Convention that had conducted a wholesale review of the Constitution. Second, Labor was not heeding the message of the electors. Some of the sought powers (particularly the health care and family allowances aspects of the Social Services proposal) had been rejected as part of the omnibus 1944 referendum. Why, opponents asked, was the government going back to the people just two years later?

Chifley's campaign supporting the proposals was limited. By all accounts, his focus was on winning the general election, with the referendums rating only a short mention at the end of his stump speech. Even then, Chifley did not go beyond merely exhorting a blanket Yes vote. For the most part, the referendum was not on the public radar. The *Adelaide Advertiser* captured the mood: 'Referendum Hush',[25] it declared, noting that well into the election campaign Chifley had barely mentioned the referendums and, when he did, he referred only to the Social Services question.

Francis Bland, a professor of government at the University of Sydney, who was later elected as Liberal Member for the Commonwealth seat of Warringah, speculated that this was a deliberate Labor tactic. The Labor government was popular; its handling of the Second World War remaining firmly in the electorate's mind. For Bland, and for much of the press, Chifley's tactic was to sweep to referendum victory on the back of an election victory. The hope was that electors would vote indiscriminately for the government in the general election and in the referendums. Opponents sought to turn this 'small target' approach against Chifley. For Bland, the government's approach was 'audacious' and an attempt to 'catch the electors unawares'.[26] For Sir Thomas Playford, Liberal and Country League Premier of South Australia, Chifley's tactic was even more insidious. He wrote that Chifley's intention was to 'scare' voters into believing critical services would be withdrawn if the Social Services proposal failed and 'that many electors will be too indifferent to examine closely the other two amendments, and will vote "Yes", "Yes", "Yes" to all three.'[27]

It was not until four days before the referendum that Chifley turned to explaining and advocating a Yes vote in the referendums. Perhaps in response to press criticism, or perhaps realising that the referendums would be close, Chifley discussed the referendums at length in a speech in Sydney on the night of 24 September. Even then, the focus was on the Social Services question and Chifley tied it closely to Labor's electoral platform. Labor's policy was to provide free medical, dental and optical treatment. This, Chifley said, was contingent on the success of the Social Services proposal.

The press was almost unanimously opposed to all of the referendum questions. The *Courier-Mail* urged 'prudent Queensland electors' to vote No and so to oppose Labor's 'obvious' use of the referendum for 'party political expediency'.[28] The *Sydney Morning Herald* was particularly trenchant. It devoted its editorial on the day of the vote not to the election that was to occur that day, but to the referendum.

It said:

> The people have to decide … whether the balance of power within the Federation shall be radically altered …
>
> [T]he suspicion has grown that in seeking powers over industry and rural marketing, Labour is attempting, under the guise of modernising the Constitution, to whittle away such sovereignty as still remains with the States …
>
> It is difficult … to resist the conclusion that the Government's renewed demand … is inspired by the intention to prepare a still greater measure of socialisation, and to maintain the regimentation of war-time …
>
> [N]o explanation has been offered of the use which it intends to make of the sweeping legislative authority being sought. This lack of frankness characterises Labour's political as well as its constitutional approach to the electors. In essence the public is asked to accept its war record … as a sufficient reason for giving it a blank cheque on the future. [Labor] is afraid of revealing its real intentions …
>
> What this Commonwealth needs above all else, in the coming years, is the co-operation of all classes in developing the rich heritage which, by the grace of god, is ours.[29]

When Australians went to the polls on 28 September, Labor comfortably won the election. The referendum results, on the other hand, were mixed.[30] The Social Services question was successful in all six states, achieving a national Yes vote of 54.4 per cent (the closest battle was in Tasmania where the proposal scraped across the line by 1719 votes). This remains the lowest national Yes vote for a successful referendum.

The Organised Marketing and Industrial Employment proposals failed. Both achieved a national majority (50.6 per cent and 50.3 per cent respectively), but only majorities in three states (New South Wales, Victoria and Western Australia).

The referendums, which had never been a focal point of the

campaign, fell quickly from public attention. Before the poll, Labor Minister Arthur Calwell had promised that Labor would reintroduce any referendum questions that failed. But, by 1947, the Chifley government was focused on the issue of bank nationalisation. In 1948, the government again focused on constitutional reform, but not on the proposals rejected in 1946. This time the referendum question was a proposal to give the Commonwealth power over rents and prices. That question, held in 1948, failed in all six states and received a national minority of barely 40 per cent. The bank nationalisation issue then played a role in the government's defeat in 1949 and its replacement by the reinvigorated Menzies-led Coalition government. Under that government, two of the themes of the 1946 referendum – totalitarianism and communism – returned to play a major role in Australia's next referendum, the 1951 proposal on the banning of communism in Australia.

1951 – Banning communism

Australians were next asked to vote in a referendum on 22 September 1951, this time on whether to change the Constitution to permit the banning of the Australian Communist Party. The 1946 referendum had been a battle between hope (health, jobs and stability) and fear (totalitarianism, communism and unification). The 1951 referendum was just about fear. The question asked of Australians boiled down to this: which was the greater threat – communism or a Commonwealth armed with special and dangerous powers.

Two men entered the debate as saviours. Robert Menzies, Prime Minister and leader of the Liberal–Country Party Coalition government, stepped up as defender against the communist menace. Dr HV Evatt, a former High Court judge and leader of the Labor Opposition from mid-1951, stepped up as defender of the rule of law and the separation of powers.

The story of the 1951 referendum is one of two battles. There was the battle of ideas: national security or limited government? And there was the battle of personalities between Menzies and Evatt.

The story of the referendum began almost two years before, on 19 December 1949, with the swearing in of the Menzies government. While the focus of the election had been on domestic issues, both the Liberal and Country Parties went to the people with the policy of banning the Australian Communist Party. As far back as the 1946 federal election, the latter party had made a policy statement which asserted that: 'The Country Party regards the Australian Communist in the same category as a venomous snake – to be killed before it kills. Therefore, it stands foursquare for declaring the Communist Party an illegal organisation.'[31]

The new government's first major measure was the Communist Party Dissolution Bill, which was introduced into Parliament on the day that Australian forces landed to take part in the Korean War. The Bill proposed to dissolve the Australian Communist Party, prosecute its members and purge them from the Australian public service. It also enabled the Governor-General to declare other organisations unlawful that had supported or advocated communism, were affiliated with the Party, or had policies substantially shaped by members of the Party or 'communists'. Once unlawful, an association would be dissolved. This declaration power could also be used by the Governor-General to declare any person to be a 'communist' or member of the Party. Once declared, a person could not hold office in the Commonwealth public service or in industries declared by the Governor-General to be vital to the security and defence of Australia. A person wishing to contest a declaration against them bore the burden of proving that they were not a communist.

Chifley, still leader of the Labor Party, and Evatt, his Deputy and Shadow Attorney-General, decided initially to oppose the Bill. But it became clear that, if Labor did not support it, Menzies would call a double dissolution election based upon the Bill having been rejected twice by the Senate. Evatt was confident that the Bill would not survive a High Court challenge. He urged Labor to support it, trusting in the judicial backstop. With Labor support, the Bill became law in late 1950.

An immediate application was made to the High Court to stop any use of the new law, with a full hearing of the Court commencing soon after. The leading lights of the Bar appeared for the government: Barwick KC (later Chief Justice of the High Court), Taylor KC and Windeyer KC (both later Justices of the High Court). In a move that astonished many, Evatt accepted a brief from the Waterside Workers' Federation to oppose the Bill. When judgment was delivered on 9 March 1951, it was against the Commonwealth by 6:1.[32] The Court held that the Commonwealth lacked the power to pass such a law during peacetime, and in particular was not permitted to give the Governor-General an unchecked discretion to declare organisations unlawful and people to be communists.

Ten days later, on Menzies' advice, the Governor-General called a double dissolution election. The legal reason for the dissolution was not the High Court case; it was the Senate's failure twice to pass the Commonwealth Bank Bill. But the political reason was clear: Menzies wanted further electoral backing for his anti-communist policies. At the election on 28 April 1951, communism was a major issue. Evatt was opposed in his seat by Second World War hero Nancy Wake, who campaigned on the slogan 'I am the defender of freedom; Dr Evatt is the defender of communism'.[33] Evatt retained his seat by 243 votes, and the Menzies government was returned, with a reduced majority in the House of Representatives, but with control of the Senate.

After the election, Menzies immediately set out to gain the constitutional power to ban the Australian Communist Party. He first sought a referral of power from the states, but the New South Wales and Queensland Labor governments refused the request.

Menzies then introduced a proposal into Parliament to amend the Constitution by adding a new section 51A as follows:

(1) The Parliament shall have power to make such laws for the peace, order and good government of the Commonwealth with respect to Communists or Communism as the Parliament considers to be necessary or expedient for the defence or security of the Commonwealth or for the execution or maintenance of the Constitution or of the laws of the Commonwealth.

(2) ... [T]he Parliament shall have power:
   (a) To make a law in the terms of the Communist Party Dissolution Act 1950
       (i) Without alteration; or
       (ii) with alterations, being alterations with respect to a matter dealt with by the Act or with respect to some other matter with respect to which the Parliament has power to make laws;
   (b) To make laws amending the law made under the last preceding paragraph, but so that any such amendment is with respect to a matter dealt with by that law or with respect to some other matter with respect to which the Parliament has power to make laws.[34]

The parliamentary debate on the proposal established the battle-lines for the referendum. For Menzies, the question was whether Parliament should have the power to deal with the communist menace as it saw fit. For Evatt, now leader of the Labor Party after the death of Chifley on 13 June 1951, the question was whether Parliament should have a power contrary to British traditions of liberty and justice. Menzies saw the power as essential; Evatt saw it as totalitarian. With the government controlling Parliament, the Bill passed both Houses, and on 10 August 1951 the Governor-General issued the writ for the referendum. The date was set for

22 September 1951, leaving time for a six-week campaign.

Menzies was operating with the benefit of strong public support for the banning of communism. He had reason to be confident about his prospects of success at the referendum. In June, a Gallup poll put support for the proposed referendum at 80 per cent. By August, it was still at 73 per cent.[35] The No case faced an enormous challenge.

Evatt led the No campaign. The referendum was an important opportunity for him, as the recently installed leader of the Labor Party, to dent the government's popularity. Labor had clawed back five seats at the 1951 election, and another eight at the next election would put Labor back in power. In addition to his political motivations, Evatt had a strong personal dislike of the proposal. He saw the constitutional change as an attack on fundamental legal principles. Evatt's campaign was monumental for the day. Over the six weeks, he traversed Australia, travelling more than 22 000 kilometres. Even opponents would acknowledge Evatt's superhuman efforts, with Menzies later describing Evatt's campaign as having all the intensity of a general election.[36]

Menzies took charge of the Yes campaign. Perhaps distracted by government or convinced of the referendum's popularity, Menzies gave Evatt almost three weeks head start – a decision he would later regret. His campaign commenced on 4 September 1951 with a rousing speech at Canterbury Memorial Hall in Menzies' home town of Melbourne. Menzies' motivations were complicated. No doubt he saw in the referendum an opportunity to split the Labor Party, and to tie its name and its leader indelibly to communism. Menzies, as Prime Minister and as a frequent correspondent with counterparts in the United States and the United Kingdom, may also have truly believed in the Red Menace, that communism formed a fifth column in Australia and that Australia could fall just like eastern Europe. Regardless of Menzies' motivation, what is clear is that, once he started the campaign, he expressed his opinions as forcefully and almost as tirelessly as Evatt.

The campaign was wild and raucous. Menzies' speeches were repeatedly shouted down by interjectors. In a meeting in Hurstville, in Sydney, he was confronted by interruptions of 'Heil Hitler'.[37] Menzies saw this as a plus: these interjectors, he said, were communists doing as was their wont, denying free speech and destroying liberty. After being heckled in a meeting at City Hall in Brisbane that attracted 3000 people, Menzies declared:

> It is wonderful that the only real supporters for the 'No' case
> in this campaign that I have been able to find have been
> Communists and their hangers on.[38]

In another meeting in Melbourne, Menzies' retort to an interjector was: 'He is just one of Dr Evatt's Reds: don't worry about him'.[39] This became a common theme of Menzies' campaign: opponents of the referendum were either communists or communist sympathisers. On the day before the referendum, the *Sydney Morning Herald* urged:

> Communists' right to the protection of the laws they are
> pledged to destroy cannot logically be defended. Before voting
> tomorrow, Australians of whatever political opinion should ask
> themselves whether such a dangerous and treasonable element
> ought to be accorded the privileges and immunities enjoyed by
> loyal citizens. Communists are enemy agents …
>   We are under attack as a free nation. We must defend
> ourselves, from enemies within no less than enemies without.
> There is a clear call to every patriotic Australian to rally behind
> his Government at a time of national emergency.[40]

Liberal MP William Wentworth was also explicit, describing the Labor Party as a 'transmission belt between the Communists and the Labor voter'.[41] Advertisements commissioned by the Yes campaign implied that opponents were unpatriotic. Under a picture of Australian soldiers in Korea, one advertisement stated: 'these boys are fighting communism … Vote 1 yes'.[42]

FIGURE 5.3 **Advertisement for the Yes campaign in the 1951 referendum**
Source: *Sydney Morning Herald*, 12 July 1951, p. 2.

On one level, the campaigns were about over-the-top slogan-eering. Proponents repeatedly said that there was only one issue in the referendum: do you oppose communism? Proponents used a common vocabulary of emotive words: 'smash', 'sabotage', 'cripple', 'destroy' and 'weaken'. This was what the Australian Communist Party would do to Australian democracy and individual liberty, they said, if it were not declared illegal. Opponents equally repeatedly said there was one issue in the referendum: do you oppose totalitarian-ism? Opponents also had a shared vocabulary: 'Police State', 'dicta-torship', 'control' and 'tyranny'. On one occasion, opponents even said that the powers sought by the government, far from being anti-communist, were a method of communism itself. The No campaign also had an image: Belsen, the horrific Nazi concentration camp.

Evatt described the Menzies government as 'following the road that led to the horrors of Belsen'.[43]

As much as such rhetoric may have dominated the public debate, it did represent deeper positions. The No campaign said that the new powers were disproportionate. It was one thing to give the Commonwealth the power to re-enact the Communist Party Dissolution Act; it was another entirely to give the Commonwealth a general power to make laws with respect to communists and communism. Perversely, in Evatt's view, the powers could be used to make laws *for* communism, not against communism. Alternatively, Evatt said, the powers could be used to target trade unions and religious groups, or indeed whatever and whomever Parliament deemed to be 'communists'. Evatt called on Chifley's memory. Chifley would oppose the referendum, he said: in Chifley's words, the Menzies Bill that the referendum would authorise would pave the way for 'the liar, the perjurer and the pimp to make charges to damn a man's reputation'.[44] Existing criminal laws, Evatt said, already gave more than sufficient power to respond to the threat that communism posed to the nation.

The Yes campaign replied that the powers were not unprecedented: the United Kingdom, other Commonwealth countries and even the Australian states already had these powers. In fact, proponents pointed out that it had always been Labor party policy to give the Commonwealth all the powers that the states possessed. They

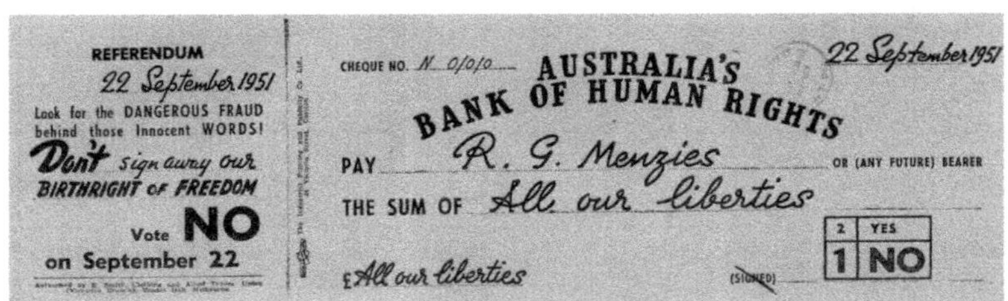

FIGURE 5.4 **Advertisement for the No campaign in the 1951 referendum**
Source: State Library of NSW, Mitchell Library, Ephemera Collection.

FIGURE 5.5 Advertisement for the No campaign in the 1951 referendum

Source: *Liberty*, No. 17, 28 August 1951, p. 1.

argued that parliamentary democracy was a sufficient check on any abuse of the powers, and that their exercise would be subject to judicial review. To this end, the campaign commissioned and published a supportive opinion from Sir Garfield Barwick and Alan Taylor, both King's Counsel.[45] Kevin Ward KC also published an opinion saying that there were adequate safeguards.[46] As to the existing criminal laws, the Yes case said that if they were sufficient to deal with the threat, the government would have used them. In any event, such laws are not preventive, and could only operate once a crime had occurred.

In addition to these legal arguments, the Yes case said that the people had already approved the exercise of these powers by electing the Menzies government in 1949 and 1951. They also said that Labor members, in opposing a referendum, were hypocrites because they had voted in Parliament for the Communist Party Dissolution Act.

Urgency was a theme of the Yes case. Action was needed now to prevent the apocalypse: vote Yes now, 'while there is still time',[47] one advertisement urged. Menzies captured the argument in saying:

> Are we, in the name of philosophical freedom, to allow enemy
> agents to defeat our defence preparations and weaken our
> economic state, so that on the appointed day we shall be unable
> to fight?[48]

For both campaigns, the other was devious and misleading. Advertisements, with some wit, labelled the No case full of 'red herrings'.[49]

The campaign split all of the major political parties. One advertisement purported to set out 'why every thinking Liberal will vote NO'.[50] A leading Young Liberal, Alan Missen, later to become a Senator, wrote in the *Argus* opposing the referendum: it was 'a totalitarian power to be given for all time'.[51] Ivor Greenwood, a prominent member of the Liberal Party, who was later to serve as a Minister in both the McMahon and Fraser governments, described the referendum as 'completely contrary to all that liberalism stands for'.[52] Labor was also internally divided. Labor had a historical connection to Catholics, and many Catholics, following the Vatican's strict anti-communist views, were viscerally opposed to communism.

Many Australians joined the debate. Religious groups played an important role. The No case drew support from Anglican clerics and even some Catholic ones. Archbishop Mannix, the charismatic Bishop of Melbourne, advocated neither side; but said that he doubted the proposal would be effective at stopping communism. Alban Moyes, the Anglican Bishop of Armidale, decried the referendum as risking a police state. For Reverend Ernest Burgmann, Anglican Bishop of Canberra, the issue was sectarian and Anglicans had a special responsibility to oppose the referendum: the question was one of British freedom (No) versus Catholic authoritarianism (Yes). In a letter published in the *Sydney Morning Herald*, he argued:

> Roman Catholics are behind the present Government in
> this proposed legislation … That Church is authoritarian in
> principle and by conviction and tireless in pursuit of its aims …
> My fellow Anglicans will use their traditional freedom, not
> lightly won, nor easily maintained and vote as they think best.[53]

Jack Lang, a former New South Wales Premier and bitter adversary of communism, came out in opposition of the referendum. The Australian Council of Civil Liberties, formed in 1935, also stepped in to oppose, as did academics such as future Governor-General Zelman Cowen, a professor of law at Melbourne University. The Yes campaign similarly drew support from prominent figures. Former Prime Minster Billy Hughes, for example, addressed 600 students at Sydney University in support of the change.

The media played a prominent role. Most newspapers promoted a Yes vote. An editorial in *The Age* described Evatt's case as based on 'theoretic deductions'.[54] For the *Sydney Morning Herald*, Menzies' speeches were 'forceful and bitingly logical', and Evatt's simply repetitious.[55] It saw Evatt's strategy as being 'the familiar lawyer's trick of trying to create a doubt in the minds of the jury – in this case, the Australian people'.[56]

As the campaign progressed, Menzies' attacks became increasingly directed at Evatt rather than the No case, prompting the *Sunday Herald* to call the referendum a 'Menzies–Evatt duel'.[57] Evatt, Menzies said, posed the real risk of dictatorship. In a speech in Brisbane, Menzies commented: 'If you were to ask anyone in Parliament House who is the best qualified person to hold the title of Dictator in Parliament the answer would be "Dr Evatt".'[58] Menzies recounted how, when he had opposed Evatt's 1944 referendum, Evatt had (according to Menzies) sent two security guards to Menzies' office the next day to rough him up.[59] Menzies started satirically referring to Evatt only as 'the learned doctor'.[60] Menzies also reminded audiences that Evatt had defended the Australian Communist Party before the High Court, had never forcefully criticised the Party and had even argued against the United Nations fighting communists in Korea.

As Menzies' campaign became personal, Evatt's became populist. The referendum, he said, was about trust and power: could you trust Menzies with more power? This enabled Evatt to remind the voters of the domestic failures of the Menzies government.[61] Despite Menzies' promises, inflation had soared; tax increases were pending; and the government had threatened to sell key assets, like Trans Australia Airlines. This was the government, Evatt said, which was now seeking more power.

On 19 September, just three days before the election, support for the Yes case had dwindled, but remained strong. A poll put the national Yes vote in the range of 53 per cent to 57 per cent. One million Australians had changed their minds since the No campaign began in August; but not enough to mean that the referendum would fail. The day before the referendum, the race had narrowed

The Leader of the Opposition, Dr. H. V. Evatt, opposing the referendum bill, said the A.L.P. believed the Government had ample powers under the Constitution, without any amendment to deal with treasonable, seditious or subversive offences.

FIGURE 5.6   Cartoon from the 1951 referendum

Source: *Sydney Morning Herald*, 24 May 1967, p. 1. Reproduced courtesy of George Lipman and fairfaxphotos.com.

even further. The *Sydney Morning Herald* reported that both sides were 'sure of victory'.[62]

As referendum day loomed, the campaigns became frenetic. Menzies travelled to Hurstville, on the corner of Evatt's electorate, to deliver his final speech. Evatt's final speech was on the Esplanade at Bondi, before 1200 people. Evatt, not known as a powerful orator, delivered what was, according to observers, a powerful, heartfelt speech. On referendum eve, the view of most of the press and commentators was that the vote would be very close.

When Australians went to the polls on 22 September, 4 687 936 formal votes were cast.[63] The referendum was narrowly lost. The national Yes vote was 49.4 per cent (2 317 927 Yes votes to 2 370 009 No votes), with majorities achieved only in Queensland, Western Australia and Tasmania. New South Wales, Evatt's home state and focus of his campaigning, recorded the lowest Yes vote of 47.2 per cent. Sydney, where the battle was particularly closely fought, was a city divided. Electoral districts north of the harbour and the blue ribbon Liberal seat of Wentworth in Sydney's east all voted Yes. Most other electorates, including Evatt's electorate of Barton in Sydney's south, voted No. The electorate of Cook, which took in Sydney University and surrounds, recorded an overwhelming No vote of 80.1 per cent, while 75.5 per cent of voters in Bradfield, in Sydney's upper north shore, voted Yes. Melbourne was even more clearly divided, with a clean fracture between east (Yes) and west (No). Menzies' electorate of Kooyong supported its representative, recording the highest Yes vote in Melbourne (65.6 per cent). The results were news worldwide, with the *New York Times* giving it front-page billing.

The press immediately began to dissect the reasons for the referendum's failure. This gave rise to a familiar list. For commentators, the referendum showed the inherent reluctance of Australians to change their Constitution, and in particular their resistance to giving more power to the Commonwealth. The question was also too wide, and the result may have been different had the Commonwealth asked just for the power to pass the Communist Party Dissolution Act. The government had mismanaged the campaign: Menzies gave Evatt too much of a head start, and should have extended his campaign beyond the capital cities. Australians wanted a chance to express their dissatisfaction with Menzies' handling of domestic issues such as inflation, credit restrictions, retrenchments in the public service and prospective tax increases. Australians were also swayed by the declarations of religious groups and university figures. Only *The Age* suggested that the people might have reached a rational judgment that the risk the referendum posed to civil rights outweighed the risk of communism.[64] For Menzies, on the other hand, the reason for the failure was simple: the people were misled by an unscrupulous No campaign.[65]

The press speculated on the ramifications for Menzies and Evatt. For Menzies, commentators said that it was a rebuff, but not terminal. Menzies had control of both Houses of Parliament, and almost three years until another election. Indeed, Menzies went on to become Australia's longest serving Prime Minister, but his government was to never again hold a referendum. Later political leaders have cast doubt on Menzies' wisdom in holding the 1951 referendum. Prime Minister John Howard, for example, a successor to Menzies as leader of the Liberal party, said in 2002 that he thought Australians had got it right in voting No in 1951.[66]

For Evatt, the ramifications were mixed. He had strengthened his position in the party (he would remain Opposition leader for another nine years). But it had also branded him, and the Labor Party, indelibly as communist sympathisers in the minds of many Australians. The onus was now on Evatt and Labor to disprove that brand, something they would find very difficult. Due in part to this, and also its own bitter internal splits, the Labor Party would remain in Opposition for another 21 years until it was led to power by Gough Whitlam in 1972. Evatt sensed these problems, but was unapologetic. In his view, the referendum was 'more important than half a dozen general elections ... an error of judgment in a referendum would tend to destroy the whole democratic fabric of justice and liberty'.[67] That may be so, but Evatt paid a heavy price. He never became Prime Minister, and decades after his death in 1965 he would still often be recalled as a defender of communism rather than for his illustrious career as a leading barrister, High Court Justice, Attorney-General, Minister for External Affairs, President of the United Nations General Assembly, leader of the Opposition and, during the 1951 referendum, advocate for the rule of law, justice and liberty.

1967 – Australia's greatest referendum?

On 27 May 1967, Australians made their most important constitutional pronouncement since 1901 when they voted to erase a racially discriminatory provision from the Constitution and to grant the Commonwealth power to make laws with regard to Aboriginal peoples. That, however, was not the only question put to Australians on that day. While the people accepted this change to the Constitution, they simultaneously rejected a proposal to break the link between the sizes of the two Houses of the federal Parliament.

The story of the two referendum proposals begins with the dying days of the Menzies government. Menzies retired from Parliament in early 1966 and was succeeded on Australia Day 1966 by his Treasurer, Harold Holt. Menzies had been reluctant to attempt constitutional reform since his failure in the 1951 referendum. Nevertheless, in 1965, the government committed to putting two questions to the people – which would ultimately become the questions on the ballot in May 1967. Holt had no special interest in the proposals, but after winning the November 1966 general election he needed to keep the Liberal Party's public commitment to put them to the people.

The Aboriginals proposal involved two components. Both of them reflected fundamental changes in Australia's conception of Indigenous people and Indigenous policy since Federation. Neither of the 1890s Conventions that debated the Constitution had included Indigenous people: cast as a 'dying race', they played no meaningful role in its drafting. While the preamble to the Constitution suggests that 'the people ... have agreed to unite', it makes no mention of Aboriginal people or their prior occupation of the lands upon which the new nation was formed.

The operative provisions of the Constitution were also premised upon exclusion and even discrimination. The Constitution made two references to Indigenous Australians (in neither case referring to them as 'people'). Section 51(26) empowered the federal Parliament to make laws with respect to: 'The people of any race, *other than the aboriginal race in any State*, for whom it is deemed necessary to make special laws'. The 1967 referendum deleted the words in italics. It also repealed section 127, which provided: 'In reckoning the numbers of the people of the Commonwealth, or of a State or other part of the Commonwealth, aboriginal natives shall not be counted'.

The original drafting of section 51(26) meant that laws about Aboriginal peoples were to be made at the state and not federal level. The practical effect of section 127 was that Indigenous people were not to be counted for the purpose of determining the size and distribution of electorates for the federal Parliament. The result was a substantial under-weighting of the Indigenous vote.

Well before 1967, national attitudes had changed. The ban on Aboriginal people voting in federal elections put in place in 1902 was removed in 1962 (though, even then, full equality at federal elections did not occur until 1983 when the law was amended to make enrolment for and voting in federal elections compulsory for Indigenous people as it is for other Australians). A sense had also emerged that national laws needed to be enacted to protect the interests of Aboriginal people, and that it was no longer acceptable to have a provision in the Constitution that was so obviously discriminatory. Rooting out this constitutionalised discrimination was an important part of changing Australia's conception of itself as a nation.

This is not to say that all discriminatory provisions were removed. No attempt has ever been made to delete section 25 of the Constitution, which provides that, for the purpose of determining how many members each state will have in the House of Representatives, 'if by the law of any State all persons of any race are disqualified from voting at elections for the more numerous House of the Parliament of the State, then, in reckoning the number of the people of the

State or of the Commonwealth, persons of that race resident in that State shall not be counted'. Section 25 lowers the population count of a state if that state disqualifies people of a particular race from voting, and thus penalises it by restricting its parliamentary representation. However, in doing so, the provision tacitly acknowledges that Aboriginal and other racial groups can be so disqualified by a state.

Attitudes had also changed on whether the Commonwealth should be able to make laws for Indigenous peoples. By 1967, the states were moving towards uniformity in Indigenous policy, but gaps remained. Why, it was asked, should an Indigenous person have freedom of movement in New South Wales, but, upon crossing the Queensland border, need permission to enter a hotel? Why did only South Australia apply internationally recognised labour standards to Indigenous employees? Why should South Australia be able to target laws at Indigenous disadvantage, but the Northern Territory was unable to do so? Above all was one issue: when it came to Indigenous disadvantage, why should the Commonwealth have all the money, but none of the responsibility?

For the media, the question was a 'simple matter of humanity … [and] a test of Australia's standing in the world'.[68] *The Age* said the question posed to Australians was whether they would yet recognise that 'Aborigines [should] be regarded as completely human'.[69]

The question put in 1967 capped decades of effort. The push for change could be traced back at least as far as the late 1920s, when the Association for the Protection of the Native Races of Australasia and Polynesia argued that:

> The method of relying upon State and Colonial Governments
> has been tried from the earliest days of colonisation, and has
> undeniably failed … It is a recognised political principal that
> the wider the area from which the governing power is derived,
> the larger the task set, the wider and more statesmanlike the

FIGURE 5.7 Advertisement for the Yes campaign in the 1967 referendum
Source: AIATSIS Digital Archive. Reproduced Courtesy of Faith Bandler.

policy is likely to be. It follows as a corollary that the Federal government is likely to deal with the whole problem more adequately than the State Governments.[70]

The dissenting report to the 1929 Royal Commission on the Constitution agreed, and recommended that the Commonwealth should have responsibility for Indigenous peoples. In 1938, the Australian Aboriginal League, together with the Aborigines Progressive Association, initiated a 'Day of Mourning', calling for Commonwealth control of Indigenous affairs and a national policy.[71]

In 1944, the Curtin government unsuccessfully sought power over Indigenous peoples in the failed Post-war Reconstruction and

Democratic Rights referendum. This proved only to be a temporary setback for the movement, and debate stepped up a notch in the late 1940s and 1950s. In 1949, Indigenous returned servicemen were given the right to vote. In 1950, the House of Representatives unanimously moved a motion that the Commonwealth Government:

a. Exercises national responsibility for Aboriginal people and cooperates with the States.
b. Works towards the social advancement as well as the protection of Aborigines.
c. Provides additional finance and effective administration.[72]

In 1957, Opposition Leader HV Evatt declared in Parliament:

the only thing to be done with the Australian aboriginal, full-blood or otherwise, is to give him the benefit of the same laws as apply to every other Australian.[73]

In 1962, the franchise was extended to all Indigenous Australians, something that strengthened the case for constitutional reform: it was absurd for Indigenous Australians to have the vote, but not the right to be counted for the purposes of determining electoral districts.

The movement for constitutional reform continued to build, culminating in the Freedom Ride in 1965 in which 30 Sydney University students, including Jim Spigelman, a future Chief Justice of New South Wales, travelled through rural New South Wales to highlight discrimination against Indigenous people. That same year, Western Australia and Queensland became the last states to guarantee Indigenous people the right to vote. By 1967, and probably well before that, debate on the issue had come to an end: there was consensus on the need for reform. The referendum could almost be described as being just a formality.

Support for the referendum came from all quarters. Every major party and many community figures supported the change. The unique national consensus was reflected in the absence of any strong or effective No campaign. Parliament produced no official No case. Letters to the newspapers ran almost unequivocally in support. Where there was opposition, it lay at the margins of the debate. Some argued a losing battle for state power: saying that power should remain with the states so they could fashion locally appropriate laws. Others took the opposite tack: the Commonwealth should have no power to make race-based laws at all, for that was the first step towards segregation and apartheid. None of these arguments had an impact. The Australian people had made up their minds to move on from the past, and had decided that voting Yes to the Aboriginals question was the way forward.

The Aboriginals question comprised half of the ballot that confronted the 5.2 million Australians who voted in 1967. The other question – the Parliament question – asked voters to break the 'nexus' between the sizes of the House of Representatives and the Senate. In the 1901 Constitution, the framers set out in section 24 that the House must be, as near as practicable, twice the size of the Senate. For most of Australian history, there had been 36 Senators (six from each state) and approximately 72 members of the Lower House (with New South Wales and Victoria taking the largest share of those). In 1949, the Labor government increased the size of both Houses. The Senate was increased from 36 to 60 members and the House from 74 to 121. Despite this increase, rapid population growth meant that Australians were represented by far fewer Commonwealth parliamentarians per head of population than had been the case at Federation. In 1901, there was about one member of Parliament for every 50 000 Australians; by 1967, that number was one per 94 000. Both major parties were reluctant to increase the size of the House because that would require a proportionate increase in the size of the Senate. Because of the Senate's system of proportional voting, the effect would be to increase the power of minor parties and possibly independents. These facts had formed the basis of a recommendation in the 1959 report of the bipartisan Joint Committee on Constitutional Review of the federal Parliament to break the nexus between the sizes of the Houses. Sir Garfield Barwick, Attorney-General in the Menzies government, did not support the recommendation, and it did not progress while he remained a Minister. However, after Barwick was appointed as Chief Justice of the High Court in 1964, the proposal was dusted off and adopted by the Menzies Cabinet in 1965.

The Parliament proposal sought to do three things: it would remove any link between the size of the Houses of Commonwealth Parliament; it would set a maximum number of Members of the House, being no more than one for every 85 000 Australians; and it would set a minimum number of Senators, being ten per state. The key to the proposal from the government's perspective was the first of these, the breaking of the nexus. The other two parts to the proposal were designed, ultimately unsuccessfully, to alleviate concerns that the proposal was an attack on the Senate.

The Menzies and Holt governments had strong political reasons for championing the Parliament proposal. There had been no redistribution of Commonwealth electoral boundaries since 1955, and one was clearly overdue. A planned redistribution after the 1961 census had been abandoned after strong opposition by the Country Party. Since 1955, there had been vast demographic changes, and by 1967 some electorates had almost 125 000 voters, while others had less than 40 000. Because of these changes, it was expected that the Liberal Party and, particularly, the Country Party would lose a swath of seats in any redistribution. To avert this, Holt had two options. With no change to the Constitution, he could increase the size of the House and the Senate. But he knew that any increase in the size of the Senate would, because of the proportionate representation system, increase the representation and power of the Democratic Labor Party (DLP), a consequence none of the major parties wanted. Alternatively, Holt could break the nexus and increase the size of the House by about 12 members, with no increase in the size of the Senate. In doing so, he would hand some seats to the Labor Party, but that would not be disastrous, given that the Coalition had 82 seats to Labor's 41. More importantly, he could act to protect the seats of sitting Coalition members. This, then, was the political calculus that underpinned the broad support for the Parliament proposal: the Liberal and Country Parties would retain seats; Labor would gain seats; and all major parties would guard against an insurgent DLP.

To recognise the political expediency behind the proposal is not to deny that there were solid arguments for the change. For its proponents, an increase in the size of Parliament was necessary for effective representative government. The parliamentarian to elector ratio was said to be too low for representatives to properly respond to their constituents' needs. Not only were parliamentarians representing many more people than in the past, they were saddled with far greater responsibilities as the Commonwealth had entered into fields that had traditionally been the responsibility of the states. If there were an increase in the size of the House so that constituents could be effectively represented, proponents argued, the question is whether that should necessarily flow on to an increase in the size of the Senate. Should an increase on one side of the equation necessarily cause an increase on the other? For proponents, the answer was No. They saw the need for a cautious increase of 12 or so Members of the House of Representatives if the proposal were successful, and a much larger growth across both Houses of up to 72 new politicians if it were not.[74]

This was the case that Holt and the leaders of the Country Party (John McEwen) and Labor Opposition (Gough Whitlam) took to the people. They had the support of all 124 members of the House and 50 of the 60 members of the Senate.

Ranged against the heavy artillery of the major parties was a motley crew of ten Senators. Most prominent were Vincent Gair, federal leader of the DLP, Frank McManus, Victorian DLP representative, and Reginald Wright, Tasmanian Liberal representative. They were supported by three other Liberal Senators, two Country Party Senators and two Independents. The No campaign mobilised quickly and rallied under a simple banner: 'no more politicians'. The claim was this: the only check on the size of the House is that a government wanting to expand the House must also expand the Senate. If you take away that check, they said, greed will lead to ever more politicians in Canberra. Gair, who took on the mantle of unofficial leader of the No campaign, raised the spectre of a House with 300 Members by the year 2000. Tacked on to the cry of 'no more politicians' was a more familiar referendum angle: the referendum was portrayed as an attack on the Senate that would also weaken constitutional protection of the small states. The Senate, they said, was the states' House; a proportionate increase in the size of the House relative to the Senate would see relatively fewer Senators in Cabinet, with less representation of state interests, and there would be few opportunities for small state interests to be effective in exercising Commonwealth power. Further, the larger the size of the House compared to the Senate, the more power the House would wield in any joint sitting of the Parliament after a double dissolution held in accordance with section 57 of the Constitution. For the Gair-led opposition, a Yes vote was a big win for politicians and the big states, and a big loss for the people. The No campaign was vigorous and astonishingly effective.

Holt, McEwen, Whitlam and the Yes campaign seemed to be taken unawares by the strength of the opposition. Their campaign began slowly and never accelerated to full speed. Holt's support was limited to recorded television and radio broadcasts. The Country Party distributed some handouts and the young Ian Sinclair (later a leader of the Country Party after it had been rebadged as the National Party) gave two broadcasts. Whitlam was the only leader of the major parties to spend extensive time on the hustings, and even he limited himself to speeches in Brisbane, Sydney and Perth. The press quickly formed the view that Holt was not committed to a campaign that had become a losing fight.

The Yes campaign stumbled from one gaffe to another. In the lead-up to the referendum, Holt instigated a fight with the Senate. The government wanted to increase postage charges, while the Senate took the popular step of saying No. The day before the referendum, Holt hinted at the possibility of a double dissolution; but it was clear that the Senate had the people on side. For the No campaign, this was manna from heaven: Holt was seen to want to undermine the body that had stood up to his arrogant, overbearing government. Whitlam did not help matters either. On the eve of the referendum, he spoke about abolishing the Senate, something that made it all the more difficult to portray the change as a mere machinery provision, as opposed to an attack on that institution.

Many people were concerned that the impending train wreck of the Parliament proposal would affect the Aboriginals proposal. As the referendum approached, the letters pages of the newspapers lit up, but the major parties barely stepped up their campaign. One letter writer to the *Sydney Morning Herald* was 27-year old future Prime Minister John Howard, who was to be pre-selected for the federal seat of Drummoyne later that year. Howard wrote in strong support of the Parliament proposal.[75] In his view, an increase in the size of Parliament was necessary to enable parliamentarians to properly fulfil their responsibilities.

Even as the press stepped up its coverage, Australians continued to report widespread ignorance and confusion about the Parliament proposal. Australians did not understand the word 'nexus'; nor did they understand the constitutional principle that the proposal was targeted at – the tying of the sizes of the Senate and House.

As referendum day approached, Holt took to targeting the No campaign, rather than to supporting the Parliament proposal. He called opponents 'childish' and spouters of prejudice and ignorance.

When Holt did speak, his focus remained on the question of the nexus. Just a fifth of his key speech delivered on the night of 15 May – about two minutes – was devoted to the Aboriginals proposal. The press reported that, by and large, the Aboriginals question was ignored by the parties.

When Australians went to the polls on 27 May, many Indigenous Australians, being residents of the Northern Territory, could not vote. It would be another ten years before a referendum was passed to give people living in the territories the right to vote in referendums.

Contrary to expectations, it rapidly became apparent from the counting of the ballots that Australians had not voted a blanket Yes or a blanket No to the questions. The Aboriginals proposal streaked ahead, and recorded the highest national Yes vote for any referendum proposal ever put to the people. More than nine in ten formal votes favoured this change. The lowest Yes vote was in Western Australia, but more than eight in ten Western Australians still supported the proposal, making it the most successful referendum ever in that state. The largest No vote of any area was recorded in the Western Australian rural district of Kalgoorlie, where 8888 or 29 per cent of the votes were against changing the Constitution. The pattern Australia-wide was for huge Yes votes in the cities and slightly lower Yes votes in rural and regional areas. The differences in attitude between electors in regional areas where there was a higher concentration of Indigenous people and those in urban areas disturbed many. The referendum's success was unquestioned, but the attitudes it revealed were disappointing to some. Who, it was asked, would vote against a proposal to count Indigenous Australians in determining electoral boundaries and to give the Commonwealth power to make laws for their welfare?

Most Australians voted the opposite way for the Parliament proposal. At final count, barely four in ten Australians would support a proposal that had the approval of the three major parties,

FIGURE 5.8 Front-page *Sydney Morning Herald* photograph run during the 1967 referendum

Source: Sydney Morning Herald, 24 May 1967, p. 1.
Reproduced courtesy of George Lipman and fairfaxphotos.com.

the bipartisan Joint Committee on Constitutional Review and much of the press. Only New South Wales returned a Yes vote, in its case one of 51.0 per cent. Every Sydney district voted Yes, including Whitlam's outer-suburban electorate of Werriwa (which recorded a Yes vote of 53.6 per cent). The results in the other states were disastrous for proponents. Victoria, Holt's home state, recorded a Yes vote of barely more than 30 per cent, which remains the lowest Yes vote ever recorded by that state. Almost two-thirds (64.7 per cent) of Holt's own Victorian electorate of Higgins voted against the proposal. Tasmanians said No in greater proportions than any other state, with close to eight in ten (76.9 per cent) voting against the reform.

The day after the referendum, Holt left to travel overseas. Rather than focusing on the extraordinary moment of national consensus recorded in the vote on the Aboriginals proposal, he focused on the Parliament failure. Rather than labelling 27 May as a victory for Aboriginal Australians, he labelled it as a 'victory for prejudice and misrepresentation'.[76] Holt blamed Australians: 'the majority of electors chose to ignore the advice of those to whom they normally look for guidance'.[77] The Parliament proposal was also the main game for the press. Page one of the *Sunday Herald* on 28 May recorded the Yes vote on Aboriginals in small-type, before blaring in big, bold capitals: 'AUSTRALIA SAYS NO ON NEXUS'.[78] The press interpreted the day as a defeat for Holt. 'Prime Minister gets his first rebuff', *The Australian* declared.[79] Alan Ramsey, writing for *The Australian*, described Holt's campaign as a 'pitifully weak effort'.[80]

Commentators put the defeat of the Parliament proposal down to a range of factors. First, there was the strong No campaign run by Gair and the DLP. As Ramsey put it:

> [The No campaign] was an enormously successful and
> impressive example of clever misrepresentation and shrewd use
> of propaganda media. It ensured not an unintelligent vote on a
> complicated and confusing issue but an ill-informed one.[81]

Second, there was the weak Yes campaign, characterised by silence and gaffes by Holt and Whitlam. *The Australian* described the situation in this way: 'it was a case of an apathetic Goliath being demolished by a David armed not with a slingshot but a highly effective stream of emotional propaganda'.[82] The large difference in Yes votes between New South Wales and Victoria had three explanations: the DLP's special strength in Victoria; the stronger Yes campaign was run in New South Wales because New South Wales would gain the most from any new seats in the House once the nexus was broken; and the fact that most of the New South Wales press supported the referendum, while most opposed it in Victoria. Above all, contemporary commentators put the referendum's failure down to a perception by Australians that the purpose of the proposal was to serve the major political parties and not the national interest. The *Sydney Morning Herald* summed it up this way in their Monday editorial after the Saturday referendum:

> The explanation is too simple. There were the obvious campaign inadequacies (how little the Country Party tried!) and blunders (Mr Holt's hint of a double dissolution almost on the eve of the referendum, and Mr Whitlam's talk of abolishing the Senate); but the politicians need to look at themselves for one of the real causes of failure. The electorate decided … to deliver a judgment on politicians and their performances by voting No.[83]

It is only over time that Australia has come to see the true significance of the 1967 referendum. The unprecedented Yes vote for the Aboriginals proposal was interpreted as a strong mandate for the making of national laws and policy on Indigenous affairs. Before the referendum, Holt gave no indication that the Commonwealth had any intention of using the power it would acquire should the referendum be successful. Soon afterwards, however, the Commonwealth convened a Federal–State Conference on Aboriginal Welfare. Over the coming decades, Indigenous affairs would become a central part of the Commonwealth political and policy landscape. The other major effect of the referendum was to strengthen Indigenous groups and their public advocacy. Many took strength from the overwhelming success of the poll. On the 40th anniversary of the referendum, the immediate reaction to the polls was reversed. The focus was all upon the Yes vote cast by Australians to remove discrimination against Aboriginal peoples and enable laws to be made on their behalf. Little or no attention was paid to the Parliament proposal, with many Australians not even realising that on referendum day in 1967 two votes had been cast.

1977 – Triple success

The genesis of the referendum held on 21 May 1977 lay in the meetings of the Australian Constitutional Convention. From 27 to 29 October 1976 at the Wrest Point Hotel Casino in Hobart, representatives of the Commonwealth, states and local government took part in a review of Australia's Constitution. The Convention produced a series of recommendations for constitutional reform, many of which had unanimous support. The Wrest Point Hotel Casino was an auspicious location for the gathering, since it had been granted Australia's first casino licence following a Tasmanian referendum on the subject in 1968.

The Commonwealth Government, led by Liberal Party leader Malcolm Fraser, committed to putting some of these recommendations to the people. This it did in May 1977, when it sent four of the proposals to the popular vote. Three of the proposals had the support of all or a large majority of the participants at the Convention. These were proposals to: introduce simultaneous elections for both Houses of Commonwealth Parliament; give Territorians the right to vote in referendums, with their votes counting towards the national tally; and to set a mandatory maximum retirement age for federal judges of 70 years.

The fourth proposal was to require that, when there is a vacancy in the Senate between elections, the replacement Senator would be from the same party. Its purpose was to codify a constitutional convention that had been accepted since 1949, but breached in the mid-1970s when New South Wales and Queensland had appointed non-Labor Senators as replacements for vacant Labor seats. The Australian Constitutional Convention had accepted the principle that the convention existed, but had rejected its codification because of technical difficulties in drafting an appropriate clause. The proposal put to the people was designed to overcome these difficulties and so was, in that sense, a product of the Convention.

Although there were four proposals, in Fraser's mind, only one counted – the Simultaneous Elections proposal. He has said that 'he was more attached to Simultaneous Elections than the others. To the extent [he] did campaign, it [was] because of that proposal.'[84] In Fraser's view, the success of the Simultaneous Elections proposal would 'be a significant improvement in Australia's democratic process'.[85]

None of the referendum proposals were groundbreaking in themselves. But the stakes were high. For most commentators, if Australians chose to vote No on 21 May 1977, it would signal the end of constitutional reform by consensus. The voters had said No to six questions put by the Whitlam government, on two referendum days, since 1973. Memories of these failures were strong. The four questions asked in 1977 were developed in a spirit of agreement, had bipartisan support and were of modest import. If these could not succeed, people asked, what could?

The proposals sailed through Parliament on the back of bipartisan support. There was a unanimous vote in favour in the House, while only a few rebel Coalition Senators voted against the proposals in the Senate. Fraser and Whitlam, just a year and a half after the constitutional crisis of 1975, spoke with one voice in support of the reforms.

Fraser and the Yes campaign marketed the four proposals in the same way: they were portrayed as sensible, fair and minimalist reforms. When asked later in the campaign to explain why there had been no sensational campaign headlines, Fraser replied: that is because 'the issues before the people [are] not dramatic'.[86] The strategy was clear: to distinguish the questions from those asked in previous divisive referendum campaigns, and to emphasise their consensual nature.

The No campaign was less coordinated. Lacking a national figurehead, it relied more on insurgency than concentrated fire-power. It did, however, quickly settle on a theme: the four proposals were 'deceptive, dangerous [and] unnecessary'.[87] The proposals were said to be deceptive in hiding their real intent, with the proposal for simultaneous elections, for example, actually being directed at weakening the Senate. They were also seen as unnecessary because Parliament and the government could already achieve many of the same objectives, albeit with some difficulty, without going to referendum. Above all, the proposals were dangerous: they meant, according to opponents, a massive transfer of power to the Common-wealth. Advertisements urged: 'Preserve power for the people – not Prime Ministers'.[88]

Beyond the slogans, the Yes and No cases developed arguments at length. For proponents, the Simultaneous Elections proposal would save government the expense and voters the annoyance of holding Senate and House elections on different days. Before 1960, House and Senate elections had always been simultaneous, except for that in 1953. But, since 1961, every election had been held separately except for those forced by a double dissolution. Holding simultane-ous elections would also ensure against the possibility that Senate elections could take place up to 11 months before the elected Sena-tors started sitting. Its greatest effect would be structural. Under the existing constitutional arrangements, the Senate in 1975 (with the assistance of Governor-General Sir John Kerr) had blocked the budget Bills in a way that forced the House of Representatives to an election. If in such a circumstance the government chose not to call a double dissolution, the Senate's blocking of supply would mean the dissolution of the House but not the Senate. Proponents of the reform claimed this was an unfair asymmetry: the Senate could force the House to an election; but the House had no reciprocal power. The proposal would ensure that, if the House was dissolved, at least half the Senate would go with it.

For opponents of Simultaneous Elections, cost savings were a non-issue. Elections, they pointed out, cost the equivalent of a couple of ice creams per elector. That was not commensurable with their democratic benefits. Opponents relied heavily on the fact that many members of the Fraser government had opposed Whitlam's Simultaneous Elections proposal in 1974. Why, opponents asked, had they changed their mind? The implication was clear, but unstated: that Fraser had short-term, political motivations – he was scared of holding a half-Senate election. Most importantly, opponents said, the proposal would weaken the Senate. Fraser, and the Yes case replied that this was incorrect: nothing in the proposal affected the Senate's powers of review. But the reply was flawed: proponents could not both argue that a reason for the change was to remove the asymmetry of power between the House and the Senate *and* argue that the referendum did not go to the Senate's powers. Both propositions could not be true. This was to become the major rift between the two sides, with repeated charges both ways of blatant misrepresentation and misinformation.

After Simultaneous Elections, Senate Casual Vacancies was the most controversial proposal. The constitutional convention that it sought to codify had existed since 1949, when proportionate representation was introduced for the Senate. Everyone agreed that the convention existed. The dispute was over its precise scope and whether it should be put in the text of the Constitution. The proposal put to the people went beyond what was the unanimously accepted convention. The convention only applied when a Senator died or resigned for bona fide reasons (such as ill health), whereas the proposal would apply in the event of any casual vacancy, including where it arose because the government chose to appoint a Senator to a plum administrative posting. The convention also only permitted a replacement Senator to be appointed until the next election; whereas, under the proposal put to the people, the replacement would be appointed for the remainder of the term of the replaced Senator, which could be two Senate elections away.

The argument for the Yes case was simple: the convention exists; it has been breached; it should be codified. The argument for the No case was equally simple: conventions should not be codified – there is a reason they are just conventions; codification necessarily causes problems of definition and may give rise to unintended consequences.

Opposition to the remaining two proposals was virtually non-existent. Proponents of the Territories proposal argued that it was only fair that Territorians who were subject to the Constitution, paid taxes and could vote in federal parliamentary elections should also be able to vote in referendums. Their opponents' strongest argument was that Territorians, being subject only to Commonwealth law, had no proper interest in voting on proposals to do with the federal balance. Why, opponents asked, should Territorians be able to vote on matters such as maintaining or increasing state power?

The Retirement of Judges proposal was being put at a time when there had been a substantial increase in the size of the federal judiciary due to appointments to the Federal Court and Family Court. The view was that life tenure was inappropriate for a large judiciary that needed to remain in touch with community standards. The proposal could also be seen as a response to the longevity of some members of the High Court, including Sir Edward McTiernan, who had been appointed to that Court in 1930 and only retired, at age 84, in 1976 after a record 46 years of service. Opposition was muted: unlike for the other three proposals, an official No case was not published. Only a few community figures stood up in opposition. One was Sir Robert Menzies, who argued that the new rule would deprive Australia of many fine legal minds. The other was Pat Lane, a professor of constitutional law at the University of Sydney.

For Lane, the proposal would provide little benefit and impose one substantial cost: it would increase the power of the government by increasing the turnover of federal judges and so the number of judges they could appoint.

Fraser took to the campaign with gusto. He was lauded by the press for his novel, 'multimedia' campaign technique, which involved talk-back radio, television and press conferences.[89] In a sign of a developing trend in political campaigns, the *Sydney Morning Herald* said:

> [Mr Fraser] is testing a new electioneering technique, which consists almost exclusively of giving radio and television interviews, interspersed with news conferences … By midday the Prime Minister has given three or four interviews on television and radio, interspersed with a news conference or two. Mr Fraser is reaching huge invisible audiences each day.[90]

When an air controller strike hit the campaign in its second-last week, Fraser did not miss a beat. He commandeered an RAAF Hercules aeroplane to fly to Tasmania in support of the referendum. Fraser promised that Tasmania would have the full support of the air force as the strike hit; and requested, incidentally, that Tasmanians vote Yes to all four proposals. Fraser travelled Australia-wide, but focused particularly on Tasmania, which he saw as the linchpin. His view seems to have been that the Yes vote in New South Wales, Victoria and South Australia was solid and the No vote in Queensland and Western Australia reasonably strong. In Tasmania the Yes vote was weak, but many voters were in the 'don't know' category. Fraser's strategy was to move them across to being Yes voters.[91]

Whitlam also hit the campaign trail, but he was much less prominent than Fraser. Whitlam publicly assured Labor supporters that a Yes vote in Simultaneous Elections would be in Labor's long-term interests. This proved counter-productive: the press reported a widespread 'contra-suggestibility' where Liberal voters expressed an intention to vote No purely because Whitlam had urged a vote of Yes.

The Yes campaign soon hit headwinds. The conservative side of politics was split, particularly on the Simultaneous Elections and Senate Casual Vacancies questions. These headwinds would be embodied in two State Premiers: Sir Joh Bjelke-Petersen, the National Party Premier of Queensland, and Sir Charles Court, Liberal Premier of Western Australia. Those two would become the figureheads of the No campaign and Fraser's major opponents.

For Sir Joh, opposition to Canberra was reflexive. It dated back at least to the Whitlam government that Sir Joh had hated with a passion. But it also extended to Fraser's Coalition government. Fraser had fought with Queensland over native title issues and over the mining of Fraser Island. Fraser felt betrayed by Sir Joh's opposition to the referendum and their relationship became increasingly hostile. When Sir Joh ran a vigorous anti-referendum campaign in Queensland, Fraser accused him of 'tilting at windmills'.[92] The slogan employed by the Queensland Government in opposition to the proposals was unreasoned, but emotive, and tapped into a basic anti-Canberra sentiment which Sir Joh had carefully cultivated: 'vote NO and protect Queensland'.[93] The Queensland Government spent tens of thousands of dollars on advertising the No case – so much, in fact, that the Commonwealth Cabinet took the unprecedented step of issuing a surprisingly strong and disparaging statement accusing the Queensland Government of misusing public funds:

> Huge sums of Australian taxpayers' funds are being spent in
> the Queensland advertising campaign that grossly distorts
> the facts of the situation … The advertisements are a blatant
> and desperate attempt to frighten the electorate away from
> progressive constitutional reforms … The State Government
> campaign is an attempt to mislead the electorate of
> Queensland.[94]

Towards the end of the campaign, Sir Joh released an anonymous, unreasoned legal opinion, saying that the Simultaneous Elections proposal could lead to the abolition of the Senate. Fraser, and the press, scoffed at the absurdity, but secretly feared that Queenslanders would follow the directions of their Premier.

Sir Charles Court's opposition was more reasoned, but no less effective. Court's motives for opposing Fraser are unclear. He had personal problems with the Fraser government, and had complained about Canberra leaking private telexes he had written. More likely, Court saw Canberra-bashing as an electoral plus in a state with traditional anti-Canberra views. Court would lose few votes in opposing the referendums, and could clothe the opposition in the language of standing up for Western Australia's rights. Court argued particularly strongly against the Simultaneous Elections proposal. In his view, the Fraser government had created a 'credibility gap' by opposing the proposal in 1974 and then reintroducing it just three years later.[95] In Court's words: '[t]o put the same proposals in 1977 is an insult to the people – and a calculated insult at that'.[96] At Court's behest, Western Australian print and broadcast media was plastered with advertisements urging a No vote.

The No campaign was also strong in Tasmania. The Tasmanian Liberal Party was officially neutral; but all Tasmanian Liberal Senators opposed the referendum, as did Independent Senator Brian Harradine.

As the campaign progressed, opposition to all four proposals, and particularly the Simultaneous Elections proposal, grew – even in Victoria, Fraser's home state. There, opposition was led by the respected Liberal Senator Sir Magnus Cormack, a former President of the Senate. The Victorian Democratic Labor Party, a diminished, but still significant political force, also came out in opposition of all four proposals. Even the Young Liberal Movement urged a No vote.

Across Australia, as opposition solidified, the Yes campaign found it difficult to generate grassroots support. Both the Liberal

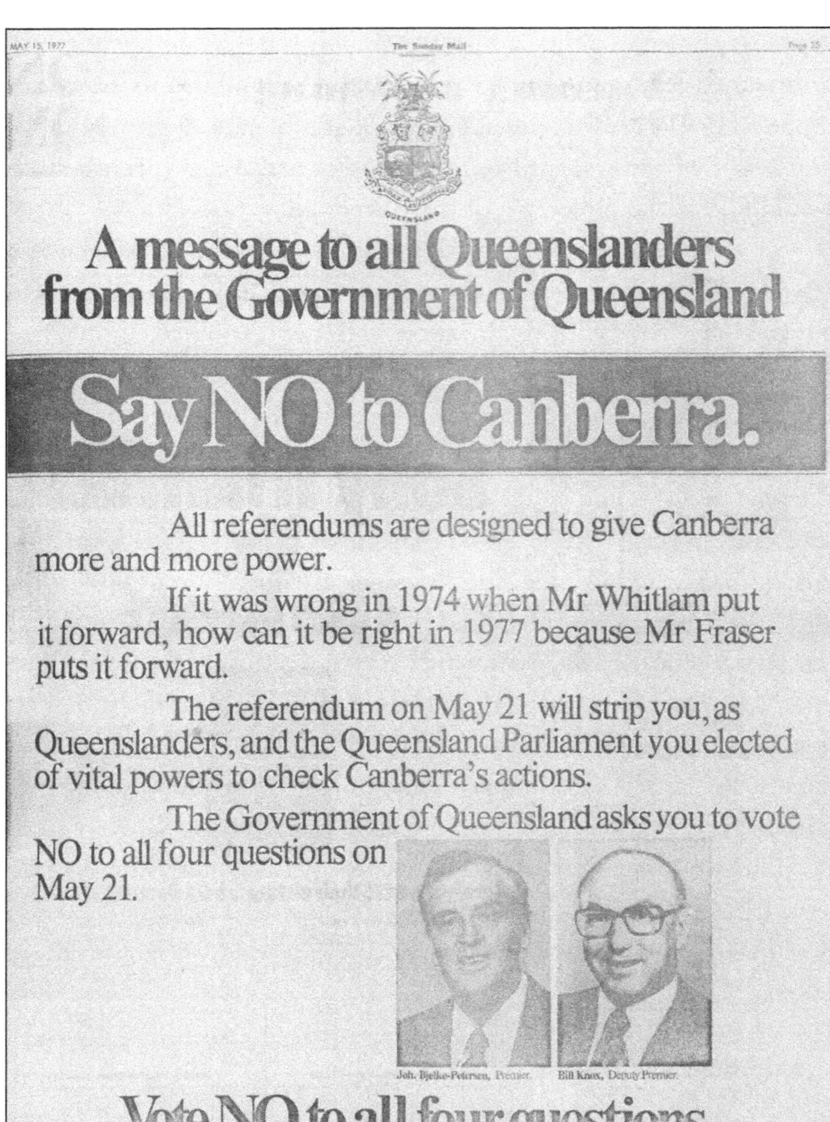

FIGURE 5.9 **Advertisement for the No campaign in the 1977 referendum**
Source: Courier-Mail, 15 May 1977, p. 25. Reproduced courtesy of J Bjelke-Petersen.

and Labor Parties reported difficulties in attracting people to hand out how-to-vote cards. In Victoria, many Liberal branches refused to do so. In Western Australia, that issue was moot: the Yes case did not even have enough money to print the cards.

In March 1977, the success of the referendums had looked guaranteed. Polling showed support of between 70 per cent and 80 per cent for all four proposals. By 19 May, three days before the referendum, support had softened, but was still strong. Simultaneous Elections was polling the lowest, with a 63 per cent national Yes vote, and with majority support in Queensland (60 per cent) and an even split (50 per cent) in Tasmania.[97] But the polls showed something else. They suggested that, as the campaign had progressed, a substantial group of people had changed from being a clear Yes to being a 'Maybe Yes'. The reason they gave for the switch was confusion due to the conflicting messages about what effect the four proposals would have. Electors simply did not know who to trust. Other people reported that they simply did not understand what the referendum was about. As the campaign reached its crescendo, Fraser travelled again to Tasmania. Appropriately, he spent the last night of the campaign where it had all begun: at the Wrest Point Hotel in Hobart.

On 22 May, Australians went to the polls. In addition to voting on the referendums, they also voted in a voluntary plebiscite on the choice of a national anthem. The plebiscite resulted in an easy victory for 'Advance Australia Fair', with 'Waltzing Matilda' running a distant second. In the referendum battle, early results were encouraging for all four questions. As counting progressed, however, and rural results came in, it became clear that the vote on the Simultaneous Elections proposal would be close. By the next morning, it was apparent that the proposal had failed. It had achieved a unique feat: a national majority of more than 60 per cent voting Yes (62.2 per cent), but not a majority of support in at least four of the six states. In New South Wales, Victoria and South Australia, not one district voted

No. Reflecting the No campaign run by Sir Magnus Cormack, the Yes vote in Victoria (65 per cent) was substantially lower than that in New South Wales (70.7 per cent). Where the proposal failed was in its lack of support in Tasmania, Western Australia and Queensland. In Western Australia (48.5 per cent) and Queensland (47.5 per cent) the results were close, but still a clear loss, while barely a third of Tasmanians (34.3 per cent) had voted Yes. Nationally, Liberal seats delivered a Yes vote on Simultaneous Elections about 10 per cent lower than Labor seats.

The same pattern repeated itself on the Senate Casual Vacancies question. New South Wales, Victoria and South Australia voted Yes by large margins of between 76.6 per cent and 81.6 per cent. Queensland (58.9 per cent), Western Australia (57.1 per cent) and Tasmania (53.8 per cent) gave strong Yes votes, but were still clearly in a different category to the other three. For the Referendums and Retirement of Judges proposals, where there had been little No case beyond a general call for a blanket No vote from opponents, the Yes vote was substantially stronger nationwide (77.7 per cent and 80.1 per cent, respectively).

Australia had achieved an unprecedented triple success in its constitutional reform efforts. But recriminations began immediately. For national politicians at least, the Simultaneous Elections proposal had been the goal. The press characterised it as a serious rebuff for Fraser and Whitlam. Fraser blamed the opposition of the Queensland and Western Australian governments.[98] For Whitlam, the failure was down to the state majority requirement. He proclaimed that there could be 'no more dramatic illustration of the restrictions and shortcomings of Australia's Constitution'.[99] Meanwhile, Court and Sir Joh were celebrating. Court triumphantly declared: 'the Constitution has come to the aid of the smaller States'.[100]

For others, there were three reasons for the failure. First, the Constitution had worked as expected in protecting the small states

FIGURE 5.10 **Cartoon from the 1977 referendum**
Source: *Sydney Morning Herald*, 20 May 1977, p. 6. Reproduced courtesy of K Molnar.

against alterations perceived to undermine their interests. This perception had been stoked by the campaign of the Queensland and Western Australian governments. Second, Fraser's reversal of views on simultaneous elections in just three years had counted against the government. The reversal smacked of political opportunism. For many, the rejection of the Simultaneous Elections proposal showed that Australians believed the Constitution was not to be played with for short-term gain. These first two factors grew from a third: there was no popular demand for simultaneous elections. The public may have been irritated by proliferating elections, but that had not translated into a call for simultaneous polls. The public did not 'own' the proposal; this made it easy for the No case to paint the question as one of political self-interest.

Focusing on the failure of the Simultaneous Elections proposal distracts from the real achievement of 22 May 1977: the success of three proposals on the one day. Universally, the press and commentators lauded this as an example of consensus-led constitutional

FIGURE 5.11 **Cartoon from the 1977 referendum**
Source: *Sydney Morning Herald*, 25 May 1977, p. 6. Reproduced courtesy of K Molnar.

reform. The Hobart session of the Constitutional Convention, involving the close consultation of three levels of government, had resulted in proposals that were broadly accepted by the groups most likely to oppose them, particularly the Opposition, the minor Parties and the states. The 1977 referendum showed that an incremental approach based upon broad political support is a viable approach to constitutional reform. As the *Sydney Morning Herald* summed it up in its first editorial after the referendum:

> Constitutional reformers need not despair. That is the clear
> moral to be drawn from Saturday's referendum results ...
> [T]he poll has shown that, with bi-partisan support,
> constitutional amendment is by no means impossible.[101]

Fraser would recover quickly from the defeat of the Simultaneous Elections proposal. He resolved the half-Senate election issue by dissolving the House early and holding a full House and half-Senate election on 10 December 1977. The public's attention moved quickly away from the remarkable feat of constitutional reform in May, distracted by the general election of later that year, which saw the first Fraser–Whitlam battle since the controversial 1975 election. In that election, Fraser was victorious, while Whitlam never recovered and resigned from Parliament in 1978. History has recorded the 1970s as a period of conflict between Fraser and Whitlam, the Coalition and the Labor Party, with few recalling that all had campaigned together in 1977 to achieve an unequalled constitutional success.

1988 – Getting to No

The third of September 1988 represents the nadir of referendum success. The Hawke Labor government put four proposals to the Australian people. All four were rejected. More important was the magnitude of the failure, with three of the questions achieving the lowest ever votes in Australian history, and the fourth not far behind. The national Yes vote percentages hovered around 30 per cent, while support in Tasmania failed even to reach that level for any of the questions.

The referendums of 1988 present a lesson in how *not* to approach constitutional reform. The Yes campaign made almost every possible error of referendum strategy, from weak leadership through to trying to do too much on the one day and in the one question. On the other hand, the No campaign was vigorous, ruthless and utterly effective. The result was never in doubt.

In 1985 Labor Attorney-General and Deputy Prime Minister Lionel Bowen established the Constitutional Commission. Bowen was, by the mid-1980s, a seasoned Labor politician. He had been a New South Wales state Labor politician for eight years before being elected to the Commonwealth Parliament in 1969. By 1972, he was a member of the Whitlam Cabinet and, when Bob Hawke was elected in 1983, was chosen as Hawke's deputy. The Constitutional Commission rose from the ashes of the Australian Constitutional Convention. The Convention had been established by Whitlam in 1972 and had great success in the 1977 referendums during the time of the Fraser government but, by 1985, was on its last legs. As its replacement, the Commission conducted the most comprehensive review yet of the Australian Constitution, delivering its final report to the Hawke government in 1988.

Each of the 1988 referendum proposals had been discussed by the Commission. Two of them – one on guaranteeing various rights and freedoms at the state level, the other on guaranteeing 'one-vote, one-value' for Commonwealth and state elections so that the size of an electorate could not vary more than 10 per cent from the average – were based on its recommendations. A third – a proposal to recognise local government – did not go as far as the Commission had proposed. The fourth – a proposal to introduce four-year terms for both the House of Representatives and Senate – departed from the Commission's recommendation. The Commission had recommended maximum four-year terms for the House (with a minimum of three years) and mandatory eight-year terms for the Senate.

Although these proposals were discussed in the Commission's Final Report, they were not actually derived from it. The Hawke Cabinet had committed to putting the four proposals even before receiving that document. These two facts – the departure from the Commission's recommendation about parliamentary terms and the fact that the government had committed to the referendums before and irrespective of the Commission's final report – would later undermine the Yes campaign. No matter how hard the government tried, it would be unable to cloak the proposals with the mantle of the Commission.

For the government, the Parliamentary Terms and Fair Elections proposals were the core of the package. The remaining two proposals – Local Government and Rights and Freedoms – were added by the government largely as 'a bit of supposed sugar'.[102] The government hoped that adding the Local Government proposal would ensure strong grassroots campaigning for the referendums. The Rights and Freedoms proposal sought to entrench at the state level a set of rights (free exercise of religion, separation of church and state, right to trial by jury and the right to compensation for government acquisitions of property) that were already recognised in the Constitution at the Commonwealth level. This strategy of adding sweeteners would, in the words of political commentator Michelle Grattan, prove 'a disaster'.[103]

The Hawke government had two motivations for holding the 1988 referendum: it saw the changes as sound, and it thought that it was a good idea for there to be constitutional reform in the bicentennial year of white settlement in Australia. The government's problem was that it did not spend enough time making the case that the referendum questions were good ideas, and the people of Australia disagreed that the bicentenary was a sufficient justification for reform. Unlike previous referendums, there was also no obvious political gain for the government should the referendums succeed. The Parliamentary Terms proposal, for example, was expected to benefit the Liberals far more than Labor; contemporary observers expected it to increase Liberal representation in the Senate. Likewise, the Fair Elections proposal was expected to benefit the Liberal Party more than Labor given that gerrymandering in Queensland had ensured National Party dominance over the Liberals in that state.

There was a good case for each of the proposals. Four-year parliamentary terms would bring greater stability to the Commonwealth Government. It would reduce the number of elections (by 1988, there had been a federal election – including half-Senate elections – every 2.3 years since Federation). The value of four-year terms had been recognised, with a number of states having adopted four-year terms for their Lower House. The proposal would also mean that the full Senate would be elected at the same time as the House, thereby arguably giving the Senate a stronger claim to an electoral mandate.

In the case of Fair Elections, entrenching 'one-vote, one-value' was seen to be essential to democracy. By virtue of complicated electoral zoning, the Queensland National Party was able to govern with a popular vote in the low 30 per cent range. This meant that the Queensland Government had only questionable popular legitimacy and that the votes of some Queenslanders were being systematically under-weighted.

The Yes campaign described the cases for Local Government and Rights and Freedoms as matters of common sense and logic. Local government was part of the Australian federal landscape, so it should be recognised in the fundamental document of Australian governance – the Constitution. The rights contained in the Rights and Freedoms proposal were already recognised at the Commonwealth level. Why should not they also be recognised at the state level?

The government had reason to think that the proposals would have bipartisan support. The Liberal Party's official policy, which it had taken to the 1987 election, was behind the Local Government and Rights and Freedoms proposals. John Howard, leader of the Opposition, had personally supported constitutional recognition of local government. The Liberal Party also stood to gain from the other two proposals. Bipartisan support was the government's hope, but it took no steps to secure a political commitment from the other major parties. Shadow Cabinet considered the proposals and even took the step of formally approving the Local Government proposal; but this decision was overturned in the full party room, which called for a blanket No campaign. Some Liberals continued

FIGURE 5.12 Advertisement for the Yes campaign in the 1988 referendum

Source: *Courier-Mail*, 2 September 1988, p. 13. Reproduced courtesy of Wayne Swan.

to support the proposals, such as South Australian Ian Wilson who abstained in the House. But, by and large, the Coalition committed to a unified response: the Labor proposals must fail. The result was the most effective No campaign seen in Australia.

Opponents had a score of responses to the Yes case. Parliamentary Terms, far from leading to fewer elections, would *increase* the number of elections. The government would know that, by dissolving the House, it could also dissolve the Senate, giving it an incentive to hold an election whenever it felt obstructed and believed it had popular support. Also, rather than increasing the Senate's clout, it would undermine that body. The government could threaten the Senate with dissolution at will should the Senate prove obstructionist. Further, the proposal would remove the protection against passing political fads which the Senate enjoyed by virtue of only half the Senate facing the electorate at each election. According to its opponents, Fair Elections was equally wrongheaded. It was wrong in principle: electoral matters were for states to decide, and there was a need for variance in the size of regional electorates because of the difficulties that parliamentarians face in servicing large geographical areas. It was also wrong in practice because, were the proposal successful, a party could still secure government with a minority of votes.

For opponents, the Local Government and Rights and Freedoms proposals were dangerous and unnecessary. Both were vague and could be interpreted broadly by the courts. In the words of Shadow Attorney-General Peter Reith, 'the legislative phraseology [was] so loose as to open up a Pandora's box of implications'.[104] Opponents raised the spectre of *Cole v Whitfield*,[105] a case just decided by the High Court that had overturned decades of case law on one section of the Constitution. Imagine, they said, what the High Court might do with a set of new provisions. Local government, opponents pointed out, was already protected in most state constitutions, while rights were already respected. All the proposals could achieve was to change for the worse a situation that was already acceptable.

For Reith, the proposals were a 'trojan horse which would extend Canberra's power'.[106] The Local Government proposal would enable the Labor government to achieve Whitlam's dream of establishing regional super-councils, while the Rights and Freedoms proposal would enable left-wing groups to reopen the legal debate about whether governments could fund religious private schools.

Outside the government, the Yes campaign had substantial support. The Australian Democrats supported all four proposals. The Australian Local Government Association was also a strong supporter, and distributed more than half a million how-to-vote cards during the campaign. Sir Maurice Byers QC, who had been chair of the Constitutional Commission and a former Commonwealth Solicitor-General, appeared regularly in support, as did Peter Garrett, then lead singer of Midnight Oil and later a Labor Party politician, who had been on an Advisory Committee of the Commission. Even some Liberals supported the proposals. The Queensland Liberal Party came out in support of the Fair Elections and Local Government proposals. *The Age*, *Sydney Morning Herald*, *The Australian* and *Courier-Mail* also lined up behind some of the proposals. There were also some supporters which the government wished it did not have. The Defence of Government Schools organisation placed an advertisement early in the campaign advocating a Yes vote on the Rights and Freedoms proposal and saying that it would reopen the challenge to government funding of private schools if the referendum were successful. Support for the proposals by the government itself was surprisingly muted. Bowen, who had primary responsibility for shepherding the referendums, was distant from the public debate: the *Daily Mirror* described his approach as 'low-key'.[107] Bowen's aim was, in his words: 'to [keep] the politicians out of it … because [he] wanted the people to judge this on the merits'.[108] Hawke, the government's most effective communicator, stayed out of the campaign until the last week, while Treasurer Paul Keating was not seen at all.

At the beginning, the cards looked stacked against the No campaign. In May 1988, support for the proposals stood at between 66 per cent and 72 per cent.[109] John Howard had been leader of the Liberal Opposition since September 1985. He had fought and lost one election in 1987. By 1988, he was far behind Hawke as preferred Prime Minister. Rivals, particularly Andrew Peacock, were snapping at his heels. Howard needed a win. He identified that, if the 1988 referendums failed, this might signal a turning point in the Coalition's fortunes. It would dispel the myth that Hawke could not lose, and it would show that the people of Australia were once more willing to listen to the non-Labor parties.

Howard appointed Shadow Attorney-General Peter Reith to lead the No campaign. Reith had risen quickly in what were dark days for the Liberal Party in the early 1980s. First elected to Parliament in 1982, he joined the shadow ministry soon after. Reith had degrees in economics and law from Monash University and was an effective parliamentary performer with impeccable conservative credentials. Despite this, no one predicted just how successful he would prove as custodian of the No case in 1988. From the minute the proposals were announced, Reith knew the broad themes his campaign would take. His first thought was that the proposals were 'no good' and 'that he couldn't believe his luck'. He knew that he could 'turn the polls and win the day'.[110]

Reith's No campaign had two basic messages, both of which were straight out of the No campaign playbook. First, he urged that there was more to the proposals than met the eye. He pointed out that, although there were only four questions, 33 separate textual changes to the Constitution were to be made. He pointed out that the title of the proposed laws (for example, Constitution Alteration (Fair Elections) Bill) was very different from the changes that were to be made (that is, providing for 'one-vote, one-value'). The Rights and Freedoms proposal said it was about protecting rights, but it was argued to be really about taking away government support from religious schools and broadcasts. Second, Reith said, these proposals were all about Canberra – about placing the states and the people under Canberra's thumb. He asked why 'should those living in Vaucluse or Turramurra tell those living in Western Australia's Kimberleys or Pilbara area' how they should run their lives?[111] These messages proved very effective. Australians who never switched on to the campaign heard the message that there was something fishy about the proposals and decided it was safer to vote No. Australians who did switch on heard the message that this was about Canberra and yet more power to politicians and decided reflexively to vote No.

The No campaign quickly gathered strong supporters. The Business Council of Australia and the Australian Chamber of Commerce began on the government's side, but, in the middle of the campaign, reversed their support. The about-turn by the Chamber of Commerce was particularly embarrassing for the government, which had featured the President of the Chamber of Commerce in the main advertisement for the Yes campaign. The Queensland National government, led by Mike Ahern, as one of the targets of the referendums, became one of their strongest opponents. It spent between one and two million dollars on a swath of advertisements, including a personally addressed letter to each voter. The Queensland Government spent so much money that the Commonwealth threatened to impose a 'fine' on the state in its next funding allocation.

Other No advocates, such as Fred Nile of the Call to Australia Party, and present Member of the New South Wales Legislative Council, were less qualified: the Rights and Freedoms proposal, he said, would result in 'Hindu idols in Martin Place' and the 'Immam of Lakemba blessing the colours of an Australian battalion'.[112] The *Sydney Morning Herald* also reported Nile as indicating that the referendum could lead to the legalisation of 'self-immolation by widows … the stoning of adulterers, the amputation of thieves' limbs and female circumcision.'[113] Most important of all the supporters the No campaign gathered was a group of Catholic Bishops and the Anglican Archbishop of Melbourne, who came out in unequivocal opposition to the Rights and Freedoms question on the ground that it threatened government aid to private schools.

Opposition was also strengthened by bungles in the Yes campaign. In the middle of the campaign, Reith initiated proceedings in the

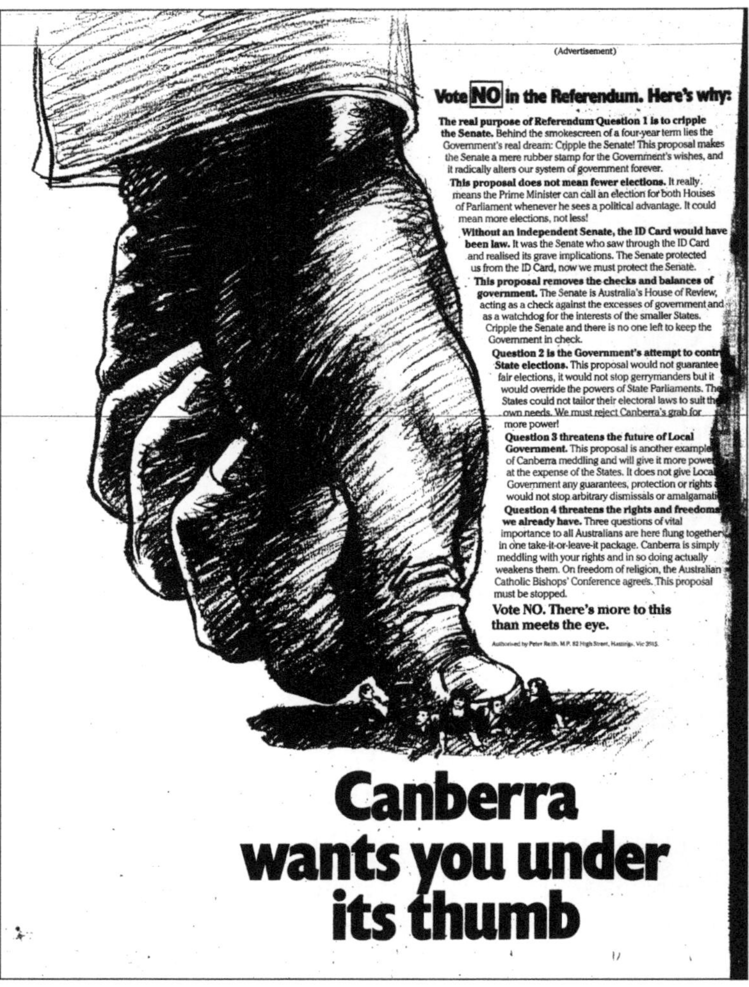

FIGURE 5.13 Advertisement for the No campaign in the 1988 referendum

Source: *The Advertiser*, 31 August 1988, p. 10. Reproduced courtesy of the Liberal Party of Australia.

High Court that led to a finding that the government had breached the *Referendum (Machinery Provisions) Act 1984* (Cth). By funding supposedly neutral advertisements, the government was found to have, in fact, advocated a Yes vote. Reith's view was that this result 'was a massive blow to the credibility of the government. It is a massive blow when a government trying to change the Constitution has its campaign declared illegal by the High Court.'[114]

In another High Court challenge, Vennard Boland, an electrician from Labrador on the Gold Coast, argued that the government had violated the Constitution by putting four separate issues in the one question on rights and freedoms. Boland's challenge was dismissed, but the mere fact of the challenge, together with the successful challenge to the referendum advertising, fed the perception that the government was seeking to dupe the Australian people.

A feature of the campaign was the battle of the legal opinions.[115] This arose from the claim by the No campaign that the Rights and Freedoms proposal threatened government subsidies for a range of services, particularly education. Sir Maurice Byers QC drafted an opinion saying that the proposal did not threaten government aid. The Yes campaign touted his advice as being particularly authoritative since he had represented the government in the *DOGS Case*[116] in which the High Court had held that the existing separation of church and state in the Constitution did not prohibit government aid to religious schools. The No campaign commissioned an opinion from David Bennett QC, then a leading member of the Sydney bar, and later to become Solicitor-General in the Howard government. The opinion commissioned by the No campaign was carefully worded: it asked whether there was 'any doubt' that the referendum could threaten government aid. Unsurprisingly, Bennett, in suitably qualified language, found that the referendum could create a doubt. The No campaign trumpeted this as the proof it needed that the government was tampering with settled protections. Keith Mason QC, Solicitor-General of New South Wales, also gave an opinion to the New South Wales Government that the Rights and Freedoms proposal could take away power from state governments. All this served to create uncertainty. If experts differed, people said, surely there was a doubt; and, if there was a doubt, it was better to stick with the status quo.

Uncertainty and mistrustfulness characterised the approach of many Australians to the referendum. A poll two days before the referendum showed that 47 per cent of voters did not know what the questions were about and did not understand them. A survey conducted for the Constitutional Commission in the year before had even found that 47 per cent of Australians were unaware that Australia had a written Constitution.[117] Polls also showed that the No campaign had been successful in its attempts to besmirch the proposals: 63 per cent of Australians believed the questions to be misleading.[118] On the eve of the referendum, it was clear that the proposals would fail. Support had dropped from around 70 per cent in May to between 36 per cent and 44 per cent.[119] The polling also showed a nation split deeply along partisan lines. On referendum eve, support among Labor voters ranged between 60 per cent and 69 per cent, while support among Coalition voters was in the range of 18 per cent to 26 per cent.[120]

Voting took place on 3 September 1988. When the votes were counted, the disaster was confirmed. National support for each of the questions ranged between 30.8 per cent and 37.6 per cent. In only one district in New South Wales (Sydney) for just one proposal (Fair Elections) was there a Yes vote. Western Australia, South Australia and Tasmania recorded no Yes votes in any districts at all. Even the Australian Capital Territory, the home of the Commonwealth Government, could muster Yes votes in its districts only in regard to the Fair Elections proposal. Constitutional reform in Australia had hit an all-time low. *The Australian*'s editorial on Monday, 5 September said it all, blaring: 'Referendum results an absolute debacle'.[121]

FIGURE 5.14 Advertisement for the No campaign in the 1988 referendum

Source: *Courier-Mail*, 3 September 1988, p. 18. Reproduced courtesy of Liberal National Party Qld.

Contemporary commentators put the unprecedented failure of the referendums down to a range of factors. First was the absence of bipartisan support. Coalition voters listened to the message from their parties. Second was the weakness and mistakes of the Yes campaign. These fed the perception that the changes were unnecessary, and even dangerous. In Reith's words, 'Lionel Bowen didn't have any fire in his belly for the proposals'.[122] Without a bipartisan consensus, a low-key, and on occasion inept, campaign was doomed to fall to trenchant and effective opposition. According to *The Age*, the 'Government ha[d] been arbitrary and arrogant in its choice of questions; the Opposition's reaction [was] one of petulant negativism'.[123] The government also failed to marshal support from the states, with even the Labor State Premiers failing to champion the proposals, and Queensland speaking out strongly against. Third was the devastating No campaign. According to Reith, 'the poor quality of the proposals, the strength of the No case and the ineptitude of the government' meant that 'even if Labor had run a good campaign, they still would have been thrashed. It attracted the biggest No vote ever because they had everything against them.'[124]

Bowen took the loss personally. 'We lost. I lost',[125] he said. Before the referendum, he had reportedly predicted that, if Australia failed to pass the four questions, 'there would be no chance of constitutional reform until well into the 21st Century'.[126] Bowen noted one positive feature of the campaign. Polls showed that many more Australians now knew the Constitution existed. Hawke acknowledged that constitutional reform was 'a lost cause for the foreseeable future',[127] but otherwise kept quiet. He had not played a major role in the campaign and was able to distance himself from the loss. Commentators expected that the referendum loss would affect Labor in two upcoming elections: the 1988 Victorian state election and the Oxley federal by-election, which had been necessitated by Bill Hayden's appointment as Governor-General. But these expectations were proven wrong, with John Cain being returned as Labor Premier and the Labor candidate winning in Oxley. Australians had quickly switched off from the referendums, but the loss did not spell the end of constitutional reform until the next century. Eleven years later, a government led by one of the players in the 1988 referendum, John Howard, would put the idea of a republic to the people.

1999 – The republic

Australian republicanism is older than the nation itself. In 1887, Henry Lawson published his verse, *Song of the Republic*, calling for an Australia free of the English Crown. Soon afterwards, a monthly called *The Republican* was launched, backed by members of the Republican Club. At the 1891 Constitutional Convention, George Dibbs, a former Premier of New South Wales, described 'the republic of Australia' as 'the inevitable destiny of the people of this great country'.[128] Sir Henry Parkes, then the Premier of New South Wales, replied: 'I have no time to talk of this question of republicanism which has been so ungraciously launched amongst us'.[129]

Australia was almost 100 years old before the republic question was put to a vote of the people. The 1999 Republic referendum was unprecedented in its size, cost and the way it captured the nation's attention. Not even the Melbourne Cup in the week before the vote and Australia's participation in the final of the Rugby World Cup in the early hours of the morning after the vote could turn the attention of politicians, the press and the people themselves from the referendum.

The story of the referendum began eight years before the vote, in April 1991, at the Constitutional Centenary Conference in Sydney. This Conference led to the formation of the Australian Republican

Movement (ARM) in July of that year. Its first chair was prolific author Thomas Keneally. He was joined by a wealth of business-people, professionals and politicians. The ARM had clear goals: to sever Australia's formal link to the English Crown and to replace the monarch with an Australian head of state. The formation of the ARM led to a conservative reaction, and on 4 June 1992, Australians for Constitutional Monarchy (ACM) was formed as a political counterbalance. Two senior lawyers, Lloyd Waddy and Michael Kirby, later justices of the Family Court and High Court respectively, were its first leaders.

In April 1993, Prime Minister Paul Keating established a Republic Advisory Committee. Its remit was to advise on options for Australia to become a republic. Keating appointed a prominent member of the ARM, Malcolm Turnbull, as chair of the Committee. Turnbull was, in many respects, an inspired choice. A member of the Sydney establishment, he had studied law at Sydney University before being awarded the 1978 Rhodes Scholarship for New South Wales. By 1993, Turnbull had already had a successful career as a barrister and investment banker. According to journalist Paul Kelly, writing in 1999, Turnbull was 'a tall poppy, clever, successful, rich, ruthless and impatient'.[130] Turnbull brought these traits, and his own money, to prosecuting the 1999 referendum. When the dust had settled, Turnbull estimated that he had spent almost $3 million on the referendum and was responsible for 80 per cent of the ARM's budget.

The Republic Advisory Committee knew that referendums were doomed without bipartisan support and it knew that getting the support of the Coalition for a cause that had been an aspiration of the labour movement from before Federation would be difficult. The Committee, therefore, locked in, as its first priority, to develop a compromise model capable of appealing to conservative republicans. The model that resulted from this spirit of compromise came to be called the *minimalist* republican model. It proposed that the

Queen and Governor-General be replaced by a President who would exercise the same powers, and be appointed and dismissed in a similar manner to the Governor-General.

This approach, centred on political compromise, had two significant effects on the referendum campaign that was to come. First, it led to a campaign that was, by and large, conducted across party lines. The campaign even saw Prime Minister John Howard openly and vigorously debating with his Treasurer, Peter Costello, and both Howard and Costello doing the same with a senior government Minister, Peter Reith. This meant that, regardless of the outcome, the referendum would challenge accepted positions on the role that party support plays in Australian referendums. Secondly, it led to a campaign that was, from the beginning, designed to achieve consensus among the political classes rather than being driven by those who would make the ultimate decision, the people of Australia. The absence of popular ownership and the failure to persuade the community of the need for the referendum and of the appropriateness of the minimalist model proved ultimately to be terminal flaws of the failed 1999 poll.

In 1995, Keating adopted an Australian republic as a core plank of the platform he would take to the 1996 election. In November 1994, the then leader of the Opposition, Alexander Downer, had mooted the idea of a people's convention to discuss the republic. When John Howard became leader in 1995, he was forced, contrary to his monarchist beliefs, to adopt as part of his platform the holding of a convention on the republic. After Howard was elected in the 1996 election, this promise became government policy. The result was the Constitutional Convention of 1998.

The Convention's composition was unprecedented in modern Australian constitutional reform. Half of the delegates were popularly elected by a voluntary poll in late 1997 (turnout was 45.3 per cent). The other half were appointed by the government, in consultation with other groups. When the delegates assumed their positions in

February 1998, they were broadly divided into three groups: monarchists (who supported the status quo), minimalists (who supported variants of the Republic Advisory Committee model) and direct electionists, who later assumed the name 'Real Republicans' (who wanted a President directly elected by the people). The composition of the Convention meant that, barring extraordinary circumstances, a version of the minimalist model would be its recommendation. This it duly was, in the form of a republic in which a President would exercise the same powers as the current Queen and Governor-General and be appointed by a two-thirds vote of the federal Parliament.

The critical question – whether the Convention should recommend the minimalist model – achieved 73 votes in favour, less than an absolute majority of the convention; but was opposed by only 57 votes (there were 22 abstentions). This was seen as a sufficient level of support to be called a majority outcome and Howard committed to holding a referendum late in 1999. The model that ultimately went to the people was, in most respects, consistent with the spirit of the model recommended by the Convention. It did, however, include some problematic additions that would play a role in the campaign. Chief among these was a provision allowing the President to be unilaterally and summarily dismissed by the Prime Minister.

The Convention had discussed one further issue: the possibility of inserting a new preamble into the Australian Constitution to express shared Australian values and history. Together with a republic, the Convention recommended the adoption of a new preamble with no legal effect, but (hopefully) with substantial rhetorical force. The preamble was to be inserted at the beginning of the Constitution, providing a broad overview of Australian history and values.

On the republic, Howard swung between passivity and hostility; on the preamble, he was constant in his support. Howard, with the assistance of Australian poet Les Murray, prepared a draft preamble. On release, it was immediately criticised as being sexist and giving insufficient recognition to Indigenous Australians. The former criticism picked up on the draft preamble's description of 'mateship' – seen by many as a masculine term – as one of Australia's core values. The latter criticism picked up on the draft preamble referring merely to the fact that Indigenous Australians had 'inhabited' the Australian continent. On this second issue, Howard was torn between acknowledging the truth (the long, undisputed history of Indigenous occupation of Australia) and maintaining the support of the National Party (who were concerned about the risks for rural landholders should a strongly worded preamble give legal or symbolic force to native title claims). The criticism hit home and Howard enlisted the services of Indigenous Democrat Senator Aden Ridgeway to assist with redrafting the preamble to better describe the relationship between Indigenous Australians and land. After rejecting words implying a legal relationship (such as 'custodianship'), Howard and Ridgeway settled on a phraseology that was emotive, but insubstantial: that Indigenous Australians had a deep 'kinship' with the land. The final text of the new preamble on which Australians voted was as follows:

> With hope in God, the Commonwealth of Australia is
> constituted as a democracy with a federal system of government
> to serve the common good.
> We the Australian people commit ourselves to this Constitution:
> proud that our national unity has been forged by Australians
> from many ancestries;
> never forgetting the sacrifices of all who defended our country
> and our liberty in time of war;
> upholding freedom, tolerance, individual dignity and the rule
> of law;
> honouring Aborigines and Torres Strait Islanders, the nation's
> first people, for their deep kinship with their lands and for their
> ancient and continuing cultures which enrich the life of our
> country;

recognising the nation-building contribution of generations
of immigrants;
mindful of our responsibility to protect our unique natural
environment;
supportive of achievement as well as equality of opportunity
for all;
and valuing independence as dearly as the national spirit which
binds us together in both adversity and success.

The Republic proposal captured national attention in a way that no previous referendum, perhaps with the exception of the Federation referendums of the 1890s, had done. As the campaigns progressed, although Australians were to be asked two questions, most commentators referred to it as the Republic referendum, with little public debate about the proposal to insert a new preamble.

When Australians entered the polling booths on 6 November 1999, they had been subjected to the most energetic referendum campaign Australia had ever seen. Parliament had temporarily amended the *Referendum (Machinery Provisions) Act 1984* (Cth) to permit the expenditure of amounts of money by special Yes and No committees and by a 'Neutral' campaign. When it was all over, the government had spent approximately $48 million on advertising for the referendums, including $7.5 million each for the Yes and No campaigns and a further $33 million of 'Neutral' government advertising by the official Neutral campaign and the Australian Electoral Commission. Outside government spending, the Yes and No campaigns had independently raised (and spent) many millions more dollars. In the view of Kerry Jones, a leader of the No campaign, not all of that was well spent: 'there was a massive waste of money in the 1999 Yes and No campaigns. The amount of money ... made me sick'.[131]

The 1999 referendum was far from perfect, but it certainly took public awareness and passion to an unprecedented level. There were four reasons for this. The issue was one that inherently aroused passion: Australians simply felt far more strongly about a republican Australia than they did about issues such as four-year terms. Second, the government, the official Yes and No campaigns and private parties spent extraordinary amounts of money on the referendum, and in doing so were able to take advantage of the full range of modern communication tools. Third, the press wholeheartedly embraced the campaign. The television and print media perceived the republic as probably *the* issue of 1999, ahead of the impending introduction of the GST and the upcoming Sydney Olympics. The result was a storm of media coverage of growing intensity as the referendum approached, much of it in favour of the change. Fourth, the government had given the issue time to build. The republic had been an issue in the 1996 election, then there had been the February 1998 Constitutional Convention, and the campaign had continued, virtually non-stop, for the next 20 months. Unlike the 1988 referendums, which had been rushed through, most Australians had had an excellent chance to listen to the arguments for and against.

The Yes campaign wanted voters to ask themselves one question: do you want an Australian head of state? The Yes campaign was, by and large, an emotive appeal. The heart of the campaign was a repeated challenge to voters: are you ready to accept Australia's destiny as a free and independent nation? A typical Yes advertisement showed footage of Bill Clinton, President of the United States, proposing a toast to Queen Elizabeth, as Australia's head of state, in front of John Howard at a dinner in Canberra in 1996. For opponents, this tendency to simplify the issue and arouse the passions was divisive and dangerous: opponents caricatured the campaign as depicting the republic as a lifestyle choice and promoting the view that opposition to the referendum was 'un-Australian'.[132]

Proponents of the republic did not rely solely on emotion. The Yes campaign argued that Australia's ties to the British monarchy were impairing Australia's relations with its Asian neighbours. Until Australia became a republic, they said, it would inevitably be perceived as white, Anglo and Eurocentric. For the most part, however, what was lacking from the Yes campaign was a sustained defence of the republic model that was being put to the people. Yes advocates swung between arguing that the proposed model was the safe, incremental option; that it was merely a stepping stone to adopting a republic with a directly elected President; and silence. Until the very end, the Yes campaign was still struggling, unsuccessfully, to make the issue about *a* republic, not *this* republic.

The establishment had, by and large, bought into the Yes case. The Yes campaign exploited the support of the rich, powerful and famous. One advertisement was headed 'Yes, yes a hundred times yes'[133] and listed names of 100 people, mostly professionals and politicians who supported the republic. Another advertisement featured Gough Whitlam and Malcolm Fraser. The advertisement included Whitlam saying 'it's time', with Fraser responding 'it is'. The Yes campaign trotted out a litany of famous figures, including former Prime Minister Bob Hawke, former Governor-General Sir Zelman Cowen and former High Court Chief Justices Sir Anthony Mason and Sir Gerard Brennan. The message the Yes campaign intended to convey was that its model was safe, respectable and worthy of a Yes vote even if voters did not understand all the details. But the No campaign, with ruthless effectiveness, twisted this message. The result was that the message the Yes campaign in fact conveyed to many people was that the minimalist model was fundamentally elitist.

The Yes campaign had supporters from across the political spectrum and the community. Kim Beazley, Labor opposition leader, was the leading Labor spokesperson. On the conservative side, key Liberal Ministers Peter Costello, Daryl Williams, Amanda Vanstone and Robert Hill, and the former National Party leader, Doug Anthony, were prominent supporters. As they had in 1988, religious people entered the debate, but this time with less effect. George Pell, then Catholic Archbishop of Melbourne, urged a Yes vote. The strongest support for the Yes campaign came from the press, which was virtually unanimous in advocating a Yes vote. The *Daily Telegraph* in Sydney even handed out stickers to all purchasers urging a Yes vote.

Some supporters of the Yes case were undeniably effective. Many lauded Peter Costello's calm persuasion, and soon after he injected himself into the debate support for the republic among Coalition voters rose by 8 per cent.[134] As the referendum got closer and the likelihood of a No vote became clearer, contributors to the print media became increasingly accusatory of voters. Steve Vizard, a media personality, called No voters a 'bloody disgrace'.[135] Rupert Murdoch declared that a No vote showed a 'loss of self-respect'.[136] The effect was to make No voters even more intransigent, and to confirm the impression held by many that the republic was an elitist conspiracy.

The No campaign had two main messages that it repeated ad nauseam, with great success. 'Vote No to the politicians' republic', opponents urged, and, if you 'Don't know, vote No'. With these two messages, the No campaign was able to appeal to monarchists, direct electionists, sceptics, the ignorant and the apathetic. Unsurprisingly, this ragtag coalition comprised a majority of Australians. Of these two messages, the assertion that the 1999 model was the politicians' republic was the most prominent. The idea was that this republic provided for a President selected and approved by politicians and removable at their whim. This tapped into a deep Australian cynicism of the political class. If the 1988 No campaign had given evidence that this was a fruitful area to tap into, the 1999 No campaign conclusively proved it. Any referendum will have the support of Parliament, so almost any proposal can be portrayed as a 'politicians' proposal'. In an ordinary election, this does not matter: voters must ultimately vote for a politician. But in a referendum, voters need not: a No vote can be a vote against all politicians. In 1999, the No campaign was unmoved by the irony that, typically, the claim that the referendum proposal was designed to suit politicians' ends was itself propagated by many politicians opposed to the reform.

The No campaign was effective in debunking the simplified position advocated by the Yes campaign that the referendum was about the monarchy. The No case in the official pamphlet urged: 'Vote No to THIS Republic'. As Kerry Jones said: 'the current system and the monarchy are not on trial. This republican model is.'[137] This tied in with the third message of the No campaign, one which again had been tried and tested on the battlegrounds of prior referendum campaigns: Vote No because the Yes campaign is trying to deceive you. 'Don't be duped', exhorted Kerry Jones, 'the more [you] see of this referendum, the less [you] will like it'.[138] Opponents pointed out that, in just one question, Australians were being asked to make 69 changes to the Constitution. Opponents, of course, did not clarify that the vast majority of these were merely changing the word 'Governor-General' to 'President'.

Parts of the No campaign, both official and unofficial, were clearly scaremongering. David Flint, then Chairman of the Australian Broadcasting Authority, claimed Australia's spot in the Commonwealth of nations would be jeopardised, prompting a retort from the Secretary-General of the Commonwealth.[139] Others claimed that the referendum would change the flag: one advertisement sponsored by the Australian National Flag Association ominously noted that 'many of the Republican leaders are the leaders of the "change the flag" organisation'; therefore, it concluded, 'if the Republic succeeds our flag will go'.[140] Others estimated a cost of close to $900 million (based on unrevealed assumptions) to change the head of state.[141] Still others raised the spectre of Hitler-like presidencies under the minimalist model (without acknowledging that the proposed model contained more safeguards against that than the existing system).[142] Len Harris, the One Nation Senator from Queensland, asserted that the referendum would extinguish Crown land, allowing claims by

FIGURE 5.15 Advertisement for the No campaign in the 1999 referendum

Source: *The Advertiser*, 5 November 1999, p. 24. Reproduced courtesy of Kerry Jones.

Indigenous people to native title across vast swaths of Australia.[143] The claims made by some associated with the No campaign reached such a level of duplicity that Tim Fischer, former National Party leader, changed from being an opponent of the referendum to being neutral so as to 'jump on those more crazy elements that have entered the debate'.[144] This kind of scaremongering was more pronounced in the No campaign, but by no means limited to it. Supporters of a republic urged that a No vote would damage Australia's interests and undermine its foreign policy in Asia.[145] On occasions, supporters descended into crudity, printing t-shirts, for example, saying 'Give an Australian the head job'.[146] Kerry Jones, a leader of the No campaign, now describes much of the campaigning as 'hysterical scaremongering' and reflects that she 'would not want to see that hysteria and tomato-throwing repeated again'.[147]

Of course, most supporters of the No campaign did not descend to this kind of misleading advocacy. Many were well-respected Australians, including former Governor-General Bill Hayden, former politicians Phil Cleary and Ted Mack, former High Court Chief Justice Sir Harry Gibbs and New South Wales Supreme Court Judge Ken Handley. Government Minister Peter Reith entered the debate as the most prominent direct electionist sitting MP. John Howard, though known to be a monarchist, took a back seat for much of the campaign, but stepped up his opposition in the last week. Most prominent in the No campaign was Kerry Jones, head of the ACM and leader of the No campaign, who formed the counterpoint to Turnbull. She had been a music teacher and performing arts consultant, but by 1999 her full-time job was opposing a republic. Where Turnbull was polished but distant, Jones was jarring but relentlessly effective. Jones was no 'Aussie battler', but she appeared so in relation to Turnbull, and the No campaign turned this to its advantage.

Sitting outside the official campaigns was the 'Neutral' campaign. This campaign was charged with informing Australians about the current system of government, the referendum process and the actual questions. It had $4.5 million in funding and was managed by a panel of eminent Australians. The Neutral campaign was balanced but, for many, showed the danger of having three, uncoordinated, chaotic campaigns running at the same time. While the Yes campaign was running strongly on the conservative nature of the minimalist proposal, the Neutral campaign symbolised the referendum as 'Australia at the crossroads'. While both Yes and No campaigns were debating who really was Australia's head of state (the Queen or the Governor-General), the Neutral campaign said that both were. The intent of the Neutral campaign was laudable; but it also had undeniable problems in its execution. In Kerry Jones' opinion, the Neutral campaign simply 'didn't hit anyone and had no effect'.[148]

The campaigns, and many groups sitting outside the official campaigns, resorted to innovative strategies to engage Australians. Local governments and the Constitutional Centenary Foundation organised for more than 2000 Australians to participate in local constitutional conventions. A deliberative poll was held at Old Parliament House (opposition to the referendum among participants dropped from 50 per cent to 19 per cent over the course of the poll). Schools, such as the Catherine McAuley School at Westmead in Sydney, organised for students, who were too young to vote in the referendum, to debate and then cast a mock vote. Liberal politician Tony Abbott staged a walk through Bourke Street Mall in Melbourne accompanied by two campaign workers dressed as Bananas in Pyjamas, sporting the slogan 'vote no to the banana republic'.[149] (The stunt caused an outcry from the ABC, which threatened legal action for breach of copyright.) Books supporting one or the other side, published in time for the referendum, canvassed arguments for and against at length. Australians were exposed to an unprecedented level of information about the referendum, and this translated into unprecedented levels of awareness about the question.

As referendum day approached, it was clear that the Yes campaign faced an uphill battle. Australians wanted an Australian head of state, but were not sure about the model on offer. The response of many in the Yes campaign was the 'Yes and More' message: if the referendum were successful, this would not foreclose the possibility of another referendum some time after to adopt a different kind of republican model. In other words, the model on offer was the 'basic' model, and Australians could choose to add new features as time went on. The Constitutional Convention itself had recommended that, if Australians voted Yes, the system should be reviewed within three to five years of its adoption with a view to possibly holding a further referendum to refine the model. Immediately, the Yes and More campaign ran up against an equal and opposite force: the No and More campaign. This message was propagated, in particular, by Reith who argued that Parliament knows that Australians want a republic, so, if Australians vote No, there will soon afterwards be another referendum on a different republican model. Commentators immediately pointed out that a second referendum would not likely be held in the foreseeable future. For Turnbull, the failure of those advocating No and More to acknowledge this was 'absolutely disgraceful cynicism'.[150] Despite this, the No and More message got through. On referendum day, it was clear that many Australians who voted No did so with a belief that their vote would not kill off the idea of an Australian republic for the foreseeable future.

The referendum of 1999, more so than any previous poll, was characterised by comprehensive, highly accurate polling. When Australians voted on 6 November 1999, both campaigns knew that, although only 9 per cent of Australians supported keeping the Queen as head of state,[151] the referendum was almost certain to fail. Women (36 per cent Yes; 58 per cent No) were far less likely to support the referendum than men (49 per cent Yes; 49 per cent No).[152] The less educated and the lower a person's socio-economic status, the more likely they were to oppose the referendum. One poll put opposition by those with incomes under $30 000 at close to 75 per cent.[153] Polls also showed strong awareness of the republic issue, with one survey by *The Age* in the week of the referendum showing only 12 per cent of respondents not knowing how they would vote.[154] This compared to the Preamble to Constitution question, in regard to which 40 per cent of respondents said they had never read or heard anything about it.[155]

By the end of counting on the night of the referendum, it was clear that Australians had decisively voted No to both the Republic and Preamble to Constitution questions. The Preamble to Constitution question never had a chance, achieving less than 40 per cent of the national vote (39.3 per cent). The Republic question fared better, achieving a 45.1 per cent Yes vote, but it was still the 15th least successful referendum question asked of Australians. Only 43 of 144 districts nationwide voted Yes. Of the states and territories, only the Australian Capital Territory supported the model which had been caricatured as the politicians' republic, returning a Yes vote

FIGURE 5.16 **Cartoon from the 1999 referendum**
Source: *Sydney Morning Herald*, 14 November 1999, p. 22. Reproduced courtesy of Alan Moir.

of 63.3 per cent. Of the states, Victoria was the most supportive. It barely scraped under the line, with a Yes vote of 49.8 per cent and a margin of less than 10 000 votes. Queensland voted overwhelmingly No, with 62.6 per cent voting the proposition down.

Voting was characterised by two features. First, a deep division between the wealthy, educated, inner-city areas, which generally voted Yes, and the rest of Australia, which generally voted No. Second, some of the strongest Yes votes came in blue-ribbon Liberal seats and the strongest No votes in poorer Labor and National Party seats. Nationwide, the most supportive federal electoral districts were Grayndler, North Sydney, Sydney, Wentworth, Batman, Higgins, Kooyong, Melbourne and Melbourne Ports – all wealthy urban seats. Both leaders of the major parties 'lost' their seats: Howard's electorate of Bennelong voted Yes; Beazley's electorate of Swan voted unequivocally No. Nationwide, Labor seats were more likely to vote Yes than Coalition seats, but the issue was clearly one that did not split along party lines.

Referendum night saw the irony of the Australian rugby union team appearing in the grand final of the World Cup at Twickenham in England. John Eales' Wallabies were successful (beating 'the Old Republic', France). Their victory saw Queen Elizabeth, recently reconfirmed as Australian monarch, presenting the William Webb Ellis world champions' trophy to Australia's captain, prominent republican John Eales.

The reasons for the failure of the 1999 referendum have been widely dissected and analysed, not least because many believe a similar question will be put to the Australian people at some future time. The following two reasons stand out. First, the Yes campaign was simply unable to meet its burden of persuasion. Its burden was difficult: it had to educate Australians about the existing system; argue that the present system was flawed; and argue that the minimalist model was the right solution. Failure was inevitable if proponents could not overcome the ignorant and apathetic (by explaining the existing system), monarchists (by arguing that the present system was flawed) and those who supported different republican models such as direct election (by arguing that the minimalist model was the right one, or at least the right start). The Yes and More argument, which sought to neuter the third of these, was made too late and with insufficient force.

Secondly, not enough Australians felt ownership over the republic model that they were being asked to vote for. Many people asked how the referendum would affect what they perceived to be their real day-to-day needs. Obviously, the republic was never going to have a direct bearing on those issues; yet the Yes campaign failed to convince enough Australians that they had needs that the republic could satisfy. Australians, as in 1988, did not buy the argument that constitutional reform was necessary because a constitutional milestone (the centenary of Federation) was approaching. The perception that the referendum process and the model chosen were elitist entrenched the view that the republic was unnecessary and, perhaps, dangerous. *The Australian*, on 8 November 1999, led with the headline 'One Queen, two nations'.[156] This summed up the defining feature of the results: the elites had said Yes, the rest No.

Of course, many other factors contributed to the referendum's failure. The opposition of Prime Minister John Howard was important. No referendum has ever succeeded without bipartisan support, let alone over the dissent of the Prime Minister. In the words of Turnbull: 'there is only one person who could have made … November 6 a landmark in our history, and that of course is the Prime Minister'.[157] The flaw in the model – which allowed the Prime Minister to unilaterally dismiss the President – also opened the proposal to needless challenge. The statements – some accurate and some misleading – made by people associated with the No campaign hit home. The leadership of the campaigns was also significant: there was a view that Turnbull was a net negative for the Yes campaign and Jones was a net positive for the No campaign. Many commentators at the time also believed that the No campaign had won a series of tactical battles. For example, only the No campaign placed a television advertisement in the minutes before the Melbourne Cup horserace on the Tuesday before the referendum.

Whatever the reason, the outcome was clear: Australians had rejected the republican model put to them in 1999. On referendum night, Turnbull declared Howard to be 'the Prime Minister who broke this nation's heart'.[158] Much of the press followed this line, depicting Howard as obstructionist and anachronistic. Howard was, however, to have the last laugh. On referendum night, he said: 'the thing is over, the free vote is finished and we [must] all get on with the job of responding to things that are of direct and immediate interest to the Australian people'.[159] The result was to put the republic off the agenda for the rest of his long period as leader.

The 1999 referendum, along with the dismal defeat of 1988, have cast a long shadow over the prospects of constitutional reform. The view of the 1999 referendum that has taken root is that change to the text of the Constitution is almost impossible in Australia. The result can be seen in the decade that followed. Between 2000 and 2010, Australians did not once go to the polls to vote in a referendum – the first decade without such a vote in Australian history. By 2010, 33 years had passed since the last amendment to the Australian Constitution. The constitutional drought had long set in.

6

A LABOUR OF HERCULES?

Is the record bad?

In 1951, still smarting from his failure in the Communism referendum, Prime Minister Robert Menzies said:

> The truth of the matter is that to get an affirmative vote from the Australian people on a referendum proposal is one of the labours of Hercules. For this last referendum showed us ... the amount of sheer hard lying that goes on in the course of a referendum campaign designed to alter the Constitution and the amount of muddled thinking and speaking that can proceed from minds that are supposed to be improved by university degrees is quite baffling to me.[1]

Australians have approved eight out of 44 referendum proposals in over 100 years, a success rate of about 18 per cent. There is a persistent view that this is a bad record. Arguably it is. If these questions have been vetted by Parliament and the government, and represent the best ideas of Australia's political institutions, surely they should be expected to fare better when put to the people?

In fact, as a question of the rate of constitutional change, Australia does not fare *too* badly on some international comparisons. The United States has amended its Constitution 27 times in around 220 years, but ten of those amendments (the 'Bill of Rights') came in one go immediately after the formation of the United States and are often considered as being part of the original document. Take out those ten amendments, and the United States has amended its Constitution just 17 times in around twice as long as Australia has been a nation. That is the same rate of constitutional change as Australia.

On other international comparisons, Australia fares less well. Canada has amended its Constitution ten times since 1982, the year in which Canada gained the power to amend its Constitution without approval from the United Kingdom Parliament. The South African Constitution has been amended 16 times since its adoption in 1996. That is twice as many changes as Australia has made over the course of a century. Australia's performance also compares unfavourably to a broader selection of countries. Between 1989 and 1999 alone, 56 per cent of member states of the United Nations made major changes to their constitutions. Remarkably, of the states making such changes, more than 70 per cent adopted a completely new constitution.[2]

Focusing on just the rate of constitutional change does not tell the whole story. Many people think that what Australia has been singularly unable to do is to make major constitutional changes. On only three occasions has Australia amended its Constitution to grant a significant new power to the Commonwealth Parliament – despite constant attempts to do so. Australia has not granted any significant new human rights – again, despite several attempts to do so. Three of the eight successful proposals (1928, 1946 and 1977

(Senate Casual Vacancies)) ratified a situation that already existed in practice – meaning, in effect, that they did not amount to much of a change at all. The three proposals adopted in 1977 were put to the people, in part, because they were perceived to involve the least possible change to the status quo.

In contrast, since 1789, the United States has changed its Constitution to include a set of fundamental rights, to abolish slavery and, through the 14th Amendment to the United States' Constitution, to give a very significant new power to the national government to protect individual rights across the nation. Even since Australia became a nation, the United States has successfully amended its Constitution to guarantee the right to vote to women and people over the age of 18 and to abolish poll taxes. These amendments have resulted in major change to the structure of the United States government. In recent years, the United Kingdom has amended its constitutional arrangements to fundamentally change the House of Lords, to introduce a Bill of Rights, to integrate more closely with the European Union and to devolve power in Scotland. In comparison, the changes to Australia's Constitution have largely involved tinkering around the edges. Only the referendum held in Australia in 1967 to grant the Commonwealth power over Aboriginal peoples and to delete racially discriminatory references in the Constitution might be thought to be a nation-changing amendment.

One possible explanation for the lack of change to Australia's Constitution, and for the fact that the changes that have been made have largely been minor, is that greater change has not been needed. This suggests that the people have got it right in so often voting No because of the enduring soundness of the document. There is some strength in this argument.

Over the course of a century, Australia has developed into a prosperous nation and is one of the oldest continuous democracies in the world. The Australian Constitution has played an important role in this. Since 1901, it has withstood crises and the passage of time to produce an effective foundation for economic, social and cultural development and has fostered a stable democracy responsive to and representative of the people. The important role played by the Constitution is perhaps only apparent when our experience as a nation is compared to that of other nations, such as Fiji, where the lack of a stable legal system has led to social and economic discord.

Nevertheless, a century is a remarkably long time for any framework of government to endure largely unchanged. There are many areas, such as the idea of a republic, where proposals for constitutional reform remain hotly contested. On the other hand, there are areas, such as now obsolete provisions of the Constitution, where there is a broad consensus of opinion that the Constitution needs revision. Many sound proposals for change have been recommended by conventions, committees and parliamentarians, but have never made it to the floor of Parliament or to a referendum. One example of reform often mentioned across all sides of politics and in the community is the need for constitutional change to produce a more effective federal system of government. The Constitution sets down a division of power between the federal and state tiers of government devised in the 1890s. That division has itself been subject to radical change through High Court interpretation and changes in government practice. Nevertheless, it is fair to say that the current division of power brought about by the Constitution bears little relationship to contemporary problems like water scarcity and the need for national standards in areas like health and education.

When it comes to our federal system, as with some other areas, it cannot be said that the Constitution continues to operate with the efficiency and effectiveness that it did in 1901. No legal document could. Indeed, it is remarkable that the Constitution operates as well is it does given its age and the massive shift in aspirations and values from those of the drafters more than a century ago. The bottom line is that there are important areas where constitutional change is clearly needed. In this respect, the referendum process has not

FIGURE 6.1 **Cartoon from the 1988 referendum**
Source: *Sydney Morning Herald*, 5 September 1988, p. 16. Reproduced courtesy of Alan Moir.

lived up to the expectations of the founders of the Constitution that the document would be amended over time to reflect contemporary needs.

This gets us to the central question of this chapter: why has the referendum process proven unable to provide an effective means of updating the Constitution? People have been trying to explain why referendums in Australia fail since the first ever loss in 1910. The record reveals two things. First, there is no single explanation for the failure; instead, a series of overlapping factors have operated individually or in combination to scupper even the best of constitutional reform intentions. Secondly, the key to changing the Constitution is straightforward: get both the proposal and the process right.

In this chapter we discuss a range of factors that contribute to the failure of referendums: the attitudes of the Australian people, government error, committed opposition, opposition to centralised power, Labor's inability to achieve success, the double majority requirement and the quality of the campaigns. We then look at the issue from the opposite perspective: what are the features of the referendums that have succeeded?

The Australian people

It is sometimes said that the principal cause of referendum failure is the Australian people themselves. The people are said to be ignorant about the Constitution or the proposal, or inherently averse to change. The results can reflect each of these points, but only in part.

DON'T KNOW, VOTE NO

Surveys of the Australian public show a disturbing lack of knowledge about the Constitution and Australian government. Rather than being engaged and active citizens, many Australians are woefully ignorant of even the most basic aspects of government. This has been demonstrated over many years. For example:

- A 1987 survey for the Constitutional Commission found that almost half the population did not realise Australia had a written Constitution,[3] with the figure being nearly 70 per cent of Australians aged between 18 and 24.[4]
- The 1994 report on citizenship by the Civics Expert Group[5] found that only one in five people had some understanding of what the Constitution contained, while more than a quarter named the Supreme Court, not the High Court, as the 'top' court in Australia.

Such surveys reveal that the problem is not just a lack of knowledge among Australians, but also false knowledge. For example, it seems that most Australians wrongly believe that we have a national Bill of Rights. A 2006 Amnesty International Australia poll of 1001 voters by Roy Morgan Research found that 61 per cent of those polled think Australia has such a law. The level of error was undoubtedly derived in part from the frequent references to Bills of Rights in popular culture, including American television programs.

These problems are exacerbated during referendum campaigns. A lack of knowledge, or false knowledge, on the part of the voter, can translate into a misunderstanding of a proposal, a potential to be manipulated by the Yes or No cases and even an unwillingness to consider change on the basis that 'don't know, vote No' is the best policy. Overall, the record shows that when voters do not understand or have no opinion on a proposal, they tend to vote No. Polls from the 1999 referendum showed that many people had not read the official pamphlet distributed by the Commonwealth to explain the proposals, and that people who had not read the pamphlet were far more likely to vote No. Polling in the lead-up to the 1967, 1977 and 1988 referendums also suggested that those who did not know which way they would vote shortly before the referendum swung heavily into the No column on the day of the vote.

This constitutional illiteracy makes it hard for people to understand why a proposal for change has been made and how it fits into the broader context of government. This undoubtedly creates opportunities for the No campaign. An example of this was the 1999 referendum, when the No campaign relied on the simple argument: 'don't know, vote No'.

Lack of knowledge about the Constitution also feeds an argument by the No campaign that the proposal is deceptive. No campaigns have, in effect, argued: 'don't understand the proposal? That's because it's tricky, and the government is trying to deceive you into giving it more power.' This claim was put with great effect by the 1988 No campaign.

Ignorance also makes it difficult to refute unscrupulous No campaigning. In 1977, the Yes case found it difficult to respond to Sir Joh Bjelke-Petersen's assertion (supported by unsigned legal advice) that the Simultaneous Elections proposal could lead to the obliteration of the Senate. An adequate response to this claim needed to explain the Senate's current constitutional protections, including the technically obscure special majority provisions in section 128. This is a very difficult message to convey through the mass media.

In this sense, referendums are different from ordinary elections. Sometimes, Australians say that they do not understand the policies that the parties present during an election campaign, or that they do not understand how those policies will affect them. But Australians do not have the option of voting No in an ordinary election. Australians must vote *for* something: for a party or an individual; otherwise, they cast an informal ballot. Referendums are different. A No vote, made in confusion or ignorance, can lead to the failure of the referendum.

Some people blame Australians for their constitutional illiteracy. We disagree. In our view, it is a challenge to be overcome through education and other means. We discuss this further in the next chapter.

Further, even if too many Australians do not understand their system of government, it would be wrong to infer that they are constitutionally *indiscriminate* when it comes to referendums. Where Australians have voted on multiple proposals, commentators have often predicted that the popularity or unpopularity of one will dictate the result of the others. In other words, that Australians will, unthinkingly, vote Yes or No to all of the questions put to them. The people have repeatedly proven this view wrong.

In 1910, Australians considered two measures designed to improve Commonwealth–state financial relations (the State Debts and Finance proposals). The people easily approved the State Debts proposal (which secured approval in five states and almost 55 per cent of the national vote), but rejected the Finance proposal. In 1946, the view of the commentariat was that the popularity of the Social Services proposal would ensure the success of the other two proposals. It did not. The same view was expressed in 1967 (that the Aboriginals proposal would carry the Parliament proposal) and in 1977 (that Simultaneous Elections would be carried by the others). In each case, the pundits were proved wrong.

In addition, where the No campaign has called for a blanket No vote, this has not necessarily translated into an unthinking across-the-board No vote. In 1988, the No campaign advocated a blanket No, and even though all four proposals failed, there were substantial divergences in support between the proposals. For example, at least one in five people who supported the Fair Elections proposal rejected the Rights and Freedoms proposal. There was a similar divergence in the No votes between the 1999 Republic and Preamble referendums.

IF IT AIN'T BROKE, DON'T FIX IT

A No vote can reflect what psychologists call 'status quo bias': people tend to prefer continuity to change. There are two reasons for this status quo bias. First, people are more averse to losing things they have, than they are desirous of gaining things they lack. 'Loss aversion' means that, regardless of whether constitutional change promises great benefits, if there is a risk that change will come with costs, people will overweigh the costs. Second, people care more about benefits that they can get immediately and that are more probable than benefits that (even though greater) are distant and uncertain. Constitutional reform often promises a lot, but what it promises is distant and debatable, whereas the benefits of the status quo are clear and given.

This popular aversion to change has a rational basis. After all, unintended consequences pose a greater risk when it comes to constitutional change than in the case of ordinary legislation.

Unlike ordinary laws, Parliament and a double majority vote of the people is required to reverse bad constitutional reform. Aversion to change may also reflect an assessment that things are already working well or that, though there are problems, the proposed change is not the right one. Alternatively, it may reflect an assessment that changes to Australia's constitutional landscape can, through High Court decisions or intergovernmental agreement, occur incrementally and without the risk of entrenching a principle in the text of the Constitution.

No campaigns have repeatedly tapped into this status quo bias: constitutional change is forever, they urge, so do not risk this one. When constitutional reform is perceived to not be in response to a particular problem, then this argument has even greater bite. This was the case in the 1988 referendums. The No campaign pilloried the proposals as being unnecessary and hastily concocted as a symbolic gesture for the bicentenary. Opponents of the 1988 Rights and Freedoms proposal asked Australians: 'Do your rights feel at risk? If not, then vote No, lest the amendments change that.'

VOTE NO TO THE POLITICIANS' PROPOSAL

No campaigns have repeatedly charged that referendum proposals are *politicians'* proposals. This taps into a national distrust of politics and politicians. The charge is difficult to refute and is often true. It is hard to refute because, by definition, at least a majority of politicians in Commonwealth Parliament must have supported the proposal for it to get to a referendum, and they would be unlikely to give such support if the idea were contrary to their interests. It is also often true: Parliament and the government are the gatekeepers of constitutional reform, and it is unsurprising that most referendums have been tailored to their interests, such as by seeking extra powers for the Commonwealth.

A related charge is that a proposal is being championed for partisan reasons. The message is that the proposal has short-term, political motivations rendering it inappropriate for entrenchment in Australia's Constitution. The perception of partisanship influenced the rejection of the Whitlam government's 1974 (Simultaneous Elections) proposal. In ordinary circumstances, the proposal may have appeared as valid, long-term structural reform. But, in 1974, with rising tensions between the Labor-controlled House of Representatives and the Coalition-controlled Senate, the reform was easily characterised as being a strategic move by Whitlam to shore up his own position. This may explain why the proposal received just 48.3 per cent of the national vote in 1974, but 62.2 per cent three years later when it was put to the people by a Fraser government that controlled both Houses of Parliament.

STATE INTEREST

The figures clearly show that the failure of some referendums reflects a rational assessment by voters that, though the change may be in the national interest or the interests of some states, it is not in the interests of that voter's state. This can be exasperating, particularly where the proposal is perceived to be for the greater good. But it is to be expected and not always a bad thing: section 128 was drafted to protect federalism, and in particular the interests of the smaller states, as much as it was drafted to suit national needs.

The smaller states have tended to reject measures perceived to weaken the power of the Senate. From 1967 to 1988, the people voted on a series of proposals that were portrayed as an attack on the Senate. These were the proposals in 1967 (Parliament); 1974 (Simultaneous Elections); 1977 (Simultaneous Elections); 1984 (Terms of Senators); and 1988 (Parliamentary Terms). The only three states that supported any of those proposals were New South Wales, Victoria and South Australia. Of the five proposals, New South Wales supported four, Victoria two and South Australia one. The people of Tasmania, Australia's smallest state by population, clearly believed they had the most to lose from any attack on the Senate. They recorded the lowest Yes vote among the states in each of those referendums. In 1967, Tasmania recorded just 23.1 per cent in favour; in 1974, 41.4 per cent; in 1977, 34.3 per cent; in 1984, 39.3 per cent; and, in 1988, 25.3 per cent. Similarly, with the 1974 (Mode of Altering the Constitution) question, the government sought to weaken the power of small states over the referendum process by amending section 128 to require the approval of only three states, not four. The proposal was defeated, but received substantially stronger support in New South Wales and Victoria (greater than 50 per cent in both) than the remaining states (which clustered in the low to mid-40 per cent range).

Despite repeated attempts to change the structure of the Senate, Australians have approved only two of these proposals. One of these was the 1906 referendum, which was perceived to be entirely innocuous and dealt with the day that Senators would take their seats. The other was the 1977 (Senate Casual Vacancies) referendum. This weakened the power of the states in the casual appointment process by removing the ability of the states to depart from established convention; but it did not affect the power of the Senate. Even in the successful 1977 referendum, the big-state, small-state divide played out with support in Queensland, Western Australia and Tasmania being 20–30 per cent weaker than support in New South Wales and Victoria.

Assessments of state interest also work in reverse: the bigger states often say No to proposals that are perceived to strengthen the smaller states at their expense. For example, in 1910, the Commonwealth proposed a mechanism for distributing the surplus revenue of the Commonwealth. The effect would have been to redistribute money from the larger, wealthier states to the smaller, poorer states. Three of the four smaller states (Queensland, Western Australia and Tasmania) voted for the proposal, while New South Wales and Victoria were staunchly opposed.

Government error

FAILED YES CAMPAIGNS

Very often, the Yes campaign has been muted or has suffered from poor leadership or inadequate political management. Many Yes campaigns have only 'switched on' in the last two or three weeks of the referendum campaign, long after the No case has built substantial support and momentum. Even in the successful referendums of 1928, 1946 and 1967, the government did not begin an effective campaign until late in the piece, thereby giving the No campaign a free rein in the early stages.

Why has government campaigning been muted? There are four reasons. First, it has often reflected a misjudgment of the effectiveness of the No case. Menzies in 1951, Holt in 1967, and Fraser in 1977, all expressed surprise at the strength of their opponents. Second, the government may, as in 1988, run a weak Yes campaign so as not to be seen to be politicising the referendum. Third, and most importantly, the government has other priorities. A referendum is always just part of a government's day-to-day obligations. Budgets must still be developed; foreign affairs must continue to be conducted; and the national economy must be managed. Governments also have limited political capital. In 1988, for example, the Hawke government was marshalling major structural reforms to the Australian economy at the same time as the referendum: it was not surprising that Prime Minister Bob Hawke and, particularly, Treasurer Paul Keating, the government's two most effective performers, took a back seat in the campaign. Fourth, when governments engage in a referendum, they unlock a complicated political calculus. They may want constitutional reform; but, not surprisingly, they want electoral success more. Where a referendum fails and the referendum is perceived to be associated with the government, the result is seen as a rebuff to the government. The effect can be this: if the government sniffs a risk of defeat, it has an incentive to distance itself from the proposals by running a low-key campaign. Any loss can be brushed off as a decision of the people on the quality of the proposal, not a decision of the people on the government. This seems to have been at least part of the reasons for the Hawke government's lacklustre 1988 campaign.

By contrast, opponents can often be full-time No campaigners. In Australia, this position is exacerbated by restrictions on the Commonwealth's funding of referendum campaigns. The government is limited in what it can spend; many opponents, particularly state governments, are unrestricted. This would be fair if there were an equal number of proponents and opponents outside the Commonwealth Government and those groups were willing to expend equivalent resources on the campaign. But constitutional reform involves changing the status quo. Those with a vested interest in the status quo have often proved willing to expend far more time and energy to oppose change than those supporting the change. An example of this was the 1967 (Parliament) proposal. The Democratic Labor Party knew it was fighting for its survival as a political party, and it fought the referendum tooth and nail with a vigour that surprised the lethargic Holt government. The scaremongering was effective and was a significant contributor to the substantial No vote in Victoria.

TOO MUCH IN ONE QUESTION

Referendums tend to fail when governments try to do too much in the one referendum question. The reason for this is simple: questions containing multiple ideas aggregate opposition. When a popular idea is attached to an unpopular idea and presented as one question, the unpopular idea can drag them both down. Alternatively, where two popular ideas are wrapped up in the one question, some people may oppose one idea, while others oppose the other, with the result that both groups vote No to the whole package. The effect is that two ideas which, independently, would have majority support may fail.

Labor's Attorney-General, HV Evatt, recognised this risk when Cabinet was debating the 1946 referendum proposals. The original recommendation was to put the three ideas in the one question. Evatt argued against this on the ground that it would ensure the referendum's failure. The proposals were separated and Evatt was proved right by the fact that the Social Services proposal was only narrowly accepted (despite having bipartisan support), while the remaining two proposals were defeated.

Doing too much in the one question has dragged down many proposals. In 1911, the Fisher government sought greater legislative powers. Some of the powers it sought were popular, others unpopular. The government put them all into the one question, and the referendum only received 40 per cent of the national vote. Two years later, in 1913, the government separated out the proposals into different questions. The resulting six referendums all failed, but only narrowly, with all six receiving more than 49 per cent of the vote.

In the 1919 (Legislative Powers) and 1944 (Post-war Reconstruction and Democratic Rights), the Hughes Nationalist and Curtin Labor governments, respectively, acted as the Fisher government had done in 1911 in combining both popular and unpopular questions in the one proposal. On these latter occasions, however, even more powers were added to what was already a controversial proposal. Some of the powers the governments added were ones that had already been independently rejected. Unsurprisingly, both referendums failed. The official No case made a point of this in the pamphlet:

> The Labor Government … is asking you to give it additional powers in a Bill which contains seventeen proposals, but allows you one vote only … You [may] favour some powers and reject others. But the Government, by giving you one vote only, insists that you shall take them all or leave them all.[6]

In 1988, the Hawke government tied the success of a reputedly popular idea (four-year terms for the House of Representatives) to a reputedly unpopular idea (four-year terms for the Senate) in the Parliamentary Terms proposal. The government did the same thing with the 1988 (Rights and Freedoms) proposal. In the one question, the government asked for the protection of property rights, religious rights and criminal trial rights. In both cases, the result was a boon for the opposition, and led to the defeat of the proposals. This was particularly evident in the case of the Rights and Freedoms proposal: church groups advocating a No vote opposed only religious rights, not property or criminal trial rights.

When a government puts multiple ideas in the one question, this does not of course guarantee the failure of the proposal. The successful 1946 (Social Services) and 1967 (Aboriginals) referendums both contained multiple ideas. But those referendums had unique factors. The 1946 (Social Services) referendum ideas were united by a popular common theme: the Commonwealth should be able to provide benefits to the people across a range of areas. The 1967 (Aboriginals) referendum, though it contained two ideas (removal of constitutional discrimination against Indigenous people and giving the Commonwealth the power to make laws for Indigenous people), was united around the same concern and was commonly perceived in any event to be primarily about just the first of those ideas.

DOING TOO MUCH ON THE ONE DAY

The record shows that government should not try to ask too many questions on the one referendum day. Where a government asks multiple questions on the one day, some of which have broad support, but some of which are divisive, opponents of the divisive proposals may choose to run an indiscriminate, across-the-board No case. This may be based on the view that some voters may find it easier to understand a blanket call for a No vote. Opponents chose a blanket No strategy in 1974, 1988 and 1999. In 1988, the tactical decision to run a blanket No case was particularly blatant: two of the four proposals that the Coalition opposed were part of the policy the Coalition had taken to the 1987 election.

Of course, as we have discussed above, voters do not, as a rule, indiscriminately respond to these calls for a blanket No vote. Nevertheless, it is clear that some voters do respond in this way. The 1988 referendums suggest that a call for a blanket No vote works where the No campaign can weave a compelling narrative providing a reason for rejecting all of the referendum proposals in one go. In the case of the 1988 referendums, opposition was united by the theme that the proposals were about more power to Canberra. This resonated with voters, regardless of its truth. Though there was some variance in the proposal-by-proposal vote, and despite the fact that many Opposition members privately or publicly supported some of the referendums, voters clearly responded to the No campaign's call for a blanket No vote: all four proposals received only between 30 per cent and 38 per cent of the national vote. The 1974 referendums also support the view that a call for a blanket No vote can be effective: the No vote in those referendums was remarkably consistent nationwide, with opposition of approximately 52–53 per cent for all four proposals, despite each being very different. Opposition was also almost identical in each state across each of the proposals.

If governments risk a blanket No campaign, why do they continue to put many proposals (some popular, some unpopular) on the one day? There are two reasons. First, governments typically have many ideas for constitutional reform, but realise they have limited opportunities to push for them. This leads to a proliferation of proposals at the one referendum. Second, there has been a persistent view that a government which wants a difficult proposal passed should run it on the same day as a popular proposal in the hope that the popularity of the latter will rub off on the former. This tactic was used in 1946, 1967, 1977 and 1988, but has never been successful. The press and the No case have always called the government on the tactic, often to the detriment of the more popular proposal. In 1988, the tactic backfired spectacularly. The Rights and Freedoms question was added as a sweetener. It was thought that Australians would not reject the ideas contained in it. But, when the Catholic Bishops rejected it outright, it turned into a liability for the whole referendum package.

Committed opposition

Committed opposition by a major group is deadly for referendums. Malcolm Turnbull, leader of the 1999 Republic Yes campaign, has summed up the problem this way:

> [Former Liberal Party Attorney-General] Daryl Williams once observed, wisely, that for a referendum to be successful it needed to have almost no opposition, which means it must command either universal support (like the Aborigines referendum in 1967) or be so technical as to arouse no opposition, such as the retirement age for judges, senate vacancies and so on.[7]

THE OPPOSITION

No measure has passed without bipartisan support. The results suggest that committed resistance by the Opposition, whether Labor or non-Labor, is sufficient to kill a referendum.

Why is bipartisan support essential? There are two reasons. First, bipartisan support knocks out the most effective potential leader of a national No campaign – the national Opposition. The Opposition typically has Australia-wide reach, a capable grass-roots organisation to get out the vote and strong influence over the voting tendencies of supporters. Second, bipartisan support suggests a proposal is safe, consensual and fair and, therefore, appropriate for entrenchment in the Constitution. It is unsurprising that, where possible, Yes campaigns have shouted out that they have cross-party support.

When referendums have not had bipartisan support, results in electoral divisions have often split down party lines. In 1944, for example, not one non-Labor electorate voted for Labor's referendum seeking postwar reconstruction powers, and the Labor electorates that voted No were marginal seats Labor had won back from non-Labor parties in the 1943 election.

The closest referendum that did not have bipartisan support was the 1951 (Communism) referendum, which received 49.4 per cent of the national vote and support in three states. The No campaign was led by Labor under the command of HV Evatt (although many members of the Labor Right provided only tepid opposition). Before Evatt and Labor commenced their vigorous opposition, support for the proposal was stratospheric, with some polls putting it at 80 per cent or higher. Nevertheless, the proposal fell to trenchant and committed attack from Evatt and Labor.

Of course, bipartisan support at the national level, even if necessary, is not sufficient for referendum success. The Nationalist government's two 1926 referendums had support from the Opposition Labor Party, but neither achieved more than 44 per cent of the national vote. The 1937 (Aviation) proposal also had support across all the national parties, but failed. In both cases, support by the major parties at the national level did not translate to support from the *state* branches of those parties.

Where the major parties support a proposal, dissidents can actually portray this as a negative. What could the major parties agree on, opponents ask, except more power to politicians and more power to 'Canberra'? This charge was levelled against the 1967 (Parliament) and 1977 (Simultaneous Elections) proposals, both of which had bipartisan support, but both of which were open to the claim of Commonwealth aggrandisement.

Bipartisan support also runs the risk of what has been called 'contra-suggestibility': if your enemy supports it, then you should oppose it. Contemporary commentators argued that, in 1977, just two years after the 1975 constitutional crisis, Labor supporters were turned off the Simultaneous Elections proposal by the fact that Fraser supported it, and Coalition supporters were turned off by Whitlam's support.

INTERNAL GOVERNMENT DISSENT

Some proposals, though they have had bipartisan support at the leadership level of the national parties, have not had unanimous support among all parliamentary members of those parties. In these circumstances, dissidents can take on a 'maverick' quality that can allow them to assume the mantle of protectors of the people against the politicians. This has proved appealing to voters.

Dissident Coalition Senators ran successful, guerrilla campaigns against both the 1967 (Parliament) and 1977 (Simultaneous Elections) referendums. In 1967, Tasmanian Senator Reginald Wright led the Liberal backbench campaign and Tasmania returned an astonishingly low Yes vote of just 23.1 per cent. In 1977, Victorian Liberal Senator Sir Magnus Cormack and the entire Tasmanian Liberal Senate team turned against their party leadership. Victoria voted Yes, but recorded a vote almost six percentage points lower than New South Wales. (That compared with a 1.5 percentage point difference between New South Wales and Victoria in the Simultaneous Elections referendum just three years earlier.) Tasmania was a disaster for the Yes campaign, recording a vote in favour of change of just 34.4 per cent, by far the lowest state tally.

THE STATES

State governments and state political parties have often played a prominent role in the No campaign. State-based groups may oppose a referendum for several reasons. First, they may oppose out of an enlightened assessment of state or national interest. Referendums weakening the Senate may harm small states, and those centralising power may mean that local problems in small states get less attention. State leaders may also genuinely disagree that the proposal is in the national interest, and feel less need to toe the party line to support the idea. Second, state leaders may oppose out of a base self-interest. The balance of power between the Commonwealth and the states is a zero-sum game: more for Canberra means less for the states and, more importantly, less for state politicians. Third, they may oppose out of an opportunistic parochialism.

The effect of state-based opposition explains a number of referendum failures. In 1926, the Bruce Nationalist–Country Party government sought broad powers over industry, commerce and essential services. Labor was concerned that the conservative government would use these powers to wrest back gains won by the labour movement in the preceding years. Nevertheless, the federal parliamentary Labor Party chose to support the proposals on the ground that, just as they could be used by non-Labor, they could be used by Labor when it was in government. All of the state political parties (both Labor and non-Labor) failed to step into line behind their national branches, and ran strong No campaigns. The Federal Labor Executive realised the strength of the state-based opposition and advocated a conscience vote by Labor supporters. The result was that, though the proposals had bipartisan support at the national level, neither achieved more than 44 per cent of the vote nationally. The results were particularly poor in the states where opposition had been strongest (Victoria, Western Australia and South Australia), which returned between 25 per cent and 37 per cent Yes votes.

State government opposition also affected the Curtin government's 1944 referendum. At the 1942 Canberra Conference, the government reached an agreement with the states to support the referendum, but the Premiers of New South Wales and Tasmania reneged as political circumstances changed. When the referendum was put, New South Wales (45.4 per cent) and Tasmania (38.9 per cent) both dutifully voted No. The result in New South Wales was particularly telling because the referendum's principal champion, HV Evatt, was from New South Wales, yet the state's vote was significantly lower than that in Victoria (49.3 per cent), which had voted largely in lockstep with New South Wales in the three referendums seeking greater Commonwealth powers just two years later.

In 1977, state governments again led the No campaign, this time against the referendum to introduce simultaneous elections. Queensland and Western Australia, respectively under the premierships of Sir Joh Bjelke-Petersen and Sir Charles Court, plastered the media with advertisements for the No campaign. The referendum achieved a 62.2 per cent national Yes vote, with heavy majorities in New South Wales, Victoria and South Australia. The opposition in Queensland and Western Australia was, however, effective, with both recording Yes votes of around 48 per cent. (Tasmania also voted overwhelmingly No following a strong No campaign from dissident Liberal Senators.)

Sometimes, state-based opposition has come from the state Opposition parties, and can have a significant effect on an otherwise popular proposal. An example of this was the 1928 (State Debts) referendum. The proposal was approved in all six states. It achieved particularly strong support in Victoria (87.8 per cent) and Queensland (88.6 per cent) and substantially less support in New South Wales (64.5 per cent) and Western Australia (57.5 per cent). Contemporary commentators put this down to the fact that the governments of Victoria and Queensland urged supporters to approve the proposal while, in New South Wales and Western Australia, the leaders of the Opposition (Jack Lang and Sir William Mitchell) urged the proposal's defeat.

State-based opposition can also backfire when voters perceive that it has base motivations. In 1988, the Bjelke-Petersen National Party government in Queensland ran a vigorous and expensive No campaign to the four proposals. This was largely motivated by a perception that the Fair Elections referendum was targeted against gerrymandering by Bjelke-Petersen's party. Queenslanders did not take their state government's advice and, in fact, voted more strongly for the four proposals than any other state. With voters snubbing the advice of their government, the proposal that fared best in Queensland was the Fair Elections question.

OTHER GROUPS

Opposition by minor parties and significant interest groups also affects referendum success. In 1967, the No campaign to the Parliament proposal was vigorously led by Vince Gair, leader of the Democratic Labor Party. The proposal fared particularly poorly in the Party's home state of Victoria, which returned a Yes vote of just 30.9 per cent, more than 20 per cent lower than the Yes vote in New South Wales. This disparity between Australia's two largest states is anomalous in the context of other referendums which have been perceived to weaken the Senate's powers: in the four subsequent referendums on Simultaneous Elections and Parliamentary Terms, the widest divergence between the two was less than 5 per cent.

Opposition by interest groups helps explain voters' different approach to the 1973 referendums put by the Whitlam government, one on Prices, the other on Incomes. The former received 43.8 per cent of the vote, the latter received 34.4 per cent. The federal Opposition ran a blanket No campaign to both. What explains the fact that at least one in five people who voted Yes to Prices voted No to Incomes? A significant part of the answer was the advocacy of the Australian Council of Trade Unions, led by Bob Hawke. The Council strongly opposed the Incomes proposal and ran a nationwide campaign. Victoria (33.4 per cent), Hawke's home state, recorded a substantially lower Yes vote than New South Wales (40.3 per cent).

In 1988, involvement of church groups and independent schools affected the reception of the Rights and Freedoms proposal.

Catholics who attended mass before the referendum were provided with a pamphlet urging a No vote authorised by a group of Catholic bishops, who feared that religious rights would place funding of independent schools at risk. The Rights and Freedoms proposal recorded the lowest Yes vote of the four proposals put that day and, indeed, the lowest Yes vote ever recorded in Australian history.

THE MEDIA

The media has also played a role in the success and failure of constitutional reform. Of course, the media has not always had a major impact on the final result: most of the mainstream press supported the 1999 referendum on the republic, but it still failed.

Sometimes, however, the position of the press does help explain the figures. In 1967, the Parliament proposal attracted substantially more support in New South Wales (51 per cent) than in Victoria (30.9 per cent). This is easily the largest gap in voting patterns between Australia's two largest states on any of the referendums that have been seen to affect the relative powers of the Senate and the House of Representatives. Part of the explanation for this difference is the committed opposition of the Democratic Labor Party, which had a strong power base in Victoria. But this is only part of the explanation: in the 1967 federal election, the Democratic Labor Party achieved 17 per cent of the first-preference Senate vote in Victoria and 5 per cent of that vote in New South Wales. The media provides the remainder of the explanation: the two major Victorian newspapers both opposed the referendum, while three out of four of New South Wales dailies supported it.

Opposition to centralised power?

Australians have shown themselves generally unwilling to give more power to the Commonwealth. Just three of 24 proposals to do so have been successful. The last time a government sought more power for the federal Parliament was the 1973 Prices and Incomes proposals, neither of which received more than 45 per cent of the vote. This has led many commentators to conclude that governments should not seek new powers through referendum: failure is almost guaranteed, and the same result might, in any event, be achieved through referral of power from the states, intergovernmental agreements or evolving High Court interpretation of the Constitution.

Every failed referendum to centralise power has had one or the other of two features: a lack of bipartisan support or strong opposition from the states. Sometimes, the proposal has had both, with the government facing a daunting coalition of Opposition and state party machines.

Most proposals to centralise power have not had bipartisan support. There are two reasons for this. First, most referendums to centralise power were held in the first half of the 20th century, a period in which non-Labor parties were usually ideologically opposed to centralisation, whereas Labor supported a unification of power in the Commonwealth. Twenty of 24 referendums to centralise power were held in that period. Several of these were asked by non-Labor governments, but these referendums typically had only mixed support from the national non-Labor parties and often outright hostility from the state non-Labor parties. Second, where the government asks for a new power, it is invariably associated with a particular policy that the government wants to implement once it achieves the new power. That policy is, in turn, almost always one which divides the major parties. The Opposition, though it may not oppose the new power per se, may oppose the referendum to block the policy associated with the new power.

Of the 24 referendums seeking new powers, only eight have had bipartisan support at the national level. Those eight were the 1910 (State Debts), 1919 (Legislative Powers), 1919 (Nationalisation of Monopolies), 1926 (Industry and Commerce), 1926 (Essential Services), 1937 (Aviation), 1946 (Social Services) and 1967 (Aboriginals) proposals. Three of those eight were successful. The remaining five (the sets of two proposals in 1919 and 1926 and the 1937 (Aviation) proposal) confronted strong opposition from other quarters.

In 1919, members of Billy Hughes' own Nationalist government provided only lukewarm support for the two referendums – one seeking a basket of new legislative powers, and one seeking specific powers over monopolies. Nationalist members took this stance because of a general opposition to centralisation and, in particular, to laws designed to break up monopolies. The state-based Nationalist parties ran strong campaigns against the referendums. So too did John Prowse, the one Country Party representative who ran in the 1919 election held on the same day as the referendum. Even Labor's support at the national level was only tepid: though Labor supported the powers, it rejected the fact that Hughes had sought them only temporarily and that they were conditional on the holding of a Convention in 1920 to discuss their continuation.

In 1926, both Labor and non-Labor combined at the state level to oppose the referendums, which sought powers over industry and commerce, and essential services. Non-Labor opposed the proposals on the grounds of an ideological aversion to centralisation. Labor opposed on the grounds that it believed the Nationalist–Country Party government would use the new powers to implement business-friendly policies.

In 1937, the Aviation proposal had bipartisan support, but faced opposition from states motivated, in part, by an ideological commitment to decentralisation and, in part, by a desire to retain power over aviation for themselves. Even so, the proposal came very close to succeeding, winning two states and 53.6 per cent of the national vote. It would have passed if it had achieved just over 5000 more Yes votes in Western Australia and about 40 000 more Yes votes in New South Wales.

There has been no big-state, small-state divide when it comes to referendums to centralise power. Every single state has voted Yes in at least four referendums to enhance Commonwealth power. Belying its past attempts at secession from the Commonwealth, Western Australia has been the most supportive of referendums to centralise power. Western Australia was the only state to vote Yes to the two 1911 referendums. It also voted Yes to all six of the 1913 referendums, both of the 1919 referendums and the 1944 referendum. Tasmania has been the most reluctant to approve more power for the Commonwealth. It voted Yes only in the 1910 (State Debts), 1946 (Social Services), 1951 (Communism) and 1967 (Aboriginals) referendums. It is unsurprising that there is no big-state, small-state divide. Referendums to centralise power are not inherently adverse to small-state interests. Indeed, small states may perceive that with national responsibility will come national funding, resulting in better services in smaller states with smaller tax bases. That proposition would hold true at least so long as the Senate remains an effective protector of state interests by ensuring that small state issues achieve national attention and that national laws do not discriminate against them.

Where referendums to centralise power have had bipartisan support and have not attracted strong state-based opposition they have been successful, sometimes astonishingly so. The 1967 (Aboriginals) referendum, which gave the Commonwealth power over Indigenous affairs, remains Australia's most successful referendum, with a national Yes vote of over 90 per cent.

When it comes to referendums that centralise power, the challenge is not so much that the referendum is one about Commonwealth power, it is to find a proposal on which cross-party, inter-jurisdictional consensus can be achieved, and to shepherd that consensus through the process of constitutional reform. This may be difficult, but the record suggests that it is not impossible.

Labor's failure

Labor governments have found it particularly difficult to sponsor successful constitutional reform. As we have set out in chapter 4, Labor's failure rate has been 96 per cent, with only one referendum success out of 25 attempts.

The reason for this record is simple: Labor has been unable to achieve bipartisan support for its referendums. Non-Labor has supported only one in 25 of Labor's proposals. Unsurprisingly, that was Labor's successful referendum: the 1946 (Social Services) proposal. In contrast, Labor has, at the national level, supported 14 of non-Labor's referendums and declined to oppose three more (the two 1926 proposals and the 1999 (Preamble to Constitution) proposal). Seven of the 14 referendums that the Labor Party has supported from Opposition have been successful.

The real question is not why Labor has been so unsuccessful at proposing referendums; it is why Labor has been so unsuccessful at getting non-Labor to buy in to its reform agenda. There are several reasons for this. First, the majority of Labor's proposals (15) have sought greater Commonwealth powers. Non-Labor has traditionally had an ideological opposition to this centralisation. Second, non-Labor's opposition to centralisation has tied into a narrative it has built that the Labor Party is a radical constitution-wrecker. This narrative has formed an important theme in many No cases drafted by non-Labor politicians. An example of this is the No case to the 1946 (Industrial Employment) proposal, which depicted the Labor government as

> [r]esponding to the pressure of the Communists ... who are
> out to smash, not only our other democratic institutions, but
> in particular the system of Arbitration we have so carefully
> constructed.[8]

In the opinion of Malcolm Fraser, former Prime Minister of Australia, the challenge for Labor for much of Australia's history is that it has been very easy to simply say: 'Labor wants more power; it wants socialism.'[9]

Third, non-Labor has simply been more willing to oppose referendums opportunistically – either so that it can defeat the proposals it fundamentally opposes by running a blanket No campaign, or for short-term partisan gain. An example of the former was the 1988 referendums, where the Liberals opposed all four questions despite already having taken public positions supporting two of them. An example of the latter is the flip-flopping of the Coalition over simultaneous elections, opposing it in 1974 (when proposed by the Whitlam Labor government), supporting it in 1977 (under Fraser) and then opposing it again in 1984 (when proposed by the Hawke Labor government). In contrast, Labor has on occasion been willing to support non-Labor referendums, even when it realises those referendums will have adverse short-term ramifications. An example of this was federal Labor's support for the 1926 Bruce government's referendum on industry and commerce, even though Labor assessed that, with the new power, the Bruce government would implement policies with which Labor disagreed.

The double majority requirement

The record suggests that the need to achieve not only a national vote, but also a majority popular vote in a majority of states, has been important to the number of failed referendums, but not enormously so. Referendums in Australia have tended to be lost not because of the double majority requirement, but because they have been genuinely unpopular. Conversely, successful referendums have tended to be overwhelmingly successful: seven of the eight successful referendums have been supported by all six states.

How has the four-state majority requirement affected referendum success? If approval of just three states were needed, three more referendums would have been successful: the 1946 (Organised Marketing), 1946 (Industrial Employment) and 1977 (Simultaneous Elections). Those would have been important changes; and the adoption of the 1977 proposal would have made it unnecessary to ask the 1984 (Terms of Senators) and 1988 (Parliamentary Terms) question. The record of change would have improved to 11 of 42 referendums (from the present 18 per cent success rate to a 26 per cent success rate). That is significant; but it would still mean that three in four referendums in Australia had failed.

What if the requirement for a state majority at all did not exist, and the requirement were only for a national majority? If this were the case, four more proposals would have succeeded: the three outlined above where three out of six states supported the proposal and the proposal in 1937 to give power to the Commonwealth to legislate with respect to aviation, which failed because only two states supported it. This would have meant a record of 12 successful referendums of 42, or 29 per cent of the total.

The campaigns

The relative strength of the No and Yes campaigns has played an important role in referendum success and failure. Sometimes, this has been a matter of leadership. Many people perceived the 1951 referendum as a battle between Evatt and Menzies. Evatt's campaigning was relentless, a fact reflected in the referendum result. Similarly, in 1999, the referendum campaign was, for many, embodied in the battle of Malcolm Turnbull and Kerry Jones. An Australian academic, Clive Bean, has argued that Turnbull cost the Yes case approximately 1.4 per cent of the vote, while Jones gained the No case approximately 0.1 per cent.[10]

The effectiveness of No campaigns is also related to the challenges faced by proponents and opponents of change. The No campaign usually has the easier task: it must only convince people that it is safer to stick with the status quo. In contrast, the Yes campaign must make a case for change, meaning that the Yes campaign must first explain the status quo, expose its problems, and identify one option as *the* solution. The Yes campaign must be educative and persuasive. This can be a very difficult task and means that the Yes campaign almost always bears the greater persuasive burden.

The 1999 referendum demonstrates the difficulties that can be faced by the Yes campaign. Proponents had to: first, explain the workings of the existing system of executive government; second, argue that Australia should no longer be a constitutional monarchy; third, argue for the minimalist republic model; and, fourth, argue against direct election of the President. This meant that, in addition to bearing the burden of educating Australians about difficult concepts (such as the reserve powers of the monarch and the Governor-General), the Yes campaign was open to attack from a coalition of monarchists (who rejected the second argument) and direct electionists (who rejected the third and fourth claims).

The No campaign's persuasive burden is lessened further by an important dynamic of referendums: a No vote, for many people, is an expression of disillusionment, disenfranchisement or disengagement. This is borne out both in voting statistics and in the standard slogans of many No campaigns. In terms of the statistics, the record suggests that Australians who are not engaged tend to vote No. In terms of slogans, No campaigns have increasingly relied on the themes that the referendum proposal either fails to engage with the real issues affecting Australians or that the referendum is really a plot to increase the power of politicians. This means that No campaigns are in an especially persuasive position: they can both pick up on preference for the status quo and also pick up on inherent dissatisfaction with the status quo.

No campaigns have also often exercised a licence to be unscrupulous, drawing on exaggerated, mutually inconsistent arguments against change. The No campaign has not by any means had a monopoly on such campaigning, but the record suggests that it has more often been willing to sow confusion and rely on hyperbole than the Yes case. This is, no doubt, a reflection of the fact that the No campaign need not argue for anything and stands to benefit the most from popular confusion about the Constitution and the proposed change.

The self-fulfilling constitutional drought

Most recently, the failure of constitutional reform has become self-fulfilling. The historical difficulty in securing approval has made governments reluctant to even consider putting more proposals for reform. The period from 2000 to 2010 was the first decade since 1901 when no proposal for constitutional reform was put to the people. The absence of any referendum during this period was in stark contrast to the often intense public debate during that decade about the state of the Federation, human rights, the structure of federal Parliament and a range of other constitutional issues. Despite such debate and constitutional reform often being a necessary part of any solution, it was never seriously on the agenda as a response to such issues.

The closest that the Howard government came to a referendum was to moot reform of the Senate in 2003, but it quickly took the issue off the table. Kevin Rudd came to power in 2007 with a promise to examine constitutional change in areas such as the recognition of Indigenous peoples and local government, the republic, fixed four-year terms for the federal Parliament, co-operative federalism and control of the nation's hospitals, but Rudd did not take steps to progress such reform during his time in office. Throughout the 2000s, constitutional reform has been perceived to be too difficult and too costly and perhaps even as risking too much political damage for the government. Proposing a referendum is now often perceived as mere political posturing in an endeavour to secure parliamentary or intergovernmental approval for a particular policy.

The difficulty, or even impossibility, of constitutional reform has become part of the accepted political landscape in Australia – something that has made constitutional reform even more difficult to achieve. When constitutional reform is perceived to be out of the ordinary and unfamiliar, and when proponents of reform must first educate Australians about basic constitutional principles because there is no recent history of national constitutional deliberation, the approval of the people becomes even harder to secure.

What makes a successful referendum?

Most discussion of referendums tends to focus on the reasons why referendums have failed. This is no doubt because more than four out of five referendums have been rejected at the ballot box. Much less has been said about what characterises successful referendums. There is a good reason for this: they share no obvious theme. If anything, they are characterised by a negative: the features contributing to referendum failure have been absent.

THE 1967 (ABORIGINALS) REFERENDUM

This was Australia's most successful referendum, securing majorities in all six states and an astonishing national majority of more than 90 per cent. Five factors guaranteed its success. First, there was no official No case. This reflected the broad parliamentary consensus on the point. It also, of course, took away a major forum for scaremongering. Only the 1967 (Aboriginals) and 1977 (Retirement of Judges) referendums have had a Yes case, but no No case. Those have been, respectively, the first and third most successful referendums in Australian history. (The second most successful referendum – the 1906 (Senate Elections) referendum – had neither a No case nor a Yes case.)

Second, there was consensus between the Commonwealth and the states. The states had been consulted and signed on to the reform even though it gave a new power to the Commonwealth.

Third, there was a unique national consensus on the referendum. This was both cause and effect of the consensus between the parties and between the Commonwealth and states. The debate preceding the referendum, and its result, shows that by 1967 Australians were ready to speak with one voice in a referendum they perceived to be about moving away from the discrimination against Indigenous people set out in the Constitution.

Fourth, the referendum was preceded by extended national deliberation. In 1944, the Chifley government had unsuccessfully sought a similar power to legislate for Aboriginal people as part of the omnibus Post-war Reconstruction and Democratic Rights referendum question. There had been some debate on the issue at that time. In the years after 1944, debate continued. Schools, universities and the media provided forums to debate the place of Indigenous people in Australia's Constitution. By 1967, Australians were well informed and ready to go to the polls. This was reflected in the surprising absence of extended debate on the question during the referendum campaign itself. Australians, it seems, had already made up their minds.

Finally, by 1967, although important differences remained, much Indigenous policy was already uniform. The Ministers' Conference between the states had resulted in a progressively more national policy, albeit one that remained state-controlled. There was also no indication that the federal Holt government would seek any significant shift in that policy if it gained power over the area. The result was that giving control to the Commonwealth was not seen as likely to result in major change. Australians were voting for incremental reform – to change the practicalities of the system by giving direct responsibility to the Commonwealth, without changing the system itself.

THE 1977 REFERENDUMS

The 21st of May 1977 was the most successful referendum day in Australian history. Australians voted Yes to three questions. No other referendum day has managed even two. The successful 1977 proposals received between 73 per cent and 80 per cent of the national vote. Two of the three successful proposals (Senate Casual Vacancies and Referendums) limited the powers of the states. The third successful proposal (Retirement of Judges), on one view, limited the power of the Commonwealth by preventing it from stacking the High Court with judges who would remain there for life.

Why were these proposals so successful? Three factors were important. First, all four proposals put in 1977 had been the subject of extensive debate at the 1976 Hobart sitting of the Australian Constitutional Convention. As we have set out in chapter 5, the Senate Casual Vacancies proposal was, in fact, rejected by that Convention, but not for any fundamental reason. The Convention accepted the principle, but raised technical concerns with how to enshrine it in the Constitution. The proposal ultimately put to the people was designed to overcome these concerns. The Fraser government relied heavily on the claim that the proposals were the result of consultation, negotiation and compromise. This no doubt was an important persuasive tool. But the fact of prior agreement also meant that the states were, by and large, locked in to support the reforms. Only two states – Queensland and Western Australia – opposed the referendums. And, in those states, opposition was only really directed at the Simultaneous Elections and Senate Casual Vacancies proposals.

Second, the three successful proposals shared an important feature: they involved only minimal change. The Senate Casual Vacancies proposal codified a constitutional convention that was widely thought already to exist: in effect, it involved no practical change at all. The Retirement of Judges proposal was an incremental reform, with a significant, but not wide-ranging, effect. The Referendums proposal changed the calculus for determining a national majority in referendums through the inclusion of votes cast in the Australian territories, but it did not change the requirement for majorities in a majority of states. In other words, it too was an incremental reform.

Third, the government committed itself wholeheartedly to making the case for reform. Fraser travelled Australia-wide, made full use of the available media and campaigned tirelessly for a Yes vote. Perhaps only Evatt, opposing the Communism referendum in 1951, has campaigned as relentlessly as Fraser did in 1977. The government was fully committed to the referendum, and this showed in the results.

OTHER SUCCESSFUL REFERENDUMS

The 1910 (State Debts) and 1928 referendums both made important changes and received widespread support. These referendums – which dealt with voluntary financial arrangements between the Commonwealth and the states – had one feature in common. Like the 1977 proposals, they arose from a lengthy period of Commonwealth–state consultation. This led to an extraordinary commitment from the states to the reform. In 1928, state Premiers took the unprecedented step of positively *calling* for a constitutional change that would, on one view, give the Commonwealth a new power. The 1928 referendum had an added feature: it ratified an agreement that already existed. Australians had already road-tested the idea of a loan council, and clearly liked what they had seen.

The referendum proposal that succeeded with the smallest portion of the national vote (54.4 per cent) was the 1946 (Social Services) referendum. It was approved in all six states, but with low majorities in each. Three features underpinned its success.

First, the referendum sought a range of new powers, many of which were not, in fact, new. The Commonwealth had already been wielding the powers; all that had changed was that their exercise had been called into question by a High Court decision. This meant that, like the 1928 referendum, the 1946 referendum sought to ratify a pre-existing arrangement.

Second, the proposal came about through negotiation and compromise among the major parties. No government before or since has been willing to have its referendum proposal amended on the floor of Parliament by an Opposition Party. But that was what the Chifley Labor government did in 1946 when it allowed Menzies to make changes to the Bill proposing the referendum. This locked the Opposition leadership into support for the proposal, and sent a clear message to Australians that the question was not purely a partisan issue.

Third, the kinds of powers the Commonwealth Government sought were perceived, in large part, to be powers for the spending of money, rather than the making of regulations. In other words, they were beneficial, not coercive. This meant that, like the 1967 referendum, the states did not loom as major opponents: from their perspective, it meant that the Commonwealth would assume some of their expenditure burdens.

One more series of successful referendums in Australia's history is worthy of mention: the series of votes on Federation at the end of the 19th century. In terms of Yes votes, those referendums were not the most successful ever. But, in terms of adopting major alterations to Australia's mode of government and making changes that created both winners and losers, the votes on the draft Constitution had unparalleled success.

These referendums displayed all the essential conditions for referendum success. The draft Constitution was developed with the input of the people of Australia, having been debated at town meetings across the country. Popular groups outside the major political parties, such as the Australian Natives' Association, had a prominent role in the debate. The second Convention to draft the Constitution held over 1897–98 comprised representatives directly elected by the people of five of the six colonies. By the time of the actual votes taken over 1898–1900, deliberation had been long and deep. When Australians entered the polling booth, they had already had time to get used to the idea of being a federated nation.

The draft Constitution had opponents, but the framers showed great skills of negotiation. They involved opponents in the process and, ultimately, made them advocates of the change. New South Wales Premier George Reid had been a leading opponent of Federation. But, in consultation with him and the New South Wales Government, the proponents of Federation made amendments to the draft Constitution. Reid subsequently became one of the Constitution's most prominent supporters, and ran on a platform expressly supporting Federation in the 1899 New South Wales colonial election.

There was a vigorous No campaign against the Australian Constitution, but the proponents of nationhood were adept and unrelenting. Some of Australia's greatest orators, Sir Edmund Barton, Sir Alfred Deakin and Sir Henry Parkes, propelled the Yes campaign forward to success.

All the elements of successful constitutional change were there in the 1890s: popular ownership of the process; deliberation and education; consultation and compromise; and smart, effective management of the Yes case. That process brought about the Australian nation and its new Constitution in 1901. Soon after, and at intervals since, Australians have been willing to say Yes to further change. What has been critical to success in each case has been careful management of the process of getting to Yes.

7

GETTING TO YES

Getting it right

Australia has a grand tradition of reform, ranging from its experiments with referendums and direct democracy in the 1890s to the floating of the dollar, deregulation and the other economic reforms of recent decades. Australia also has a tradition of world-leading governance arrangements: in 1901, it became one of the world's first federations, and in 1902 was the second country to give women the right to vote.

At least in recent times, this tradition has faltered when it comes to reforms that require changes to the Australian Constitution. Constitutions are meant to change, slowly perhaps, but still they are meant to change. They must adapt to meet new circumstances, new technologies, new ways of dealing with old problems and new societal standards. Australia has found it difficult to change its Constitution, even when there has been broad agreement that reform is necessary. When constitutional amendment is rejected because the proposal is faulty, unnecessary or dangerous, everyone agrees that is a good result. But when constitutional reform that is necessary and valuable is rejected because of bad management of the process, there is a serious problem.

The costs of this are high. Australia's Constitution affects the nation's future and the quality of life and long-term prosperity of its people. Its impact may be borne out over the longer term, but there is no doubt that Australia's system of government brought about by its constitutional structure has a profound effect on the economy, society and the attainment of social justice. Outdated or unworkable constitutional arrangements can make policy reforms impossible or too difficult. It can also place the burden of constitutional 'reform' on the High Court, a body never intended to bear that load.

The political stakes are high when it comes to constitutional reform. A failed referendum is expensive for taxpayers, is often a major blow to the government and can discourage other reform proposals. The results of this are plain to see in Australia today, which has just experienced the first decade since Federation without any referendum being put to the Australian people, and has not had a successful referendum since 1977.

Australia needs to rethink the way it manages the process of constitutional reform. Rather than repeating the mistakes of the past, attention needs to be paid to why so many referendums have failed, and how the few successes have been achieved. There are many important lessons that can be learnt from the century of attempts to amend the Australian Constitution. The record shows that reform can be achieved if it is built upon five pillars:

1   bipartisanship;
2   popular ownership;
3   popular education;
4   sound and sensible proposals; and
5   a modern referendum process.

In this chapter, we set out a new model for managing the constitutional reform process. We first set out the bodies that should manage the process of systematic constitutional review, be responsible for generating and encouraging debate about ideas for reform and facilitate an informed, popular vote. We then look in detail at each of the five pillars for constitutional success. Our hope is that this might inspire rethinking, debate and an improvement in efforts at constitutional change. There is no doubt that constitutional reform is achievable if it is approached in the right way.

The institutions of constitutional reform

A CONSTITUTIONAL REVIEW COMMISSION

Constitutional reform in Australia has often been approached in an ad hoc manner according to the immediate political needs of the government. The results can be seen in the referendum record. Rather than seeing public funds and reform energy wasted on failed short-term proposals, it is far more sensible to invest funds earlier in the process to generate better ideas that are more likely to attract popular support.

Australia should establish a small, ongoing Constitutional Review Commission charged with reviewing the Constitution, generating proposals for constitutional reform, consulting with the public on draft proposals and, after consultation, recommending them to Parliament. The Commission's agenda of constitutional review should comprise topics recommended for its consideration by:

- any Australian government, Parliament, or parliamentary committee, whether these be at the Commonwealth, state or territory level;

- local government bodies;
- other forums of constitutional debate, such as prior Constitutional Conventions;
- members of the public; and
- the Commission itself.

The Commission has the potential to receive a large number of ideas, and should be encouraged to promote an inclusive, open debate about constitutional reform. The Commission would be expected to exercise its judgment on which ideas to progress and what priority to give them as part of its work program.

The membership of the Commission will be critical, and must be broad and inclusive. Former parliamentarians, local government representatives and constitutional experts should all be involved. So too should members of the broader Australian community. The Commission should be appointed not only by the Commonwealth Government, but also by other Australian governments. There should be an opportunity for the Opposition and minor parties within the federal Parliament to have a say on the Commission's membership. There is no point in creating a body that is incapable of bringing about broad political and community support for whatever proposals it puts forward.

A Constitutional Review Commission of this kind would bring trained scrutiny to Australia's most important law, as well as a connection to the Australian people. There is precedent for sustained, expert review. Bodies such as Reconciliation Australia and the Australian Law Reform Commission are expert in their fields and can speak with sufficient authority to move governments to act.

The Constitutional Review Commission must not suffer the same fate of prior, short-term Australian constitutional review bodies. It should be a regular (not temporary) part of the nation's political life with a membership selected in a way that brings legitimacy and authority. The idea is to create a body capable of producing good ideas and of bringing about a political commitment from the Commonwealth, the states and Australia's main political parties.

A CONSTITUTIONAL CONVENTION EACH DECADE

The recommendations of the Constitutional Review Commission should feed into a regular, popular Constitutional Convention, convened once each decade or 'half-generation'. The Convention should consider the recommendations of the Constitutional Review Commission as well as proposals put to it by the federal Parliament, a majority of the states or by petition of a large number of individual Australians. The Convention should be charged with debating proposals for constitutional reform and recommending proposals to the federal Parliament for submission to a referendum.

Whether elected or appointed on each occasion, the Convention must be broadly representative. It should be large enough to give its recommendations legitimacy and small enough to allow for meaningful debate and compromise. Australia's most successful Conventions have followed this model of inclusivity and practicality: representatives to the 1897–98 Conventions were, by and large, popularly elected in representing their states; and Australia's next most successful Convention in terms of referendum outcomes (the 1973–85 Constitutional Convention) involved broad representation across many stakeholder groups. Both, though broadly representative, were small enough to allow for real debate.

In other cases, it will be appropriate to hold a Convention to consider a specific issue, as was the case with the 1998 Convention on the republic. This will be a matter for individual governments based on an assessment of the nature of the issue and the timing of the constitutional reform cycle. These should, however, be the exception, and only ever in addition to the systematic deliberation promised by the regular Convention model.

A regular Constitutional Convention would provide a much-needed means of regular community engagement in constitutional reform. It would also build an expectation of debate about change and provide a consultative mechanism. This would allow careful consideration to be given to constitutional issues in an environment not dominated by the pressures of short-term political needs.

A REFERENDUM PANEL

Just as there is a need for a systematic, consensual approach to initiating proposals for constitutional reform, so too is there a need for a similar approach to managing the way in which those proposals are put to the people. Australia should establish a Referendum Panel to oversee public education initiatives in the lead-up to a referendum. Its role should include:

- developing and distributing neutral information about the referendum in a way that promotes community participation and enables Australians to cast an informed vote;
- overseeing any Yes and No committees to ensure that they make appropriate use of any public funding; and
- reviewing and reporting on the accuracy of factual claims made during the referendum.

As with the Constitutional Review Commission, the composition of the Referendum Panel will be of great importance. The Panel should:

- have a small membership;
- be appointed by the Prime Minister in consultation with the leader of the Opposition, other national party leaders and the states;
- include a representative of the Australian Electoral Commission; and

- include members who are widely respected and known to be impartial on the issues being debated in the referendum, such as former Governors-General, State Governors and High Court Judges.

A Referendum Panel of this kind was recommended in late 2009 by the House of Representatives Standing Committee on Legal and Constitutional Affairs in its inquiry into the holding of referendums.[1]

The first pillar – bipartisanship

THE NEED FOR BIPARTISANSHIP

Bipartisan support has proven to be essential to referendum success. Referendums need support from the major parties at the Commonwealth level. They also need broad support from the major parties at the state level. The history of referendums in Australia provides many examples of proposals defeated by committed opposition from a major party at either the Commonwealth or state level.

The proponents of constitutional reform have long known of the need for that bipartisan support. The challenge has always been how to achieve it. It is very easy for a federal Opposition to decide to oppose a referendum. Defeating the government at a referendum not only stymies the government's agenda, but can inflict lasting electoral damage. In this way, referendums can operate like by-elections. They can be a useful means for an Opposition to generate a negative public reaction to the government. Equally, they can enable voters to indicate their dissatisfaction in a way that does not threaten the government's hold on power. State-level parties can also find it easy to oppose a proposal. They can have strong political incentives to champion local state interests over the national interest, and no need to secure support from the residents of other states.

There is no easy solution to the problem of partisanship, and clearly partisanship is an important feature of any democracy. Australia's political system assumes that politicians will seek to win general elections and, in so doing, will support or oppose measures with a keen eye to their own prospects. The problem is that the issue of constitutional reform requires a different approach to ordinary politicking. Constitutional reform, by definition, is for the long term – a successful referendum cannot be done away with just by a change in government. Where partisan objections to constitutional reform spring from deep, enduring ideological differences, they are valuable additions to the reform process. But when such objections spring from short-term electioneering, they can engender a spoiling game that does not serve Australia's long-term welfare.

SECURING COMMITTED BIPARTISAN SUPPORT

To secure bipartisanship, it is not enough merely to involve a range of political groups in the process; the process must also commit those groups to reform. This can be very difficult to achieve. In 1920 and 1929, the Commonwealth thought it had reached agreement with the states on proposed reforms, but several states backed out and the Commonwealth ultimately never put the proposals to the people. Similarly, in 1977, Queensland and Western Australia extricated themselves from an 'agreement' reached at the Hobart Conference to support simultaneous elections. The problem in each of those cases was not a failure of 'involvement', but a failure to achieve a binding political commitment.

Our model – of regular review by a Constitutional Reform Commission and regular deliberation by a Constitutional Convention – is aimed at securing and locking in bipartisan and cross-jurisdictional support. The broadly representative composition of the institutions is targeted at ensuring that they are and are perceived to be inclusive, expert and, to the greatest extent possible, non-partisan.

The objective is to develop sound proposals for reform and to achieve a political commitment from political parties and governments. This should follow from the authority with which the institutions will speak. The Commission's authority will emanate from the fact that it is an entrenched part of Australia's political landscape. It will result also from the fact that it will include community representatives and be non-partisan and expert within its field. The Convention's authority will derive from the media and public attention its deliberations will attract, and the legitimacy it will derive from its broad representation of the community.

Ultimately, nothing can guarantee commitment. All that can be done is to design a process that makes such commitment more likely to be achieved and that raises the political costs of any group seeking to renege on its support. Our proposed model provides a framework for achieving this.

The second pillar – popular ownership

THE PROCESS CANNOT BE MONOPOLISED BY POLITICIANS AND THE ELITE

Just as deadly as partisan opposition is to constitutional reform is the perception that a reform idea is a 'politicians' proposal'. From the 1967 Parliament proposal, which was felled by the cry of 'no more politicians', to the Republic referendum, which was killed off by the claim that it was the 'politicians' republic', Australians have consistently voted No when they believe a proposal is motivated by politicians' self-interest. This reflects a well-known undercurrent of distrust of Australian politicians. The constitutional design of Australia's reform process exacerbates this problem. Politicians, and only politicians, can initiate constitutional reform through the federal Parliament. This renders every referendum proposal at risk of being perceived as self-serving.

Of course, the people's elected representatives should have an important role in the constitutional reform process. Changes to the Constitution directly affect the practice of national politics, and politicians are expert at debating new laws. The views of politicians may also be expected to be broadly representative of the people and their individual states. These are all reasons for involving politicians in the reform process. But none of them is a reason for giving politicians a monopoly over that process; nor is any of them an argument against erring on the side of reducing the role of formal politics in the process.

A further risk to referendum success is the charge of 'elitism'. The law and practice of the Constitution is far removed from the lives of most Australians. On the other hand, the Constitution is part of the daily lives of many people who hold privileged positions in Australian society, particularly politicians, lawyers and judges. When constitutional reform is perceived to be the preserve of these privileged groups, it becomes easy to portray the proposals as elitist, unnecessary and self-indulgent. There can be debate about the abuse of the term 'elite', but it undoubtedly captures a mood of alienation and disenfranchisement among Australian voters. When that mood exists, as the Republic referendum demonstrated, it can prove terminal for a reform proposal. 'Elites', however defined, will play a role in the process of reform. Expertise and education should be valued, and constitutional law and practice are complex. What must be guarded against is proposals for reform springing from an exclusive group that has a self-perceived monopoly on expertise and education.

It has long been recognised that popularly constituted bodies like conventions can be a good way of ensuring broad involvement in the process of constitutional reform. In 1944, former Prime Minister Robert Menzies said:

Fundamental changes in the Constitution will never be passed

in Australia if they proceed from any party ... Some changes
have a chance of being made in Australia if they proceed
from a popular convention, which has had abundant time and
opportunity to consider problems that have to be faced and to
form reasonable conclusions in respect of them.[2]

Menzies departed from his own prescription in the 1951 referendum on communism and was handed a stinging defeat. Sir Robert Garran, who had witnessed the 1897–98 conventions, agreed in his 1968 memoirs *Prosper the Commonwealth*:

[Proposals] framed and proposed to Parliament by a convention
elected by the people for that purpose, would have a far better
chance of acceptance at a subsequent referendum than any
amendment framed and introduced by the Government of the
day.[3]

Menzies' and Garran's prescription continues to hold true today.

POPULAR OWNERSHIP

Popular ownership is often used as a catch-cry, with little content. That is because popular ownership is an outcome, and an unquantifiable outcome at that. There is no one way of engendering popular ownership. What will always be essential, however, is popular participation, both in the process of generating ideas, and the consultation and deliberation that follows.

Beyond broad statements of inclusive participation, what is needed is:

- extended national debate and consultation on any proposal (it should not be forgotten that it took decades to convince a far smaller number of Australians of the benefits of Federation);
- debate and consultation occurring across a wide variety of forums, including: in all the states; in both urban areas and the

regions; and across a variety of age and ethnic groups. It should not be possible for Australians to feel that they have not had a chance to 'have their say';

- a process that is open and responsive. It is not enough to consult about a preconceived outcome; consultation must be meaningful;
- a process that makes full use of available media; and
- above all, a commitment that public engagement will permeate and drive the whole process.

These are all central elements of our Commission and Convention model.

Achieving popular ownership is a major challenge, with no easy short cuts available. It is difficult to get a large, diverse nation to sign on to a proposal for constitutional reform. But there are means by which this may be achieved. Australians need more than a veto at the ballot box; they must have a genuine say in shaping reform itself.

PLEBISCITES

Plebiscites are a useful tool in the government's toolkit for generating popular ownership of reform proposals. As we have set out in chapter 1, plebiscites are non-binding popular votes on a particular idea.

Australians have voted in plebiscites on three occasions, twice on whether to introduce conscription and once on Australia's national anthem. In the context of referendums, plebiscites allow for a 'staged' process of reform. Plebiscites can be used to determine popular support for a series of ideas and to build support for a successful proposal. They can build agreement on basic principles before proceeding to the complexities about which there may be more debate. They allow the government to test the national mood on broad propositions, such as whether Australians want a republic.

Once agreement has been reached around a broad proposition, but there remain a number of possible changes that could be made to bring this into effect, plebiscites can also be helpful at arriving at the final model. People might, for example, agree that Australia should become a republic; but that does not indicate what kind of republic to adopt. The traditional referendum process, built around binary Yes and No votes, is ill-suited to complex, non-binary choices. Plebiscites can serve a selective function in allowing voters to choose between the different options that might then be put to them in a referendum.

When used well, plebiscites can create a sustainable mood for change. People are much more likely to do something when they have already said in advance that they will do it. Psychologists call this 'commitment bias'. In the same way, when people have supported a proposal in a plebiscite, they can be expected to be more likely to also support a referendum proposal of a similar kind. Plebiscites are also useful when they are unsuccessful. Failed plebiscites can nip proposals in the bud that would never be successful at referendum. Further, whether successful or unsuccessful, plebiscites provide a forum for educating Australians about the Constitution and about the particular proposal.

The challenge with plebiscites is that they are not cheap to hold on a national basis, and can require similar levels of energy and commitment to a referendum, without actually producing the reform. These difficulties are compounded if a plebiscite is unsuccessful. Plebiscites should be used selectively. There must be a clear identified need such as a basic principle around which to build agreement or a way that the plebiscite can facilitate the narrowing of choices for a later referendum.

Some people think that the merely advisory nature of plebiscites invites a shallow response from the electorate. This was not Australia's experience with the Conscription and National Song plebiscites. Debate, particularly on the Conscription plebiscites, was deep and, though voting was voluntary, the turnout was high. If Australians truly believe their vote will count – that it will commit politicians to act and that the question is relevant and meaningful – plebiscites

FIGURE 7.1 Cartoon from the 1999 referendum
Source: The Advertiser, 5 November 1999, p. 16. Reproduced courtesy of O Atchinson.

have been shown to work.

POPULAR OWNERSHIP AND THE REFERENDUM PANEL

The importance of popular ownership does not end once a proposal is ready to be put to the people. The passage of a Constitution Alteration Bill by the federal Parliament signals the beginning of the most important phase for popular participation. Ensuring popular engagement in the referendum process should be a cornerstone principle for the Referendum Panel.

This may mean using innovative strategies to engage people, including:

- deliberative polls. This involves gathering together a large number of citizens, providing each with background material and briefings by experts and then giving them a chance to debate the issue. Issues Deliberation Australia conducted a successful deliberative poll on the republic in 1999, with most attendees reporting a substantial improvement in their understanding of the issues and many indicating that their views on the reform had changed; and

- citizens' assemblies, where the issues are publicly debated in local communities Australia-wide.

Engagement may also mean using a wide range of different kinds of communication, including:

- the vast array of social networking applications that facilitate communication;
- mobile phone applications, including SMS; and
- information, such as pictures and diagrams, in addition to text in the official pamphlet.

These are not substitutes for more traditional methods of communication, and they are not ends in themselves. Technology is only useful when it is used as an effective means to ensure that Australians have a genuine opportunity to be engaged in the process of constitutional reform.

The third pillar – popular education

It is not enough for information about referendums and the Australian Constitution to appear after a Bill to amend the Constitution has been passed by the federal Parliament. That is too late to properly educate Australians about the Constitution so that they are well placed to cast an informed vote at a referendum. As Kerry Jones, leader of the 1999 No campaign and now Executive Director of the Constitution Education Fund Australia, has said, 'for a referendum to be successful, you need an informed population, who are *already* engaged and interested'.[4]

It is clear that there is a need for an ongoing process of educating Australians about referendums and the Constitution. The government's obligation to educate Australians about the Constitution and constitutional reform is a corollary of the obligation that the law places on Australians to vote in referendums. Alfred Deakin, a former Prime Minister and one of the people who drafted Australia's Constitution, said: 'It is our duty, when we ask electors to vote for or against momentous proposals of this kind, to give them the best material we have in order that they may form an independent judgment'.[5]

Misunderstanding of the Constitution means that people can cast a Yes or No vote to a proposal in a way that does not reflect their real beliefs. Of course, the more likely result is that people will vote No out of concern about what the proposal might do, even where they would have supported the proposal had they fully understood it. A lack of popular knowledge about the Constitution also places the burden on the proponents of change to, first, explain the Constitution and then, only once that is done, make the positive argument for change. Opponents of change need do neither, and can instead rely upon familiar calls such as 'don't know, vote No'.

Governments will never be entirely effective at educating Australians about the Constitution and the referendum process. The Constitution is a complex document. People can spend many years studying it and still have only an imperfect understanding. The basic principles that illuminate it – federalism, representative government, responsible government and more – are vague and contested ideas. Australia's Constitution is also not particularly approachable – it is well known for being long, verbose and, on its face, only marginally relevant to the day-to-day needs of Australians.

The project of educating Australians about the Constitution

may be difficult, and it will never be perfectly completed, but it is a project that must be undertaken. Australians deserve access to the information they need to understand their system of government and any proposal for reform. They must be given the opportunity to cast an informed vote.

The Constitutional Review Commission, in coordination with the Australian Electoral Commission, should be required to develop and implement programs for the ongoing general constitutional education of Australians of all ages. This educative function will be greatly enhanced by regular public consultation by the Commission around specific proposals, and the focused national debate that would occur during Constitutional Conventions. The Referendum Panel, once established, should be responsible for the education of Australians about particular proposals once they have passed through the federal Parliament.

The fourth pillar – sound and sensible proposals

As important as it is to get the process of generating proposals right, it is equally important to get the proposals themselves right. By and large, the Commission and Convention model will help ensure good proposals.

Former Howard government Minister Peter Reith, who managed the 1988 No campaign, has said that good proposals begin from a 'feeling for the constitutional temper of the Australian people. You need a genuine problem and a reasonable solution, a solution which does not appear to be politicians just grabbing more power'.[6]

But it may not be enough for reform proposals to make good sense. They may also need to be smart. This means that they should be framed in a way that acknowledges and responds to the mistakes that have been made in past attempts at constitutional reform. They should also be framed in a way that takes account of what we know about how to appeal to people's sense of the long-term interest. In this section, we set out some ideas for structuring successful constitutional reform proposals.

DIFFERENT PROPOSALS, DIFFERENT QUESTIONS

Different ideas should not be lumped together in the one referendum question. The history of referendums in Australia shows that this is a recipe for failure. The effect is to ensure that opposition to individual ideas is aggregated against the joint proposal.

Of course, where proposals for reform are interdependent and unseverable, then they must be contained within the one question. No one could have suggested that it would have been possible to separate out different parts of the 1999 Republic proposal. But, where proposals are not interdependent, they should not be treated as such.

SUNSET PROVISIONS

Australians are conservative when it comes to referendums, but they are not unthinkingly so. Aversion to constitutional change is, indeed, rational. All policies and new laws risk unintended consequences. The risks with constitutional change are far greater given their potentially broad-ranging impact and the fact that such change is so hard to undo.

One response to this natural conservatism is to make the reform proposal itself more conservative. In some situations, constitutional reform could be subject to a sunset provision. That would involve the people voting on a proposal to reform the Constitution, but also giving the people an option to roll back the reform after a period of time if it is not working. The proposal could, for example, be to give a new power to the Commonwealth for a period of ten years, after which point another referendum would be held to determine whether to continue the power. Governments worldwide do this all the time when introducing major reforms, and Australian governments regularly include sunset provisions in important legislation. In appropriate cases, the same strategy should apply to referendums.

SUNRISE PROVISIONS

Vested interests pose a major challenge to referendum success. Law reform almost always alters existing rights and redistributes resources. In the case of constitutional change, this redistribution can be very significant and long-term. The challenge this poses for constitutional reform is that history shows that committed opposition to a proposal by any major interest group can be fatal – the greater the redistribution threatened by the proposal, the greater the risk of committed opposition.

The Australian Constitution, if it is to respond to changing circumstances, must sometimes be altered in ways that cause real structural change to society. The issue is how to get people to sign on to reform that is good, but may be unpleasant. Reform proposals can be structured in a way that encourages people to focus on long-term interest, not short-term advantage. One way of doing this is by using sunrise provisions. A sunrise provision is one which provides that the law will not take effect until some specified point in the future.

Sunrise provisions are not new in Australia. The framers incorporated into the Constitution a host of arrangements, particularly in relation to trade and finance, to maintain the status quo for a specified period after 1901. These helped secure the agreement of the states to the major changes that would follow.

When constitutional reform is subject to a sunrise provision, change is not immediate; it is deferred for a period of time, perhaps even a generation. The effect is to encourage Parliament and the electors to concentrate on the long-term interests of the nation and to elevate the debate beyond the temporary. Vested interests will, of course, still exist and may oppose the law. But their opposition may be more muted, and the sway of their arguments lessoned.

COMPLEX ISSUES, COMPLEX CHOICES

Referendums often involve issues that are more complex than a Yes or No answer. The choice is not between No Change and Change. It is between No Change and a range of means to progress. In 1999, for example, the choice was not between constitutional monarchy and the minimalist model; it was between constitutional monarchy and a range of possible republican models. Similarly, it is possible to imagine a range of models for changing parliamentary terms of politicians, or for introducing a Bill of Rights.

This complexity is not recognised by the current Yes and No system. The Yes and No system simplifies the issue and gives a substantial 'leg-up' to the No campaign. The No campaign can become a coalition of those who support the status quo and those who oppose the status quo, but also oppose the suggested change. The No campaign can target just the specific proposal; the Yes campaign must set its sights on both the status quo and on any alternative proposals.

It is important to recognise that there is a value in Australia's present system of binary Yes and No voting. It means that when Australians vote to change the Constitution, they speak clearly and with one voice. The more choices there are, the more divided the country may appear. Sometimes, like in 1967, it is important that if Australia says Yes, it shouts it. When an issue goes to Australia's national identity, a vote for change should be unequivocal.

However, not all referendums go to national identity. When they do not, there can be much to gain from introducing some kind of 'multiple-choice' voting into the referendum process so as to recognise the complexity of the choices involved. Multiple choices visibly demonstrate to voters the coalition of voices calling for reform. They force the No campaign to meet its proper argumentative burden – arguing against a range of reasonable changes, not just a specific change. And they allow a full spectrum of views to be put to the

Australian people – binary choices give the impression that excluded options are illegitimate. No one thinks it is problematic that general elections give voters a range of choices; why should it be different for referendums? Multiple-choice referendums are also not unprecedented. New South Wales, Queensland and Tasmania have all given voters a set of choices in state referendums. So too did the Commonwealth in the plebiscite to decide Australia's national anthem.

It is important, though, to get the multiple-choice model right. Under section 128 of the Constitution, it is necessary for a double majority to 'approve' the proposal. It is not clear that this requirement is consistent with the system of preferential voting used in Australian elections. That system could also create a risk that a successful reform could be caricatured as a 'second-best option'.

A better option is the Swiss model of multiple-choice referendums. Under that model, the various reform options are enshrined in different Bills before being voted on by the people on the same day. The people are asked to vote:

- on a series of Yes or No questions in which the status quo is pitted against each of the reform options (just like a normal referendum); and
- in a second multiple-option plebiscite in which they are asked to choose between the reform options.

If only one option gets a majority vote against the status quo, then that option becomes law after receiving the Royal Assent. If more than one option gets a majority vote against the status quo, the government then advises the Governor-General to assent to the Bill that has received the highest level of popular support in the second multiple-option plebiscite. Alternatively, the individual Constitution Alteration Bills could be drafted so as to expire if they are not favoured in the second ballot. The result is that the approved model satisfies the requirements of section 128 of the Constitution, but that the people are given more choice in the public debate and on referendum day.

STATES AS FIRST MOVERS IN CONSTITUTIONAL REFORM

Australians are more likely to agree to change the Constitution when they both understand the change and have directly experienced the issue at the heart of the question. The successful 1928, 1946, 1967 and 1977 (Senate Casual Vacancies) referendums show this: each, to a greater or lesser extent, ratified pre-existing arrangements. Four out of eight of Australia's successful constitutional changes effectively involved no change at all.

There is a lesson in this: constitutional change is easiest when it codifies a principle that has already been tried and tested. This has long been acknowledged in the United States, where national constitutional reforms have often followed constitutional or legislative change in a majority of the states, thereby giving people the time to assess new ideas on a smaller scale. For example, before the United States amended its Constitution in 1920 to guarantee women the right to vote, female suffrage had already been recognised in 29 states.

Successful state reform makes the effects of national constitutional change much less of an unknown. It makes change incremental, rather than abrupt. It also tends to turn those states that have adopted the reform (and people in those states) into advocates of the reform. The states are a logical place to 'test' potential nationwide reforms. The effects of good reform are easier to see; the consequences of bad reform are less widespread. Further, because states usually do not require a referendum to reform their Constitution, constitutional change at the state level is often much easier to achieve.

The fifth pillar – a modern referendum process

Australia's present system for the holding of referendums is set out in the *Referendum (Machinery Provisions) Act 1984* (Cth) (Referendum Act). That law was adopted in 1912, and has changed little since then. It was designed at a time when voting was not compulsory, Australia's population was far smaller and far less diverse, and the print media and public speeches were the dominant modes of communication. The system is showing its age and is not suited to contemporary Australia. To modernise Australia's referendum process, the Referendum Act should be changed to:

- abolish expenditure restrictions on the Commonwealth Government;
- rethink the official Yes/No pamphlet; and
- continue the Yes and No committees from the 1999 referendum.

These changes are reflected in the late 2009 recommendations of the House of Representatives Standing Committee on Legal and Constitutional Affairs in its inquiry into the holding of referendums.[7]

ABOLISH EXPENDITURE RESTRICTIONS ON THE COMMONWEALTH GOVERNMENT

The Referendum Act prohibits most Commonwealth expenditure on advocating a Yes or No vote in a referendum. Australia's history of referendums shows that this restriction can allow the public debate to be monopolised by groups that have an interest in opposing reform or, even, in confusing voters. This, for example, was what happened in Western Australia and, particularly, Queensland during the referendum campaign of 1977. As that campaign shows, state governments, which are free of any such spending restrictions, can use their own resources to advocate an outcome without the

Commonwealth being able to mount an effective response.

The decision to hold a referendum is a considered decision of the federal Parliament. The Commonwealth Government should not be prevented from spending money informing electors of the arguments for and against constitutional reform. The check on this (and the quid pro quo for removing restrictions) should be a principle of even-handedness: where the Commonwealth does spend money, it must spend equal amounts on the Yes and No campaigns.

RETHINK THE OFFICIAL YES/NO PAMPHLET

It is important that Australians are informed of the pros and cons of constitutional reform. Unfortunately, the history of constitutional reform in Australia shows that there are problems with the Commonwealth informing voters solely through 2000-word Yes and No cases prepared by parliamentarians.

The way in which the Yes and No cases are currently developed means that the focus is on winning the argument at all costs, not on informing people. That fosters partisanship, exaggeration and misinformation. All can be fatal to constitutional reform.

The way in which the official pamphlet is now structured means that, virtually from the outset, Australians are encouraged to divide into two camps – to be either for or against a proposal. Adversarialism does have value – it can force people to really think about an issue. But adversarial rhetoric should not be the only information the Commonwealth Government provides in the official pamphlet.

The Yes and No cases in the official pamphlet have a role to play. However, the cases should be preceded in the official pamphlet by neutral material prepared by the Referendum Panel. That material should include a clear explanation of the proposal and a clear explanation of its context, including where it fits into the constitutional structure.

The kind of work that the Referendum Panel would undertake in preparing the voter's booklet is not unprecedented in Australia.

Most Bills introduced into Parliament are now accompanied by 'explanatory memoranda' prepared by public servants that set out the general purpose and effect of the Bill.

There are also similar examples in other countries. For example, in the state of Oregon in the United States, the Secretary of State produces a 'voter's pamphlet' for each elector before referendums. The pamphlet includes an explanatory statement about the referendum drafted by a committee of five citizens. The citizens are selected by proponents and opponents of the reform. The statement is limited to 500 words. After it has been drafted, the citizen panel submits it for a period of public comment before preparing the final version.

The official Yes/No pamphlet also needs to move on from being just a print-based publication. Print remains a very important source of information, but Australians are increasingly getting information from other sources. Research more than a decade ago on the 1999 referendum showed that over 80 per cent of respondents had received the Yes/No pamphlet and only 51 per cent had read some of it.[8] Today, few Australians would expect to receive information on a referendum only in print form. Presenting information only in this form risks not engaging with a large segment of the population that now expects to receive information about public affairs online.

The Referendum Panel should be permitted to use all available methods of delivery to distribute the Yes/No pamphlet and other information about the referendum. Those methods should include radio, television, email and the Internet. The available methods of delivery should not be specified and narrowed. Just as communication technologies have changed over the last century, so may we expect them to continue to change in the future.

In addition to the method of delivery, the timing of delivery is critical. The present approach – according to which the pamphlet can be delivered just 14 days before the referendum – leaves insufficient time for true deliberation and may mean that some people never even see the official pamphlet. If referendums are to be successful, then information, deliberation and citizen engagement need to be at the core of the referendum process from the beginning. This means that the official pamphlet should be delivered at least a month before the referendum.

YES AND NO COMMITTEES

The 1999 republic referendum introduced the experiment of having publicly funded Yes and No committees take part in the public debate. The Referendum Act should allow for such committees to be used in future referendums.

Information and advocacy produced by the Yes and No committees should be subject to the oversight of the Referendum Panel. That supervision should extend only to ensuring statements of fact are not inaccurate, deceptive or misleading before release to the public. To give a greater role to the Panel would risk its neutrality and stifle public debate.

Getting to Yes

Successful referendums are an infrequent part of the Australian landscape, and indeed have been non-existent for over three decades. This needs to be remedied. Whatever a person's view about the scope of change that is required, it is undeniable that the Constitution does need some change if it is to continue to best serve the interests and aspirations of the Australian people.

In this chapter, we have set out a new approach to how Australia might go about holding referendums. The nation's long history of such polls demonstrates the many pitfalls, as well as how the chances of success can be maximised. As this book has shown, the drivers of referendum success can often be found long before a referendum is put to the people, such as when ideas are debated and proposals are first conceived. This reflects the fact that Australians need more than a veto at the ballot box. They need a process that enables them to cast a confident, informed vote on changes that they have had an opportunity to debate and learn about long before they are asked to sit in judgment.

All this demonstrates that a successful referendum needs more than a good idea for reform. It also needs a sound process. Referendums need exceptional leaders and communicators who can weave constitutional reform into a narrative of Australian history and culture. But leadership cannot be guaranteed and, in any event, is only part of the story. What is also crucial is ensuring that the processes of reform are right. At the heart of this must be a system of regular constitutional review providing opportunities for public engagement and education.

Above all, future referendums in Australia should be based upon a willingness to trust the people. If nothing else, the people wield an unreviewable veto, and taking them for granted makes it likely that they will exercise this power. It should come as no surprise that Australians have said No over and over again to proposals that they do not feel ownership of, or do not understand. The lesson is not to despair at the prospects of constitutional reform, but to change the way that Australia goes about the process. If we followed a different path, we could be much more confident of the chances of getting to Yes.

SECTION 128 OF THE AUSTRALIAN CONSTITUTION

128. Mode of altering the Constitution This Constitution shall not be altered except in the following manner: –

The proposed law for the alteration thereof must be passed by an absolute majority of each House of the Parliament, and not less than two nor more than six months after its passage through both Houses the proposed law shall be submitted in each State and Territory to the electors qualified to vote for the election of members of the House of Representatives.

But if either House passes any such proposed law by an absolute majority, and the other House rejects or fails to pass it, or passes it with any amendment to which the first-mentioned House will not agree, and if after an interval of three months the first-mentioned House in the same or the next session again passes the proposed law by an absolute majority with or without any amendment which has been made or agreed to by the other House, and such other House rejects or fails to pass it or passes it with any amendment to which the first-mentioned House will not agree, the Governor-General may submit the proposed law as last proposed by the first-mentioned House, and either with or without any amendments subsequently agreed to by both Houses, to the electors in each State and Territory qualified to vote for the election of the House of Representatives.

When a proposed law is submitted to the electors the vote shall be taken in such manner as the Parliament prescribes. But until the qualification of electors of members of the House of Representatives becomes uniform throughout the Commonwealth, only one-half the electors voting for and against the proposed law shall be counted in any State in which adult suffrage prevails.

And if in a majority of the States a majority of the electors voting approve the proposed law, and if a majority of all the electors voting also approve the proposed law, it shall be presented to the Governor-General for the Queen's assent.

No alteration diminishing the proportionate representation of any State in either House of the Parliament, or the minimum number of representatives of a State in the House of Representatives, or increasing, diminishing, or otherwise altering the limits of the State, or in any manner affecting the provisions of the Constitution in relation thereto, shall become law unless the majority of the electors voting in that State approve the proposed law.

In this section, "Territory" means any territory referred to in section one hundred and twenty-two of this Constitution in respect of which there is in force a law allowing its representation in the House of Representatives.

Appendix 2

REFERENDUM PROPOSALS

1 SENATE ELECTIONS
12 DECEMBER 1906

A proposal to make minor amendments to the system of rotation of Senators. The most significant change was for Senators' terms to end on 30 June and commence on 1 July (instead of ending on 31 December and commencing on 1 January).

RESULT: CARRIED (nationally and in all states)

2 STATE DEBTS
13 APRIL 1910
A proposal to give the Commonwealth the power to take over any public debts owed by the states, whether those debts were created before or after Federation.
RESULT: CARRIED (nationally and in five states)

3 FINANCE
13 APRIL 1910
A proposal to alter section 87 of the Constitution, which provided that in the ten years after Federation, and until the federal Parliament otherwise provided, the Commonwealth was to distribute at least 75 per cent of its net revenue from duties of customs and of excise between the states. It was proposed to alter this to provide for the distribution of a fixed amount to the states on a per capita basis.
RESULT: Not carried nationally (but in three states)

4 LEGISLATIVE POWERS
26 APRIL 1911
A proposal to give the Commonwealth greater power to legislate in respect of trade and commerce, corporations, labour, employment, and monopolies.
RESULT: Not carried nationally (but in one state)

5 MONOPOLIES
26 APRIL 1911
A proposal to give the Commonwealth the power to nationalise any industry that both Houses of Parliament declared to be the subject of a monopoly.
RESULT: Not carried nationally (but in one state)

6   TRADE AND COMMERCE
31 MAY 1913

A proposal to give the Commonwealth the power to make laws in respect of trade and commerce.

RESULT: Not carried nationally (but in three states)

7   CORPORATIONS
31 MAY 1913

A proposal to give the Commonwealth the power to make laws in respect of corporations.

RESULT: Not carried nationally (but in three states)

8   INDUSTRIAL MATTERS
31 MAY 1913

A proposal to give the Commonwealth a general power to regulate industrial disputes, and to give a Federal Court the power to prevent disputes from arising and spreading.

RESULT: Not carried nationally (but in three states)

9   TRUSTS
31 MAY 1913

A proposal to give the Commonwealth the power to make laws with respect to trusts.

RESULT: Not carried nationally (but in three states)

10 NATIONALISATION OF MONOPOLIES
31 MAY 1913

A proposal to give the Commonwealth the power to nationalise monopolies.

RESULT: Not carried nationally (but in three states)

11 RAILWAY DISPUTES
31 MAY 1913

A proposal to give the Commonwealth jurisdiction over industrial relations in the state railway services.

RESULT: Not carried nationally (but in three states)

12 LEGISLATIVE POWERS
13 DECEMBER 1919

A proposal to give the Commonwealth powers for three years with respect to trade and commerce, corporations, industrial matters and trusts.

RESULT: Not carried nationally (but in three states)

13 NATIONALISATION OF MONOPOLIES
13 DECEMBER 1919

A proposal to give the Commonwealth the power for three years to nationalise monopolies.

RESULT: Not carried nationally (but in three states)

14 INDUSTRY AND COMMERCE
4 SEPTEMBER 1926

A proposal to give the Commonwealth a general power to make laws in respect of corporations, trusts, combinations in restraint of trade, trade unions and employer associations.

RESULT: Not carried nationally (but in two states)

15 ESSENTIAL SERVICES
4 SEPTEMBER 1926

A proposal to give the Commonwealth the power to protect the public from an interruption to essential services.

RESULT: Not carried nationally (but in two states)

16 STATE DEBTS
17 NOVEMBER 1928

A proposal to ratify an existing agreement between the Commonwealth and states in respect of public debts and allow the Commonwealth and states to enter into new agreements.

RESULT: CARRIED (nationally and in all six states)

17 AVIATION
6 MARCH 1937

A proposal to give the Commonwealth the power to make laws in respect of air navigation and aircraft.

RESULT: Not carried (national majority but only two states)

18 MARKETING
6 MARCH 1937

A proposal to insert a new section 92A into the Constitution to make any law with respect to marketing exempt from section 92. Section 92 provides that 'trade, commerce, and intercourse among the States … shall be absolutely free'.

RESULT: Not carried nationally or in any state

19 POST-WAR RECONSTRUCTION AND DEMOCRATIC RIGHTS
19 AUGUST 1944

A proposal to give the Commonwealth the power to make laws with respect to 14 new matters for a period of five years. The new matters included: the rehabilitation of ex-servicemen, national health, family allowances and Indigenous Australians. The proposal sought also to give the Commonwealth power to protect various human rights, including freedom of speech and freedom of religion.

RESULT: Not carried nationally (but in two states)

20 SOCIAL SERVICES
28 SEPTEMBER 1946

A proposal to give the Commonwealth the power to make laws with respect to maternity allowances, widows' pensions, child endowment, unemployment, pharmaceutical, sickness and hospital benefits, medical and dental services (but not so as to authorise any form of civil conscription), benefits to students and family allowances.

RESULT: CARRIED (nationally and in all six states)

21 ORGANISED MARKETING
28 SEPTEMBER 1946

A proposal to make laws relating to the marketing of primary products unrestricted by section 92.

RESULT: Not carried (national majority but only three states)

22 INDUSTRIAL EMPLOYMENT
28 SEPTEMBER 1946

A proposal to give the Commonwealth the power to make laws with respect to the terms and conditions of industrial employment.

RESULT: Not carried (national majority but only three states)

23 RENTS AND PRICES
29 MAY 1948

A proposal to give the Commonwealth the power to make laws with respect to rents and prices.

RESULT: Not carried nationally or in any state

24 COMMUNISM
22 SEPTEMBER 1951

A proposal to ratify a statute struck down by the High Court dissolving the Communist Party of Australia and to give the Commonwealth the power to make laws with respect to communists and communism.

RESULT: Not carried nationally (but in three states)

25 PARLIAMENT
27 MAY 1967

A proposal to remove the requirement contained in section 24 of the Constitution that there be a link (a 'nexus') between the sizes of the House of Representatives and the Senate.

RESULT: Not carried nationally (but in one state)

26 ABORIGINALS
27 MAY 1967

A proposal to delete section 127 of the Constitution, which provided that Indigenous people were not to be counted in reckoning Australia's population and to allow the Commonwealth to make laws in respect of Indigenous people.

RESULT: CARRIED (nationally and in all six states)

27 PRICES
8 DECEMBER 1973

A proposal to give the Commonwealth a power to make laws with respect to prices.

RESULT: Not carried nationally or in any state

28 INCOMES
8 DECEMBER 1973

A proposal to give the Commonwealth a power to make laws with respect to incomes.

RESULT: Not carried nationally or in any state

29 SIMULTANEOUS ELECTIONS
18 MAY 1974

A proposal to ensure House of Representatives and Senate elections were held on the same day.

RESULT: Not carried nationally (but in one state)

30 MODE OF ALTERING THE CONSTITUTION
18 MAY 1974

A proposal for referendums to be submitted to residents of the Australian Capital Territory and the Northern Territory (whose votes would be counted towards determining the national tally) and to allow a referendum to be successful if carried with a national majority and in only three states.

RESULT: Not carried nationally (but in one state)

31 DEMOCRATIC ELECTIONS
18 MAY 1974

A proposal for the size of electorates to be determined by their total population, rather than the number of eligible voters.

RESULT: Not carried nationally (but in one state)

32 LOCAL GOVERNMENT BODIES
18 MAY 1974

A proposal to give the Commonwealth power to borrow money for, and make financial grants to, any local government body.

RESULT: Not carried nationally (but in one state)

33 SIMULTANEOUS ELECTIONS
21 MAY 1977

A proposal to ensure House of Representatives and Senate elections were held on the same day.

RESULT: Not carried (national majority but only three states)

34 SENATE CASUAL VACANCIES
21 MAY 1977

A proposal to ensure that, as far as practicable, casual vacancies in the Senate would be filled by Senators from the same political party as the person originally elected.

RESULT: CARRIED (nationally and in all six states)

35 RETIREMENT OF JUDGES
21 MAY 1977

A proposal to set a compulsory maximum retirement age of 70 years for all federal judges.

RESULT: CARRIED (nationally and in all six states)

36 REFERENDUMS
21 MAY 1977

A proposal for referendums to be submitted also to residents of the Australian Capital Territory and the Northern Territory (whose votes would be counted towards determining the national tally).

RESULT: CARRIED (nationally and in all six states)

37 TERMS OF SENATORS
1 DECEMBER 1984

A proposal to allow for simultaneous elections for House of Representatives and Senate elections and to change Senators' terms so that they were no longer of a fixed duration.

RESULT: Not carried (national majority but only two states)

38 INTERCHANGE OF POWERS
I DECEMBER 1984

A proposal to allow the Commonwealth and the states to voluntarily refer powers to each other.

RESULT: Not carried nationally or in any state

39 PARLIAMENTARY TERMS
3 SEPTEMBER 1988

A proposal to create four-year maximum terms for members of both Houses of the federal Parliament.

RESULT: Not carried nationally or in any state

40 FAIR ELECTIONS
3 SEPTEMBER 1988

A proposal to guarantee Australian citizens the right to vote and to introduce a 'one vote one value' system at the Commonwealth and state levels.

RESULT: Not carried nationally or in any state

41 LOCAL GOVERNMENT
3 SEPTEMBER 1988

A proposal to recognise local government in the Constitution.

RESULT: Not carried nationally or in any state

42 RIGHTS AND FREEDOMS
3 SEPTEMBER 1988

A proposal to guarantee the rights to trial by jury, freedom of religion and just terms for the acquisition of property at the state level.

RESULT: Not carried nationally or in any state

43 ESTABLISHMENT OF REPUBLIC
6 NOVEMBER 1999

A proposal to constitute an Australian republic with a President appointed by Parliament.

RESULT: Not carried nationally or in any state

44 PREAMBLE TO CONSTITUTION
6 NOVEMBER 1999

A proposal to insert a new preamble into the Constitution.

RESULT: Not carried nationally or in any state

NOTES

CHAPTER 1 • THE PEOPLE'S VOICE

1   *Commonwealth of Australia Constitution Act 1900* (UK).

2   *Official Record of the Debates of the Australasian Federal Convention*, Melbourne, 9 February 1898, 759 (Isaac Isaacs).

3   Andrew Inglis Clark, *Studies in Australian Constitutional Law* (1901) 21.

4   Australian Electoral Commission, *Australian Referendums 1906–1999* CD-ROM (2000) (emphasis in original).

5   *Local Government Act 1993* (NSW), section 16.

6   John G Matsusaka, 'Have Voter Initiatives Paralyzed the California Budget?' *USC Law and Public Policy Research Paper* No. 03-24 (November 2003).

7   Donald S Lutz, 'Toward a Theory of Constitutional Amendment', in Sanford Levinson (ed.), *Responding to Imperfection: The Theory and Practice of Constitutional Amendment* (1995) 237, 261.

8   Australia's Constitution would then rate 5.5 on Lutz's scale based on the need for bicameral absolute majority approval (1.25), executive approval (0.5) and approval by a majority of people in a majority of states (3.75). The Constitution of the former Yugoslavia would have been harder to amend than Australia's, but it is no longer in existence.

9   Geoffrey Sawer, *Australian Federalism in the Courts* (1967) 208.

10   See *His Holiness Kesavananda Bharati v The State of Kerala and Others* All India Reporter 1973 Supreme Court of India 1461.

11   John Quick and Robert Garran, *Annotated Constitution of the Australian Commonwealth* (1901) 991.

12   GJ Lindell, 'Why is Australia's Constitution Binding? – The Reasons in 1900 and Now, and the Effect of Independence' (1986) 16 *Federal*

Law Review 29, 49, cited in *Australian Capital Television Pty Ltd v Commonwealth* (1992) 177 Commonwealth Law Reports 106 at 138.

13   *Theophanous v Herald & Weekly Times Ltd* (1994) 182 Commonwealth Law Reports 104 at 171.

14   Tony Blackshield, Michael Coper and George Williams (eds), *The Oxford Companion to the High Court of Australia* (2001) 356.

15   LJ Mark Cooray and Suri Ratnapala, 'The High Court and the Constitution – Literalism and Beyond', in Gregory Craven (ed.), *The Convention Debates: Commentaries, Indices and Guide* (1986) 203, 203.

16   *Official Record of the Debates of the Australasian Federal Convention*, Melbourne, 28 January 1898, 283 (Isaac Isaacs).

17   *Commonwealth Powers (Industrial Relations) Act 1996* (Vic), as now superseded by the *Fair Work (Commonwealth Powers) Act 2009* (Vic).

CHAPTER 2 • THE PATH OF CONSTITUTIONAL CHANGE

1   Interview with Malcolm Turnbull (23 February 2010).

2   JE Richardson, 'Reform of the Constitution: Referendums and the Constitutional Convention', in Gareth Evans (ed.), *Labor and the Constitution, 1972–1975: Essays and Commentaries on the Constitutional Controversies of the Whitlam Years in Australian Government* (1977) 91.

3   Quoted in Michelle Grattan and Hugo Kelly, 'Reform Hopes Dashed by Vote' *Age*, 5 September 1988, 1.

4   Quoted in Michelle Grattan and Hugo Kelly, 'Reform Hopes Dashed by Vote' *Age*, 5 September 1988, 1.

5   Michelle Grattan, 'Botched Referendums to Turn the Heat on Labor' *Age*, 5 September 1988, 13.

6   House of Representatives Standing Committee on Legal and Constitutional Reform, *Reforming our Constitution* (2008).

7   Consultative Group on Constitutional Change, *Resolving Deadlocks: The Public Response*, 8–9.

8   *Boland v Hughes* (1988) 83 Australian Law Reports 673, 674 (Mason CJ).

9   *Referendum (Machinery Provisions) Act 1984* (Cth), section 8(1).

10   *Referendum (Machinery Provisions) Act 1984* (Cth), section 8(2).

11   *Referendum (Machinery Provisions) Act 1984* (Cth), section 9(2).

12   *Referendum (Machinery Provisions) Act 1984* (Cth), section 8(1A).

13   *Referendum (Machinery Provisions) Act 1984* (Cth), section 10.

14   The referendums held outside an election were those in 1911, 1926, 1937, 1944, 1948, 1951, 1967, 1973, 1977, 1988 and 1999.

15   *Daily Telegraph*, 4 February 1895.

16   *Official Record of Debates of the Australasian Federal Convention*, Sydney, 8

April 1891, 894 (Samuel Griffith).

17   *Referendum (Machinery Provisions) Act 1984* (Cth), section 9(1).

18   W Harrison Moore, *The Constitution of the Commonwealth of Australia* (2nd edn, 1910) 600.

19   *Referendum (Machinery Provisions) Act 1984* (Cth), sections 27, 89.

20   *Referendum (Machinery Provisions) Act 1984* (Cth), section 95.

21   See *Referendum (Constitution Alteration) Act 1906* (Cth), sections 18, 23.

22   Commonwealth, *Parliamentary Debates*, House of Representatives, 4 November 1992, 2547 (Paul Keating).

23   *New South Wales v Commonwealth* (2006) 229 Commonwealth Law Reports 1.

CHAPTER 3 · REFERENDUM CAMPAIGNS

1   *Lange v Australian Broadcasting Corporation* (1997) 189 Commonwealth Law Reports 520, 561.

2   *Lange v Australian Broadcasting Corporation* (1997) 189 Commonwealth Law Reports 520, 567.

3   *Evans v Crichton-Browne* (1981) 147 Commonwealth Law Reports 169.

4   (1988) 83 Australian Law Reports 667.

5   Commonwealth, *Parliamentary Debates*, Senate, 7 June 1984, 2765 (Gareth Evans).

6   Commonwealth, *Parliamentary Debates*, House of Representatives, 16 December 1912, 7154 (William Hughes).

7   Commonwealth, *Parliamentary Debates*, House of Representatives, 16 December 1912, 7156 (Andrew Fisher).

8   House of Representatives Standing Committee on Legal and Constitutional Affairs, Parliament of Australia, *Final Report –Inquiry into the Machinery of Referendums* (10 December 2009) 61.

9   AEC Submission to the House of Representatives Standing Committee on Legal and Constitutional Affairs Inquiry into the Referendum (Machinery Provisions) Act, 19.

10   All references to text from the Official Pamphlet are sourced from Australian Electoral Commission, *Australian Referendums 1906–1999* CD-ROM (2000).

11   Commonwealth of Australia, *Official Pamphlet for the Referendums to be held on Saturday, the 31st day of May, 1913* (1913) 7, 33.

12   Commonwealth of Australia, *Official Pamphlet for the Referendums to be held on Saturday, the 31st day of May, 1913* (1913) 7–8.

13   Commonwealth of Australia, *Official Pamphlet for the Referendums to be held on Saturday, the 31st day of May, 1913* (1913) 34.

14   Commonwealth of Australia, *Official Pamphlet for the Referendums to be*

held on Saturday, the 31st day of May, 1913 (1913) 41.

15   Commonwealth of Australia, *Official Pamphlet for the Referendums to be held on Saturday, the 31st day of May, 1913* (1913) 42.

16   Commonwealth of Australia, *Official Pamphlet for the Referendums to be held on Saturday, the 31st day of May, 1913* (1913) 47.

17   Commonwealth of Australia, *Official Pamphlet for the Referendums to be held on Saturday, the 31st day of May, 1913* (1913) 52.

18   Commonwealth of Australia, *Official Pamphlet for the Referendums to be held on Saturday, the 31st day of May, 1913* (1913) 57.

19   Commonwealth of Australia, *Official Pamphlet for the Referendums to be held on Saturday, the 31st day of May, 1913* (1913) 62, 61.

20   Commonwealth of Australia, *Alteration of Constitution – Federal Referendums – The Case For and Against* (1937) 3–4.

21   Commonwealth of Australia, *The Arguments FOR and AGAINST the Proposed Alterations together with a Statement showing the Proposed Alterations* (1967) 5.

22   Commonwealth of Australia, *The Case For and Against* (1951) 12, 15.

23   Commonwealth of Australia, *Yes/No – Referendum '99 – Your Official Referendum Pamphlet* (1999) 5.

24   Commonwealth of Australia, *The Case For and Against* (1946) 24.

25   Commonwealth of Australia, *The Case For and Against* (1946) 24–5.

26   Commonwealth of Australia, *Yes or No – Referendums, Saturday 3 September 1988 – The Cases For and Against* (1988) 5, 10, 15, 20.

27   Commonwealth of Australia, *Yes/No – Referendum '99 – Your Official Referendum Pamphlet* (1999) 5.

28   Commonwealth of Australia, *Yes/No – Referendum '99 – Your Official Referendum Pamphlet* (1999) 5.

29   Commonwealth of Australia, *Referendums to be held on Saturday, 21 May 1977* (1977) 9.

30   Commonwealth of Australia, *Referendums to be held on Saturday, 21 May 1977* (1977) 9.

31   Commonwealth of Australia, *Referendums to be held on Saturday, 21 May 1977* (1977) 10.

32   Commonwealth of Australia, *Yes or No – Referendums, Saturday 3 September 1988 – The Cases For and Against* (1988) 8, 14, 18.

33   Commonwealth of Australia, *Yes or No – Referendums, Saturday 3 September 1988 – The Cases For and Against* (1988) 19, 20.

34   Commonwealth of Australia, *Yes or No – Referendums, Saturday 3 September 1988 – The Cases For and Against* (1988) 10.

35   Paul Kelly, 'The Referendums: Myths and Bogeys', *Australian*, 2 September 1988, 11.

36   Commonwealth of Australia, *Alteration of Constitution – Federal

Referendums – The Case For and Against (1937) 13.

37 Commonwealth of Australia, *Alteration of Constitution – Federal Referendums – The Case For and Against* (1937) 18.

38 Commonwealth of Australia, *Federal Referendum – The Case For and Against* (1944) 5.

39 Commonwealth of Australia, *Federal Referendum – The Case For and Against* (1944) 10.

40 *Canberra Times*, 14 August 1946, 2.

41 Geoffrey Sawer, *Australian Federal Politics and Law 1929–1949* (1963) 84, 203.

42 See *Sydney Morning Herald*, 23 August 1988, 15.

43 Greg Barns, 'The 1999 Yes Case', in John Warhurst and Malcolm Mackerras, *Constitutional Politics: The Republic Referendum and the Future* (2002) 55.

44 Greg Barns, 'The 1999 Yes Case', in John Warhurst and Malcolm Mackerras, *Constitutional Politics: The Republic Referendum and the Future* (2002) 55.

45 Commonwealth of Australia, *Yes or No – Referendums, Saturday 3 September 1988 – The Cases For and Against* (1988) 7, 13, 17, 23.

46 Commonwealth of Australia, *Yes/No – Referendum '99 – Your Official Referendum Pamphlet* (1999) 6.

47 Commonwealth of Australia, *Australian Referendums 1906–1999* CD-ROM (2000).

48 AEC Submission to the House of Representatives Standing Committee on Legal and Constitutional Affairs Inquiry into the Referendum (Machinery Provisions) Act, 17.

49 House of Representatives, Standing Committee on Legal and Constitutional Affairs, Parliament of Australia, *Final Report –Inquiry into the Machinery of Referendums* (10 December 2009) 55.

CHAPTER 4 • THE RECORD

1 These were: seven bills in 1915, for which writs were issued but later withdrawn by the Governor-General on the advice of the Hughes government; two bills in 1965, for which writs were not issued on the advice of the Holt government; and five bills in 1983, for which writs were not issued on the advice of the Hawke government.

2 On other occasions, governments have sought the same power, but have included it in an omnibus question lumped together with other powers, as in the case of the 1944 (Post-War Reconstruction and Democratic Rights) referendum.

CHAPTER 5 • EIGHT REFERENDUMS

1   Commonwealth of Australia, *Australian Referendums 1906–1999*
     CD-ROM (2000).
2   Sir Robert Menzies, *Central Power in the Australian Commonwealth:
     An Examination of the Growth of Commonwealth Power in the Australian
     Federation* (1967) 14.
3   *Sydney Morning Herald*, 21 September 1906.
4   Commonwealth, *Parliamentary Debates*, Senate, 19 September 1906, 4799,
     (Senator Drake).
5   Commonwealth, *Parliamentary Debates*, Senate, 31 August 1906, 3746
     (Senator Drake).
6   Commonwealth, *Parliamentary Debates*, Senate, 31 August 1906, 3745
     (Senator Drake).
7   Commonwealth, *Parliamentary Debates*, Senate, 31 August 1906, 3749
     (Senator O'Keefe).
8   Commonwealth, *Parliamentary Debates*, Senate, 19 September 1906, 4798
     (Senator Drake).
9   Commonwealth, *Parliamentary Debates*, Senate, 31 August 1906, 3748
     (Senator O'Keefe).
10   Commonwealth, *Parliamentary Debates*, Senate, 31 August 1906, 3743
     (Senator Drake).
11   Commonwealth, *Parliamentary Debates*, Senate, 19 September 1906, 4800
     (Senator Drake).
12   Commonwealth, *Parliamentary Debates*, Senate, 19 September 1906,
     4801–2 (Senator Millen).
13   Commonwealth, *Parliamentary Debates*, Senate, 19 September 1906, 4800
     (Senator Drake).
14   *Sydney Morning Herald*, 5 September 1928, 14.
15   *Age*, 17 November 1928, 24.
16   Commonwealth of Australia, *Australian Referendums 1906–1999*
     CD-ROM (2000).
17   *Age*, 20 November 1928, 12.
18   *Attorney-General (Vic); Ex rel Dale v Commonwealth* (1945) 71
     Commonwealth Law Reports 237.
19   Constitution Alteration (Social Services) Bill 1946 (Cth).
20   Commonwealth of Australia, *Referendums – The Case For and Against*
     (1946) 27.
21   Commonwealth of Australia, *Referendums – The Case For and Against*
     (1946) 25.
22   *Adelaide Advertiser*, 24 September 1946, 12.

23 See, for example, Dr Lloyd Ross, 'The 'Yes' Case', *Sydney Morning Herald*, 26 September 1946, 4.

24 'A Party Vote', *Courier-Mail*, 17 September 1946, 1.

25 *Adelaide Advertiser*, 24 September 1946, 10.

26 *Canberra Times*, 18 September 1946, 2.

27 *Adelaide Advertiser*, 25 September 1946, 10.

28 *Courier-Mail*, 17 September 1946, 2.

29 *Sydney Morning Herald*, 28 September 1946, 2.

30 For these figures, see Commonwealth of Australia, *Australian Referendums 1906–1999* CD-ROM (2000).

31 *Country Party Policy Statement* extracted in B McKinlay, *A Documentary History of the Australian Labor Movement 1850–1975* (1979) 691.

32 *Australian Communist Party v Commonwealth* (*Communist Party Case*) (1951) 83 Commonwealth Law Reports 1.

33 Kylie Tennant, *Evatt: Politics and Justice* (1970) 270.

34 Constitution Alteration (Powers to Deal with Communists and Communism) Bill 1951 (Cth).

35 *Adelaide Advertiser*, 20 September 1951, 3.

36 *Sydney Morning Herald*, 9 September 1951, 2.

37 *Adelaide Advertiser*, 18 September 1951, 3.

38 'Big Audience for Menzies – "Yes" Campaign in Queensland', *Sydney Morning Herald*, 7 September 1951, 4.

39 *Sydney Morning Herald*, 5 September 1951, 2.

40 *Sydney Morning Herald*, 21 September 1951, 2.

41 'Referendum on Communists – Campaign has Two Weeks to Go', *Sydney Morning Herald*, 8 September 1951, 2.

42 *Sydney Morning Herald*, 13 September 1951, 8.

43 'Distortion Cannot Hide the Real Issue', *Age*, 10 September 1951, 2.

44 'Dr Evatt: 'Conspiracy to Silence Churchmen', 11 September 1951, 2.

45 'Counsel's View of the Referendum', *Sydney Morning Herald*, 18 September 1951, 3.

46 'Senator Spooner Replies to 10 Clergymen' *Sydney Morning Herald*, 17 September 1951, 4.

47 *Age*, 18 September 1951, 4.

48 'Menzies Appeals Vote "Yes"', *Sydney Morning Herald*, 5 September 1951, 1.

49 See, for example, *Adelaide Advertiser*, 13 September 1951, 9.

50 *Sydney Morning Herald*, 12 September 1951, 10.

51 *Argus*, 22 August 1951.

52 Cited in Fay Woodhouse, *Anti Communism and Civil Liberties: The 1951 Communist Party Dissolution Referendum Debate at the University of Melbourne* (1998) 11.

53 'Anglican Bishop in Letter Urges No Vote', *Sydney Morning Herald*,
    1 September 1951, 1.
54 *Age*, 3 September 1951, 2.
55 *Sydney Morning Herald*, 5 September 1951, 2.
56 'Referendum Powers are Strictly Limited', *Sydney Morning Herald*, 18
    September 1951, 2.
57 *Sunday Herald*, 9 September 1951, 7.
58 *Sydney Morning Herald*, 7 September 1951, 4.
59 *Sydney Morning Herald*, 7 September 1951, 4.
60 *Sunday Herald*, 9 September 1951, 7.
61 See, for example, *Sydney Morning Herald*, 8 September 1951, 2.
62 *Sydney Morning Herald*, 21 September 1951, 4.
63 For these results, see Commonwealth of Australia, *Australian Referendums
    1906–1999* CD-ROM (2000).
64 *Age*, 24 September 1951, 2.
65 *Sydney Morning Herald*, 24 September 1951, 4.
66 John Howard (Press Conference, Beijing, 22 May 2002).
67 *Sydney Morning Herald*, 24 September 1951, 4.
68 *Age*, 22 May 1967, 5.
69 *Age*, 22 May 1967, 5.
70 Cited in John Gardiner-Garden, *The 1967 Referendum – History and Myths*
    (Research Brief No. 11, 2006–07) 5.
71 John Gardiner-Garden, *The 1967 Referendum – History and Myths*
    (Research Brief No. 11, 2006–07) 6.
72 John Gardiner-Garden, *The 1967 Referendum – History and Myths*
    (Research Brief No. 11, 2006–07) 6, citing Max Griffiths, *Aboriginal
    Affairs: A Short History 1788–1995* (1995) 72.
73 Commonwealth, *Parliamentary Debates*, House of Representatives, 9 May
    1957, vol 15, 1227 (HV Evatt).
74 See *Australian*, 29 May 1967, 9.
75 *Sydney Morning Herald*, 25 May 1967, 2.
76 *Australian*, 29 May 1967, 1.
77 *Australian*, 18 May 1967, 1.
78 *Sunday Herald*, 28 May 1967, 1.
79 *Australian*, 29 May 1967, 2.
80 *Australian*, 29 May 1967, 9.
81 *Australian*, 29 May 1967, 9.
82 *Australian*, 29 May 1967, 2.
83 *Sydney Morning Herald*, 29 May 1967, 2.
84 Interview with Malcolm Fraser (23 February 2010).
85 Interview with Malcolm Fraser (23 February 2010).
86 *Courier-Mail*, 16 May 1977, 8.

87   *Sydney Morning Herald*, 17 May 1977, 9.

88   *Sydney Morning Herald*, 17 May 1977, 9.

89   *Sydney Morning Herald*, 20 May 1977, 7.

90   *Sydney Morning Herald*, 20 May 1977, 7.

91   *Sydney Morning Herald*, 20 May 1977, 7.

92   *Age*, 18 May 1977, 13.

93   *Courier-Mail*, 21 May 1977, 12.

94   *Adelaide Advertiser*, 17 May 1977, 3.

95   *Age*, 16 May 1977, 10.

96   *Age*, 16 May 1977, 10.

97   *Australian*, 19 May 1977, 3.

98   *Age*, 23 May 1977, 1.

99   *Age*, 23 May 1977, 1.

100 *Age*, 23 May 1977, 1.

101 *Sydney Morning Herald*, 23 May 1977, 6.

102 Michelle Grattan, 'Botched Referendums to Turn the Heat on Labor', *Age* 5 September 1988, 13.

103 Michelle Grattan, 'Botched Referendums to Turn the Heat on Labor', *Age*, 5 September 1988, 13.

104 *Age*, 1 September 1988, 13.

105 (1988) 165 Commonwealth Law Reports 360.

106 *Sydney Morning Herald*, 1 September 1988, 6.

107 *Daily Mirror*, 5 September 1988, 8.

108 *Age*, 30 August 1988, 6.

109 *Australian*, 3 September 1988, 1.

110 Interview with Peter Reith (5 February 2010).

111 *Sydney Morning Herald*, 1 September 1988, 6.

112 *Sydney Morning Herald*, 23 August 1988, 15.

113 *Sydney Morning Herald*, 23 August 1988, 15.

114 Interview with Peter Reith (5 February 2010).

115 *Age*, 29 August 1988, 3.

116 *Attorney-General (Vic); Ex rel Black v Commonwealth* (1981) 146 Commonwealth Law Reports 559.

117 Constitutional Commission, *Bulletin*, No. 5, Canberra Publishing and Printing (1987).

118 *Age*, 3 September 1988, 3.

119 *Age*, 3 September 1988, 1.

120 *Age*, 3 September 1988, 1.

121 *Australian*, 5 September 1988, 8.

122 Interview with Peter Reith (5 February 2010).

123 *Age*, 2 September 1988, 13.

124 Interview with Peter Reith (5 February 2010).

125 *Age*, 5 September 1988, 21.
126 *Age*, 31 August 1988, 3.
127 *Sydney Morning Herald*, 5 September 1988, 1.
128 *Official Report of the National Australasian Convention Debates*, Sydney, 10 March 1891, 186 (George Dibbs).
129 *Official Report of the National Australasian Convention Debates*, Sydney, 18 March 1891, 323 (Henry Parkes).
130 Paul Kelly, 'The Severed Country', *Australian*, 6 November 1996, 29.
131 Interview with Kerry Jones (1 February 2010).
132 *Australian*, 2 November 1999, 3.
133 *Adelaide Advertiser*, 3 November 1999, 8.
134 *Australian*, 3 November 1999, 5.
135 *Australian*, 2 November 1999, 3.
136 *Australian*, 3 November 1999, 1.
137 *Sydney Morning Herald*, 5 November 1999, 15.
138 *Sydney Morning Herald*, 5 November 1999, 15.
139 *Age*, 4 November 1999, 8.
140 *Courier-Mail*, 3 November 1999, 9.
141 *Sydney Morning Herald*, 5 November 1999, 15.
142 Greg Barns, 'The 1999 Yes Case', in John Warhurst and Malcolm Mackerras, *Constitutional Politics: The Republic Referendum and the Future* (2002) 55.
143 Mark McKenna, 'The Australian Republic: Still Captive after all these Years', in John Warhurst and Malcolm Mackerras, *Constitutional Politics: The Republic Referendum and the Future* (2002) 153.
144 *Australian*, 3 November 1999, 1.
145 *Australian*, 2 November 1999, 3.
146 *Australian*, 2 November 1999, 3.
147 Interview with Kerry Jones (1 February 2010).
148 Interview with Kerry Jones (1 February 2010).
149 *Australian*, 4 November 1999, 1.
150 Interview with Malcolm Turnbull (23 February 2010).
151 *Daily Telegraph*, 4 November 1999, 1.
152 *Australian*, 3 November 1999, 5.
153 *Courier-Mail*, 3 November 1999, 19.
154 *Age*, 5 November 1999, 1.
155 *Age*, 5 November 1999, 1.
156 *Australian*, 8 November 1999, 1.
157 *Australian*, 8 November 1999, 2.
158 *Sydney Morning Herald*, 8 November 1999, 1.
159 *Sydney Morning Herald*, 8 November 1999, 7.

CHAPTER 6 • A LABOUR OF HERCULES?

1   LF Crisp, *Australian National Government* (1983, 5th edn) 40.

2   Heinz Klug, *Constituting Democracy: Law, Globalism and South Africa's Political Reconstruction* (2000) 12.

3   Constitutional Commission, *Bulletin*, No. 5 (Canberra Publishing and Printing, September 1987).

4   Reported in Constitutional Commission, *Final Report* (1988) at [1.56].

5   Civics Expert Group, *Whereas the People: Civics and Citizenship Education* (1994).

6   Commonwealth of Australia, *Alteration of Constitution: Federal Referendum – The Case For and Against* (1944) 11.

7   Interview with Malcolm Turnbull (23 February 2010).

8   Australian Electoral Commission, *Referendums to be Taken on the Proposed Laws: The Case For and Against* (1946) 27

9   Interview with Malcolm Fraser (23 February 2010).

10   Clive Bean, 'Political Personalities and Voting in the 1999 Australian Constitutional Referendum' (2002) 14 *International Journal of Public Opinion Research* (2002) 459–69.

CHAPTER 7 • GETTING TO YES

1   House of Representatives Standing Committee on Legal and Constitutional Affairs, *A Time for Change: Yes/No?: Inquiry into the Machinery of Referendums* (December 2009) 60.

2   Commonwealth, *Parliamentary Debates*, House of Representatives, 23 February 1944, 468 (Robert Menzies).

3   Sir Robert Garran, *Prosper the Commonwealth* (1968) 207–14.

4   Interview with Kerry Jones (1 February 2010).

5   Commonwealth, *Parliamentary Debates*, House of Representatives, 1913, vol 69, 7155 (Alfred Deakin).

6   Interview with Peter Reith (5 February 2010).

7   House of Representatives Standing Committee on Legal and Constitutional Affairs, *A Time for Change: Yes/No?: Inquiry into the Machinery of Referendums* (December 2009) 60.

8   Australian Electoral Commission, Submission to House of Representatives Standing Committee on Legal and Constitutional Affairs Inquiry into the Machinery of Referendums (2009) 18–19.

INDEX

9 781742 232157